MD   6/17/98

**HENRY COUNTY
LIBRARY SYSTEM**
DATE DUE

Cormac McCarthy

Twayne's United States Authors Series

Frank Day, Editor

Clemson University

TUSAS 679

CORMAC McCARTHY
Photo by Marion Ettlinger

Cormac McCarthy

Robert L. Jarrett

University of Houston–Downtown

Twayne Publishers
An Imprint of Simon & Schuster Macmillan
New York

Prentice Hall International
London • Mexico City • New Delhi • Singapore • Sydney • Toronto

Twayne's United States Authors Series No. 679

Cormac McCarthy
Robert L. Jarrett

Copyright © 1997 by Twayne Publishers

Twayne Publishers
An Imprint of Simon & Schuster Macmillan
1633 Broadway
New York, NY 10019

Library of Congress Cataloging-in-Publication Data

Jarrett, Robert L.
    Cormac McCarthy / Robert L. Jarrett.
        p.   cm. — (Twayne's United States authors series ; TUSAS 679)
    Includes bibliographical references and index.
    ISBN 0-8057-4567-X (alk. paper)
    1. McCarthy, Cormac, 1933– —Criticism and interpretation.
2. Southern States—In literature.   I. Title.   II. Series.
PS3563.C337Z74   1997   96-29644
813'.54—dc21   CIP

The paper used in this publication meets the minimum requirements of American National Standard for Information Sciences—Permanence of Paper for Printed Library Materials. ANSI Z39.48-1984. ⊚ ™

10 9 8 7 6 5 4 3 2 1

Printed in the United States of America.

Contents

Preface

In three- to seven-year intervals since the 1965 publication of his first novel, *The Orchard Keeper,* Cormac McCarthy has written novels praised for their lyric prose, innovative subject matter and characters, and dark narrative vision. The goals of this volume—only the second book-length critical study to cover McCarthy's fiction—are to introduce that fiction to new readers and, for readers more familiar with the works, to debate a series of issues raised in reviews, in Vereen Bell's *The Achievement of Cormac McCarthy* (1988), and more recently in the rapidly proliferating article-length criticism of McCarthy's fiction.

McCarthy's fiction has followed two patterns. From the beginning McCarthy has been a writer associated with regional fiction, and his career divides almost evenly into the novels based in the Appalachian South, from *The Orchard Keeper* to *Suttree* (1979), and the novels based in the Southwest, from *Blood Meridian* (1985) to *The Crossing* (1994). The second pattern is that of the maturing of McCarthy's fiction—a maturity marked by a penchant for increasingly bold experiments in form and style and by protean shifts in his subjects and narrative techniques. The first three novels—*The Orchard Keeper, Outer Dark* (1968), and *Child of God* (1973)—mix modernist and realistic narrative techniques, merging contemporary fiction with the tradition of Southern literature. In *Suttree,* his fourth and final Southern novel, he writes a highly modernist imitation of *Ulysses* that exchanges the streets of Knoxville for those of Joyce's Dublin. After a silence of six years, McCarthy's imagination abruptly shifts focus with *Blood Meridian.* Alongside the shift in regional setting to the Southwestern border formed by the geographical overlap between the United States and Mexico, the work is not a novel written under the predominantly realistic and modernist esthetic of the Southern fiction but a historical romance written under a new postmodern esthetic. Disguised as popular westerns, the first two novels of The Border Trilogy—*All the Pretty Horses* (1992) and *The Crossing*—revise the theme of the journey at the center of McCarthy's earlier fiction. While McCarthy is often a writer whose tales may not tell us what we want to hear, the pleasure of his novels lies in their imaginative and stylistic power.

The early phase of McCarthy's career is represented by his first two novels, *The Orchard Keeper* and *Outer Dark,* both of which examine the problem of writing a fiction of the New South, a region split between past and present, rural and urban, traditional and modern cultural values. In Chapter 2 I approach these novels as attempts to write a modern fiction of the hill country of twentieth-century Tennessee comparable to what the local-color realists or regionalists accomplished in the nineteenth century and to what Faulkner accomplished in his mixture of modernism and regionalism in his Yoknapatawpha fiction. In *The Orchard Keeper* McCarthy opposes the Southern present and past by means of the conflict between a series of misfits—the whiskey-runner Marion Syldar, the "hillbilly" Arthur Ownby, the fatherless John Wesley Rattner—and men such as Sheriff Gifford, who represents the dominance of law, urbanization, and modernization in the New South. In *Outer Dark,* by means of the wanderings of Culla and Rinthy Holme, McCarthy develops more fully the themes of alienation, exile, and loss— themes that were faintly introduced in *The Orchard Keeper.*

In my analysis of *Child of God* and *Suttree* in Chapter 3, I attend to the heightening alienation of McCarthy's protagonists—an alienation accompanied by a violence aimed outward by Lester Ballard and inward by Cornelius Suttree. Ballard, the necrophilic protagonist of *Child of God,* is McCarthy's first exploration of an underground-man figure and his self-imposed exile from a society external to him. Reviewers of the novel were both fascinated and appalled by McCarthy's unsentimental and unflinching portrayal of Ballard's struggle for survival against a fully imagined landscape and by his deterioration into alienation, perversion, and violence. If Ballard represents an expansion of a fictional critique of rural and historic Southern culture, this critique intensifies in the complex protagonist of *Suttree,* the highly modernist novel that is McCarthy's valediction to Southern literature. Suttree is a tour de force of psychological complexity, a modern Huck Finn living on a houseboat in Knoxville in self-imposed exile from the wealth and status of his father. Bent on self-destruction through alcohol and violence, he is nonetheless a member of an urban community and is sympathetically aware of his plight and those of others—aware in a way that Ballard can never be. Emerging from his hellish dream world at the novel's conclusion, Suttree's departure from Knoxville provisionally affirms the value of life and symbolically repudiates Southern culture and literature.

Suttree represents a crisis in McCarthy's imagination, posing the question of what comes next. McCarthy's response is *Blood Meridian; or, The*

Evening Redness in the West, a postmodern western that revises the "classic" theme of cultural conflict on the frontier. In Chapter 4 I argue that the violence of the novel's unsympathetic characters—the kid, the scalphunters, and the judge—represents the bloody historical work of nationalism during the period of Manifest Destiny. The Southwest is represented in the novel as a hostile landscape, a violent "border zone" of conflicting Anglo, Hispanic, and Native American cultures. If violence in earlier McCarthy fiction was depicted as a largely unconscious compulsion of rebellious instincts aimed against an external society, the violence in *Blood Meridian* is motivated by a complex matrix of rebellious alienation, social conflict, and a metaphysics of violence. Judge Holden, one of McCarthy's most complex and enigmatic characters, dramatizes this metaphysics, revealing warfare as the ultimate game that expresses the autonomy of the self and its will.

All the Pretty Horses and *The Crossing* achieve a more psychologically complex vision of the cultural conflict presented in *Blood Meridian.* Chapter 5 argues that both novels revise the stereotypes of the action western—the idealistic hero, the context of violence and cultural conflict, and the filmmaker John Ford's use of the harsh Southwestern landscape as poetic image—into psychologically complex postmodern fiction. John Grady Cole of *All the Pretty Horses* and Billy Parham of *The Crossing* are revisionary cowboys who flee from a modern, urbanized twentieth-century America in search of a "last, good country" to the south. Cole flees south only to be bewildered by the complexity of Mexican society, by its aristocrats who form a law unto themselves, and by the bitter nihilism of the failed revolutionary Alfonsita. If the court case that concludes the novel seems to depict Cole as representative of heroic past American values, the events on the Mexican range and in Mexican prison suggest Cole's inability to adapt to the moral complexities of love, of modern existence, or of his own life. In *The Crossing* Billy Parham brings further ambiguity to McCarthy's revisions of the western. Incorporating the quest motif of romance, this novel is structured in terms of Billy's attempts to return to its home the trapped wolf (symbol of an original Southwestern nature), to recover his father's horses, and to atone for the tragic consequences of his idealism by returning his brother's corpse to U.S. soil. In contrast to Cole, Billy ends in a conscious repudiation of himself and his idealism, recognizing its tragic consequences on his family. The novel's conclusion poses a dark anti-myth to the heroic visionary myth of West as a new start.

Chapter 6 stresses three distinctive aspects of McCarthy's fiction: the diverse and idiosyncratic styles of his narrative, the central theme of the quest undertaken through a visionary landscape, and the role of interpolated tales. I first argue that McCarthy's narrative is a mixture of diverse narrative styles and speech patterns: the lyric, the oratorical, various dialects, and the vernacular of the underclasses, each accompanied by its ideology or worldview. In his symbolic yet realistic landscapes, McCarthy alludes to the visionary merger between self and the world at the heart of American luminist painting. In the ex-priest's and blind man's tales of *The Crossing,* these landscapes and the natural world they represent are transformed into an unknowable world opposed to the self's desires. These embedded tales outline a skepticism that questions various forms of belief, yet they also, by enclosing the rhetorical structure of the narrator and hearer within the larger novel, demonstrate a paradoxical faith in narrative's power to build identity and the world itself within the borders of language.

Acknowledgments

My family, colleagues, and helpful strangers made the writing of this book possible. I should first thank my wife, Rhonda, and sons Nathan and Christopher, who cheerfully tolerated my long evening and weekend hours in exile while writing. My colleagues Nell Sullivan and Sheryl Mylan read portions of the manuscript, while Twayne's United States Authors Series editor Frank Day provided crucial feedback, support, and comments on the manuscript. Barbara Sutton's painstaking copyediting smoothed out numerous rough edges of the manuscript. Rick Wallach, McCarthy's greatest enthusiast, also provided support and contacts. I should also thank Stephen Nasser, who volunteered part of his final undergraduate spring and summer semesters tracking down reviews, and my undergraduate class in Studies in Fiction, who contributed to the development of the ideas in Chapter 4.

Other institutional and professional support deserves special mention. The writing of Chapter 6 and portions of Chapter 1 was made possible by a course release granted from the University of Houston–Downtown's Organized Research Committee and recommended by my department chair, Susan Ahern. Thanks are also due to Shirley Carter of the Knoxville *News-Sentinel* and the University Historian and University Archivist and their office staff at the University of Tennessee, Knoxville.

Finally, I gratefully acknowledge *Cañon: The Journal of the Rocky Mountains American Studies Association,* edited by Thomas W. Cutrer, for the permission to reprint in Chapter 4 sections of my article "Revisioning the Western? Three Recent Cases," originally published in the spring 1995 issue. The biography in Chapter 1 quotes a series of articles originally published in the Knoxville *News-Sentinel*; these passages are reprinted by permission of the Knoxville News-Sentinel Company.

Chronology

1968   *Outer Dark.*

1969   Awarded a Guggenheim fellowship.

1973   *Child of God.*

1976   Writes screenplay *The Gardener's Son* for PBS's Visions series.

1977   *The Gardener's Son* premieres on PBS in January; McCarthy moves to El Paso, Texas.

1978   Divorced from DeLisle.

1979   *Suttree.*

1981   Awarded a $236,000 MacArthur fellowship (the "genius grant").

1984   Ecco Press reprints McCarthy's Southern novels in paperback.

1985   *Blood Meridian; or, The Evening Redness in the West* sells only 1,500 copies.

1988   Vereen Bell's *The Achievement of Cormac McCarthy* attracts critical attention to McCarthy's novels.

1990   Inducted into the Southwest Writers Hall of Fame.

1992   *All the Pretty Horses* published, sells more than 500,000 copies in first two years of release, and wins National Book Award for fiction and the National Book Critics Circle award; Vintage Press releases *Suttree* and *Blood Meridian* in paperback.

1993   *The Orchard Keeper, Outer Dark,* and *Child of God* republished by Vintage Press.

1994   *The Crossing* and *The Stonemason.*

Chapter One

The Shape of a Career

Born in Providence, Rhode Island, on 20 July 1933, Charles Joseph McCarthy, Jr., moved in 1937 with his mother, Gladys, and older sisters, Barbara and Helen, to join Charles Joseph Senior. Since 1935 Charles Senior had been working in Knoxville as a legal clerk and attorney for the Tennessee Valley Authority. The name Cormac, the Irish version of Charles, was used inside the family to refer to both father and son. Although the son's first published writings in the University of Tennessee literary supplement, *The Phoenix,* were attributed simply to C. J. McCarthy, *The Orchard Keeper* was attributed to Cormac McCarthy.

During Cormac's childhood years in Knoxville, his father's career progressed rapidly: he was promoted to assistant general counsel in 1941 and finally to general counsel in the early 1960s.[1] Younger brothers and sisters—William, Dennis, and Mary Ellen—were born in Knoxville, while the family moved into two residences, the first on Cherokee Drive, immediately north of the Tennessee River that divides Knoxville, and the other on Sherrod Road, immediately south of the river. In 1943 the family took up residence on the extreme southeastern periphery of Knoxville in a white-frame house in a newer housing area on Martin Mill Pike, an old road wandering among wooded hills and small farms and running parallel to the road to Sevier, the county seat of old Sevier County. The boyhood home on Martin Mill Pike brought the young Cormac into direct contact with the rural Tennessee mountain areas and the mountain folk of Sevier, renamed Sevierville in Cormac's third novel, *Child of God.* Various materials of *The Orchard Keeper*—the Green Fly Inn overhanging the cliff and the boy fur trappers—are taken in part from the environs of his childhood home and his childhood hobby of trapping.[2]

No doubt the reasons for the family's choice of the home on Martin Mill Pike varied, but the location expresses the isolation of a Northeastern Irish Catholic family submerged within the South's rural and Protestant culture. Cormac would attend parochial schools, graduating from Catholic High in 1951. In the fall of 1951 he enrolled in the local campus of the University of Tennessee and is listed in the school directory as a freshman major in the College of Liberal Arts. His early academic career was indifferent at best, for in the spring of 1952 either he was asked to leave the university or he made the decision to drop out of school, perhaps to roam the country. Little is known about this period of wandering that concluded with his enlistment in the Air Force, where he served from 1953 to 1957, stationed for at least two years in Alaska. Here he began reading literature in the barracks.[3] On his release from military service, McCarthy returned to Knoxville and the University of Tennessee, enrolling under the G.I. Bill first in the College of Engineering from the 1957 to 1958 term, then majoring in business administration in his junior and senior years. He published in the school literary supplement, *The Phoenix,* two short stories, "Wake for Susan" in fall of 1959 and "A Drowning Incident" in spring of 1960. In 1960 he received his first literary award, an Ingram-Merrill Foundation grant of $125 to pursue his writing (*Volunteer Moments,* 45). In 1961 he again dropped out of school before receiving a degree. In a rare interview he admitted, "Seems I skipped around too much from one course to another."[4] From 1961 to 1964 McCarthy married Lee Holleman, a student at the University of Tennessee; had a son, Cullen; began work on what would become *The Orchard Keeper*; and left Knoxville, landing in New Orleans and in Chicago, where he worked a series of odd jobs, reportedly as an auto mechanic, and wrote on his first novel.[5] On the family's return to Sevier County, his first marriage ended, chronicled in some of the poems in Lee McCarthy's *Desire's Door,* published in 1991.[6]

The 10-year period from 1964 to 1973 suggests an ambitious, talented, and dedicated author who wrote persistently. The inauguration of McCarthy's career reads in part like the fairy tale dreamed by most aspiring writers. After finishing the manuscript of *The Orchard Keeper,* he sent the unsolicited manuscript to Random House, where it attracted the notice of Albert Erskine, Faulkner's editor. The manuscript was accepted for publication and printed in 1965 (Fields 1965). *The Orchard Keeper* received largely favorable reviews from Orville Prescott in the *New York Times,* Granville Hicks in the *Saturday Review,* and Walter Sullivan in the *Sewanee Review.* In May 1965 as a young writer of promise, McCarthy was awarded a $5,000 fellowship for travel in Europe from the American Academy of Arts and Letters. That award soon was succeeded by the prestigious William Faulkner Foundation Award for 1965 (now the PEN-Faulkner Award) and a grant in 1966 from the Rockefeller Foundation. While his first novel had not sold many copies, he had succeeded in attracting the attention of the critical establishment.

Using his travel grant to sail to Europe on the *Sylvania* in the summer of 1965, McCarthy brought with him the manuscript of *Outer Dark*.[7] On ship the first night out he met Annie DeLisle, a native of Southampton, England, who was working on the ship as a singer and dancer. A retrospective interview from DeLisle in 1990 provides a rare personal insight into an intensely private man: the two fell in love, and the tour became a whirlwind romance, with McCarthy following DeLisle, who was touring around the Mediterranean performing in shows for the English military. Nine months later the two were married in an old Norman church in Hampshire, honeymooned in Cornwall, and then set off on a European tour traveling from Paris to Geneva and around the coast of Italy back north to southern France and then to Barcelona. The newlyweds ended on the island of Ibiza, an artist's colony just off the Spanish coast, where they spent close to a year working and carousing in imitation of the expatriates after World War I (Williams 1990A, E2).[8] During McCarthy's European tour, the manuscript of *Outer Dark* was rewritten several times and sent to Random House in summer 1967. Another manuscript also was begun as early as 1966.[9]

In December 1967 McCarthy and his wife returned to America on the *Queen Elizabeth*, living in what she would call "a little pig farm" in Rockford, a small hamlet south of Knoxville. *Outer Dark* was published in 1968, again to largely favorable reviews in the *New York Times* and *Sewanee Review*. The novel also attracted the attention of Robert Coles, who wrote a particularly favorable review in the *New Yorker*. Coles's praise was balanced by a more negative review by Patrick Cruttwell in the *Washington Post Book World*. Cruttwell found the novel to be a "parody" of "very, very murky Gothic horror."[10] Few readers purchased copies of the novel. Referring to the couple's life in Rockford and later in an "upgraded barn" in Louisville, another small town in the area, DeLisle would comment that McCarthy "was such a rebel that he didn't live the same kind of life anybody on earth lived. He knew everything that there was to do in life. . . . We never had any money. We were always scrimping and scraping. He couldn't have had children, it would have driven him crazy" (Williams 1990B, E1–2). After the money ran out from a new Guggenheim fellowship, awarded in 1969, McCarthy apparently eked out a bare living on his novel advances and odd jobs to support his writing. He himself did the stonework on a new room and fireplace on the Louisville property, using bricks from James Agee's childhood home (Arnold and Luce, 6–7). Stonework of this sort would become the central theme of the play *The Stonemason* (1994).

In 1973 his third novel, *Child of God,* was published, eliciting a series of reviews that range from shocked criticism to sympathetic praise. If the shocking subject matter of Faulkner's *Sanctuary* boosted sales, these shocked reactions to McCarthy's third novel generated no more sales; in fact, none of his Southern fiction would sell more than 2,500 copies in hardcover for Random House while Ecco Press's paperback reprints of 1984 would sell only 3,000 to 5,000 copies per novel.[11] At some point in this period, McCarthy's reticence seems to have begun a transformation into a form of public withdrawal, for DeLisle notes that he would turn down offers of $2,000 and more for speaking engagements at universities—money that certainly would have seemed attractive to support his writing (Jaynes, 64).

During this period McCarthy was working on an ambitious manuscript, longer and stylistically more experimental than his first three novels; the novel would ultimately become *Suttree.* From 1974 to 1975 he became acquainted with the director Richard Pearce, who convinced McCarthy to write the screenplay *The Gardener's Son* for the Visions series on PBS. Dealing with the murder of a cotton mill owner by a poor white man during the Reconstruction in South Carolina, the film analyzes the social conditions of the South, particularly the paternalism of its new industrial oligarchy toward the impoverished working class. Starring Brad Dourif as the murderer and Jerry Hardin as the father, the film was televised in January 1977 to critical acclaim.[12]

Meanwhile, on New Year's Eve of 1976, McCarthy's personal and imaginative crisis came to a head. That evening he suddenly announced to DeLisle, "I'm leaving. I'm going." After packing his truck for a month, he took his wife to dinner, then left for the Southwest the next day (Williams 1990B, E2). In 1978 or 1979 he was divorced from DeLisle. Viewed in retrospect, McCarthy's move to the Southwest in early 1977 represents a sudden break with his past, including his family, wife, and career in Southern fiction. This wish to close out his past life emerges in the 1979 publication of *Suttree,* a novel rumored to have been begun as long as 20 years before its publication (Arnold and Luce, 8). In the conclusion of the novel, its protagonist bids good-bye to his alcoholic existence in Knoxville, thumbing a ride on the highway heading west. Suttree's impoverished lifestyle represents a symbolic break from the lifestyle and values of his well-to-do parents. To what degree the novel is autobiographical can be conjectured, not factually established. In light of Suttree's alcoholism, we do know that at some point after his move to El Paso, McCarthy abruptly stopped drinking. In a 1992 interview he would call drinking the "occupational hazard" of writing and comment that the friends still alive from the *Suttree* days "are simply those who quit drinking."[13]

Suttree again received friendly reviews, most notably Jerome Charyn's in the *New York Times Book Review.* Charyn praised the novel's "horrifying flood" of language, and Edward Rothstein in the *Washington Post* called McCarthy "some latter-day Virgil with an unabridged dictionary."[14] Ignored by the public, *Suttree* did attract the attention of Saul Bellow and the historian and novelist Shelby Foote, who for some time had followed McCarthy's career as a fellow writer from the South. Both applauded his being awarded the prestigious MacArthur fellowship for 1981. Foote commented that "I told the MacArthur people that he would be honoring them as much as they were honoring him," and Bellow, a MacArthur prize committee member, praised his "life-giving and death-dealing sentences." The $236,000 fellowship was crucial in supporting the research and writing of his next novel, *Blood Meridian,* and bankrolled his purchase of a small stone cottage in El Paso, allowing him to move from El Paso's cheap motels.[15] *Blood Meridian,* published in 1985, sold fewer than 1,500 copies as a Random House hardcover and received reviews expressing praise of the novel's language and shock at the unremitting violence. Walter Sullivan's despairing review is typical, for on the one hand he values McCarthy as "the best writer we have" in the use of detail, dialogue, and setting and depiction of life while on the other he dismisses the novel as a "single-minded celebration of rapine and slaughter, relieved only by an occasional fainthearted thrust at philosophy."[16]

McCarthy's life of anonymity continued after the publication of *Blood Meridian.* Little is known of the period between 1985 and 1992, other than that McCarthy lived a quiet existence in El Paso, writing regularly in the mornings, researching the Southwest on several trips, collecting rare books, and playing golf and pool.[17] Several accidents conspired to transform the author not only into a public figure but also into the position of one of the United States' best-selling literary authors. With the retirement of Albert Erskine, his editor at Random House, McCarthy acquired a literary agent, Amanda Urban, and shifted publishers to Alfred A. Knopf, the prestigious printing arm of Random House. A new agent, a shift in subject matter to the western, the faint trappings of a romantic plot, a more sympathetic hero, and perhaps most crucially the new publisher's enthusiasm to vigorously promote the new novel, *All the Pretty Horses*—perhaps all these factors combined in 1992 to create a seemingly overnight literary sensation.

The first installment of a proposed series entitled The Border Trilogy, *All the Pretty Horses* rapidly sold 180,000 copies in hardcover and 300,000 in paperback over a two-year period through 1994 and received a six-figure advance from director Mike Nichols for movie rights (Jaynes, 54). Reviews of the novel were almost universally positive, although as Edwin Arnold and Dianne Luce note, in its reviews the book "received less genuine consideration than most of McCarthy's earlier novels" (Arnold and Luce, 11). The novel also won the National Book Award for fiction and the National Book Critics Circle award. Almost simultaneously with *Pretty Horses,* Vintage (another publishing arm of Random House) reprinted *Suttree* and *Blood Meridian* in paperback editions. Capitalizing on the sales momentum of the new hardcover sensation and the respectable sales of these reprints, Vintage quickly released paperback reprints of the other novels in early 1993. In the meantime, Vereen Bell's *The Achievement of Cormac McCarthy* (1988) focused the attention of literary critics on McCarthy's fiction, resulting in the first McCarthy conference, sponsored by Bellarmine College in 1993. McCarthy's sequel to *Pretty Horses, The Crossing,* was published in 1994, with a hardcover first printing of 200,000 copies and largely positive reviews, capped off by Robert Hass's judgment of the novel "as a miracle in prose" in the *New York Times Book Review.*

If his westerns are esteemed by readers and critics alike, McCarthy has not become a familiar public personality. A reclusive person, McCarthy has adamantly protected his privacy since the late 1960s, granting only one significant interview from the 1970s to the 1990s. In 1990, under consideration for induction into the Southwest Writers Hall of Fame in El Paso, he agreed to the award on the condition that he not appear in person or submit to photographs.[18] Winning the National Book Award in 1992 for *All the Pretty Horses,* McCarthy refused to attend the banquet, allowing his publisher, Sonny Mehta of Alfred A. Knopf, to accept the award for him. With rare exceptions Cormac McCarthy has preferred to let his fiction, and only his fiction, speak.

Chapter Two

New Beginnings for Southern Fiction: *The Orchard Keeper* and *Outer Dark*

From his first novel, *The Orchard Keeper* (1965), to his fourth, *Suttree* (1979), Cormac McCarthy's early fiction was widely identified by reviewers as "new" Southern literature. By this term, reviewers and critics referred not merely to a literature written by a Southerner—or to a literature set in the South, populated by Southern characters, and embedded in Southern contemporary or historical culture. The term was employed more narrowly by such critics as Louis Rubin and Lewis Simpson to refer to a literature that acknowledges—and in some cases critiques—the myth of Southern exceptionalism: that is, the South's regional, cultural, historical, and economic differences from mainstream American culture. In this chapter and the next I argue for a view of McCarthy's early fiction that acknowledges its debt to twentieth-century Southern literature but sees it as reconstructing (1) that literature's assumptions about Southern culture, (2) the literary and cultural construct termed "the South" through an emphasis on the peculiar divergences of the Appalachian South from the larger region, and (3) the narrative of Southern fiction through a sensibility, style, and structure characteristic of modernism. Thus McCarthy's early fiction may be usefully regarded as a "Southern" fiction but also as an "Appalachian" or as a "modern" fiction. And this tendency of his fiction to be positioned on and to investigate overlapping borders or peripheries—whether regional, cultural, or historical—might be identified as one of its distinctive traits.

McCarthy's Contributions toward a Modern Southern Literature

Despite their disagreement on the specific merits of his early fiction, McCarthy's reviewers were virtually unanimous in assessing him as an

important new voice and a major new talent in Southern literature. Two
reviews of McCarthy's *The Orchard Keeper* might be regarded as representative of the two main viewpoints toward his early fiction. In a *New York
Times* review of 12 May 1965, Orville Prescott praises the novel's pas-
toralism as representative of a modern retreat from industrialization to
the "folkways" of "rural America."[1] Criticizing the style as flawed by
McCarthy's "humble and excessive admiration" of the flaws of
Faulkner's style, Prescott nonetheless admits the "torrential power" of
this first novel and singles out for praise its "flashing visual impact," its
"brief dramatic scenes," and its method of achieving characterization
primarily through action. Somewhat contradictorily, Prescott criticizes
the narrative as "disconnected" and lacking in motivation—characteristics largely produced by the dramatic action that he earlier praised
(Prescott, 45–46).

In a second appraisal published in the *Sewanee Review,* Walter Sullivan
displays the close, long, and ambivalent interest he would show in all
McCarthy's early fiction. Sullivan regards McCarthy's first published
work as proof that "the Southern renaissance. . . is still alive."[2] Locating
the novel squarely "in the middle of the agrarian influence," praising the
prose as "magnificent, full of energy and sharp detail," Sullivan concludes, "McCarthy is like nobody so much as he is like all the writers
who have gone before him and has sense enough to see in the land a
source of human salvation" (Sullivan 1965, 721). Sullivan, as he himself
recognized in a later analysis of McCarthy's *Child of God,* misreads as
"agrarian" the text's representation of the relation between man and
nature and errs in associating the distinctive features of the tradition of
the Southern renaissance with McCarthy. But both reviewers mark a
beginning point for the reception of McCarthy's early fiction. Both con-
cur that the prose style, despite its faults, is innovative and energetic;
that the novel's dramatic emphasis on action is deceptive, suggesting
further psychological depths to the characters; that the novel relates
character and society to the natural setting or landscape; and that the
first novel must be judged in light of earlier Southern literature.

Sullivan's association of *The Orchard Keeper* with the term "Southern
renaissance" is a crucial point, for by it he inserts the novel within a
series of literary works that constitute a cultural and literary tradition
viewed by Sullivan and other Southern critics to be at a critical stage, in
danger of dying but with possibilities for revival. In "The Profession of
Letters in the South" (1935), an essay that served as a foundation for the
academic criticism of Southern literature, Allen Tate argued that the

flowering of Southern literary culture after World War I was "temporary," existing only at the moment of crisis when Southern culture was poised at the "crossing of the ways" between modernity and consciousness of its former cultural difference.[3] A decade later in "The New Provincialism," an essay revising his earlier remarks, Tate had defined the famous Southern "renascence"—the literary awakening that was begun by the Agrarians and led to literary prominence by Faulkner—as a brief "backwards glance" at Southern culture and history. Thematically, Tate argued, this was "a literature conscious of the past in the present" (Tate, 545).

Periodical reviewers such as Walter Sullivan of the *Sewanee Review* and academic critics of Southern literature—most prominently Cleanth Brooks, Louis Rubin, and Lewis Simpson—would define three separate generations of twentieth-century Southern literature, linking Faulkner and then the novelists who succeed him back to the "Fugitives" of Vanderbilt University in the late 1910s to the middle of the 1920s. The most influential writers who originally published in the literary journal *Fugitive* were the poet-critics John Crowe Ransom, Allen Tate, and Donald Davidson. After the dissolution of the *Fugitive,* published between 1922 and 1925, these writers, along with the generation-and-a-half-younger novelist and poet Robert Penn Warren, would form the core of the 12 "Agrarian" writers whose essays are collected in the controversial *I'll Take My Stand* (1930).[4] The Agrarians combined a sense of their own difference from the Southern past in the form of literary modernism with a stance of regional and conservative defiance of modernism (Rubin 1978, 187–97). The essays in *I'll Take My Stand* take aim at various aspects taken to be characteristic of modernism, particularly industrialism's economic bases in manufacturing and consumerism and the critique of Southern segregation and religious fundamentalism.[5] The essays collected in the volume launched, renewed, or furthered the literary careers of the former Fugitives: Tate contributed an article on Southern religion that could be construed as much as a critique as a defense (155–75); Ransom witheringly critiqued the ideology of "Progress" associated in his mind with modern manufacturing, technology, and scientific materialism (1–27); and Warren, in a most inauspicious essay titled "The Briar Patch," defended segregation with remarks he later would come to regret and publicly repudiate in *Segregation* (246–64).

The second generation of twentieth-century Southern writers, crucially important to McCarthy's early fiction, might be represented by the increasingly modernist tendencies of Tate and Ransom's verse, particularly the verse after the Fugitive period. But this second generation takes sharp definition in William Faulkner's unique version of modern fiction—a fiction in which, after an abortive beginning in modernist verse, he reinterprets the patriarchal narrative of Southern history as tragedy. The final generation of Southern writers before McCarthy might be represented by the satiric realism of Flannery O'Connor, the more traditional realism of Eudora Welty, and the heroic myth of the modern defiance of the romanticized past in Robert Penn Warren.

But we can mark a dramatic change between the literary and critical reception of the first two generations of writers and the newer, contemporary writers. Once a canon of Southern literature was established, with Faulkner as leading novelist and Tate as leading poet (despite Tate's later preferred affiliation with the "moderns" rather than with the "Southern" writers), academic critics and periodical reviewers tended to assess contemporary Southern writers largely by reference to Faulkner, Tate, and the Agrarians. Acknowledging Faulkner's world preeminence as novelist and operating under Tate's thesis that the renaissance could exist only while stationed historically and literally between an earlier autonomously traditional Southern culture and a newly emergent modernism, such assessments almost invariably discredited newer writers. If the poetry of Tate, along with the fiction of Faulkner and Warren, takes up the theme of a distinctive agrarian Southern culture disappearing into modern culture and regrets that disappearance, O'Connor's and Welty's works assume the disappearance of the antebellum Southern culture and are concerned more with a realistic description—with an accompanying satiric perspective—of contemporary small-town or rural Southern culture of the mid-twentieth century. In part because of their acceptance of the disappearance of the agrarian South, the third generation of Southern novelists—Flannery O'Connor, Robert Penn Warren, and Eudora Welty—were compared invidiously to Faulkner. Thus in two book-length studies of Southern fiction, Walter Sullivan uses the fiction of Walker Percy and Cormac McCarthy to define and denounce the new generation of writers who write as contemporary writers (or as "Gnostics" or "existentialists") and represent the death of the Southern renaissance and its mode of writing.[6]

We now recognize that Tate and later critics of Southern literature overstated the unique qualities of the Southern writer's celebrated historical identity crisis from 1916 to the late 1930s.[7] Nonetheless, Tate's insight that Southern literature expressed a historical tension or identity crisis, split between a modern and a traditional Southern culture, may be usefully applied to all of McCarthy's first four novels, grounded as they are in the Tennessee countryside, culture, dialect, folkways, and characters. But the specific historical crisis that forms and informs McCarthy's fiction is different from that of his predecessors in twentieth-century Southern literature. Rather than investigating Southern history to find cultural patterns, an ideology, a system of moral values, or an agrarian lifestyle that might be continued into the present, McCarthy's early fiction reconstructs prior Southern writing in part by pointing to radical discontinuities between the present and the Southern past—discontinuities that, furthermore, could be traced within Southern culture and its history. For the moment I will trace this sense of historical discontinuity in McCarthy's fiction. Later I will demonstrate how his early novels redefine our understanding of the term "Southern" by expanding its range to include a collection of alternate lifestyles, regions, and values hitherto excluded.

The Orchard Keeper: Three Southerners' Search for Identity

Although McCarthy's first two novels, *The Orchard Keeper* and *Outer Dark,* do raise the question of the relation between the Southern past and present—undoubtedly the central theme of Faulkner's fiction and Southern fiction as a whole—both point more to an ironic disjunction rather than a tragic continuity between past and present. Of the two works, *The Orchard Keeper,* as the novel set in the contemporary South (at least of the generation immediately preceding that of the novel's publication), more fully critiques the Agrarians' and Faulkner's assumption of an essential or meaningful continuity between Southern past and present. At the opening of the novel Red Branch, a formerly insular Tennessee hamlet located on the western edge of the mountains directly east of Knoxville, has been newly connected by means of a paved highway to Knoxville and the other urban metropolitan areas of the South.[8] The novel's three main characters—the ancient hillbilly Arthur Ownby, the whiskey-runner Marion Syldar, and the young orphaned John Wesley Rattner—represent a local version of traditional Southern culture newly transformed into the unconventional by means of Red Branch's new highway connections to the urbanized South—connections stretching between Knoxville and Atlanta.

The twin motifs of connection and disconnection constitute the core of the novel. The three main characters are not connected genealogically through any familial relation but through a set of chance encounters that form the novel's unique plotting. The relationship between Ownby, Syldar, and young Rattner thus is imagined within the novel as metonymic, by contiguity in space or time, rather than through the more metaphoric identity of father and son, the metaphor by which Southern fiction usually asserts historical and social relationships. Similarly, the novel is constructed of small, disconnected scenes that sketch seemingly unrelated settings and events in the lives of disparate characters. Yet by the end of the novel Ownby, Rattner, and Syldar's disparate lives are seen to interconnect historically and psychologically. The novel's darkness derives not merely from the ending imprisonment of Syldar and Ownby but primarily from the dramatic irony that the main characters always remain unaware of their more fundamental connections. By its emphasis on such disconnections and metonymic connections, McCarthy's fiction reconstructs both modernism and Southern literature in an attempt to achieve in style, sensibility, and theme what might be termed a contemporary fiction of the South. If Quentin Compson and Ike McCaslin may be taken as Faulkner's most fully realized depictions of the "modern" Southerner—men whose tragic identity is rooted in a heroic myth of a Southern past that they can neither believe nor quite discard—then in *The Orchard Keeper* John Wesley Rattner represents the contemporary or postmodern Southerner. By the novel's end Rattner has become a figure for the Southerner-as-exile, uprooted and cut off from his genealogical past through the mysterious death of a father he has never known and trapped within a present with which he has no relation.

Representative of the earliest generation of Southerners is the novel's title character, Arthur Ownby, a man who "keeps" the dying apple orchard by shooting holes in the government tanks that disturb its isolation (*OK*, 51, 58, 93, 97) and who "keeps" sacrosanct the secret burial place of an unnamed corpse by yearly cutting fresh branches to place over the decaying remains (*OK*, 45–46, 52, 90, 138–39). While in the course of the narrative we learn a great deal about Arthur's past, we are supplied with no direct rationale for his taking on the responsibility for the preservation of the orchard or its corpse. Born before the Civil War, he bears no allegiance to or fondness for the antebellum South (*OK*, 145). He is a failure at farming and a cuckold whose memories obsessively return to his brief marriage—a marriage that concluded with his wife's abandonment of him for a roving salesman, or drummer (*OK*, 154–55). Depicted primarily through his archaic lifestyle of living off the land rather than by working in a trade or farming, Ownby resembles more Wordsworth's leech gatherer or a countercultural rebel from the 1960s than the patriarchal warriors and slave owners memorialized by Faulkner and the Agrarians. Ownby has no way of knowing the corpse he protects was Kenneth Rattner, the father of a young boy he meets on a local path and to whom he plays the avuncular role of "Uncle Ather."

The representative second-generation Southerner of the novel is Marion Syldar who, earlier during the depression along with millions of other natives of the region, had escaped the Appalachian hills to the Northern factories. On his return home to Red Branch, Syldar gains his living as a whiskey-runner, alienated from both the agrarian and mercantile Southern economy and unable to adopt Ownby's impoverished subsistence lifestyle. If Ownby is unaware that Marion Syldar is the killer of the corpse Ownby guards, he is aware that Syldar smuggles whiskey. While in bed with his wife, at the end of the third of the novel's four sections, Syldar has a brief insight linking Ownby with his own imminent imprisonment: "Suddenly he had a bile-sharp foretaste of disaster. *Why was that old man shooting holes in the government tank on the mountain?*" (*OK,* 168). Ironically, Ownby guards the corpse against violation by the government's tank partly as a ritual of propitiation of the dead man's spirit, which he believes howls at night; partly to preserve himself against a false accusation as murderer; and partly in the deluded belief that after seven years the murderer is free from prosecution for the murder of the corpse (*OK,* 228). Despite Syldar's presentiments of a disastrous connection between the two, Ownby is not responsible for Syldar's imprisonment, nor is Ownby incarcerated for Rattner's murder. Instead, both imprisonments are linked only by the connecting ground of Mr. Eller's store, for Ownby is apprehended there after trading herbs with Eller, who also recently has sold Syldar the water-contaminated gasoline that causes his car to stall on the Knoxville River bridge, resulting in his arrest for boot-legging the whiskey found in his car.

The novel's third-generation Southerner—the young, orphaned John Wesley Rattner—is perhaps the most powerful representation of the theme of disconnection in McCarthy's reconstructed contemporary fiction. History, acting through Marion Syldar's killing of Kenneth Rattner, has cut off John Wesley from his father. The neglected son of a now-dead psychopathic father and an enthusiastically religious mother (O'Connor's satires of female Protestant Southern religiosity come to mind), John Wesley is emblematic of the cultural disconnection of the contemporary Southerner. Rattner is connected to the community only tenuously through his friendship with Syldar and Ownby. Left unprotected from Sheriff Gifford by the two men's incarceration and unable to sustain himself economically through the trapping of animals and sale of their hides, Rattner flees the mountains of Red Branch to the larger America—a flight that is referred to elusively (*OK,* 233–34), never directly described, occurring only between the lines in the novel's concluding sections. Although the main action of the novel concludes with Rattner's flight and the disinterment of his father's corpse (*OK,* 234–42), in the novel's final four pages we discover a now-mature Rattner who has suddenly reappeared in Red Branch to visit his mother's grave. Between the penultimate and final chapters lies the blank of time, a silent gap of history that has separated the once-callow country youth from the almost urbane adult.

All three of *The Orchard Keeper*'s main characters are linked by their common exile from the values and lifestyles of a newly dominant urbanized South—values represented in the novel by the modernism of the state highway; by government officers such as Sheriff Gifford, Constable Legwater, and state welfare officials; and by governmental institutions such as the state bounty office (paying bounties for hawks and other wildlife), the Brushy state penitentiary, and the county tanks that Ownby resents as intrusions on the orchard and the corpse he guards there. Through the figure of John Wesley Rattner we see that the past, in the form of either Ownby or Rattner's father, is unrecoverable and unrepeatable within the present. At the novel's conclusion, Rattner seems to be offered a symbolic choice between a past that takes the form of his mother's tombstone and an alluring future in the shape of the woman in the automobile. But this choice is a momentary illusion, only apparently proffered him. Rattner can make no such choice; he merely waves at the woman, who disappears into his past with her husband, leaving Rattner alone in his present (*OK,* 245–46).

If *The Orchard Keeper* often seems to share the repudiation of "progressivism" in Faulkner's Snopeses or in the Agrarians' quest to preserve an already-outmoded agrarian economic base, the novel also rejects the Southern past. That past is represented most clearly in the images of three graves: the tombstone of Rattner's mother, his father's rotting then cremated corpse, and Ownby's living interment in an asylum. The attempt to perpetuate the past by reliving history is absurd, as John Wesley recognizes by leaving Red Branch. Rattner's recognition is dramatically represented within the novel in a scene immediately before his escape—the scene in which he attempts to recover the dead hawk he has sold earlier to the county government for bounty. Naively assuming both that the past can be preserved and that the value of hawks is fixed by a "use commensurate with a dollar other than the fact of their demise," Rattner asks, "What all do you do with em?" (*OK,* 233). The clerk replies, "Burn em in the furnace I would reckon. . . . They sure cain't keep em around here. They might get a little strong after a while, mightn't they?" (*OK,* 233) At first questioning her answer— "They burn em?"—Rattner's speech moves to a recognition of the absurdity of the modern in the declarative "And thow people in jail and beat up on em. . . . And old men in the crazy house" (*OK,* 233). Failing to repurchase his hawk, the young Rattner recognizes his inability both to reenact Ownby's life through trapping wild animals and to resist the power of the "they"—an impotence shared by Ownby and Syldar. Rattner's final response is to "retreat" into the present's irrationality by joining the "they" whose insanity he has just critiqued; hence he flees from Red Branch. This retreat is the temporal and spatial opposite of Ownby's earlier failed attempt to escape imprisonment by retreating into the wilderness of the "Harrykin" or Smoky Mountains that represent nature and the past—a failure punished by Ownby's incarceration in the asylum.

If Rattner's failure to repurchase the hawk is insufficient to underline the novel's acceptance of the absurdity of the contemporary South, the scene should be read alongside the next section's description of Constable Legwater's mad attempt to dig up Kenneth Rattner's burnt corpse in order to recover and sell a platinum plate "buried" in Rattner's skull to heal a war wound. As even Gifford recognizes, Legwater is naively attempting to recover a past that has never existed: "He wadn't no war hero. It ain't for sure it was even him, but if it was he never had no—no thing in his head" (*OK,* 240). Legwater's past is built on a naive acceptance of Mrs. Rattner's delusions about her husband's heroism, a naive belief that even Rattner's own son has repudiated. John Wesley's escape is similarly interpreted by Mrs. Rattner as a search for vengeance against his father's killer. This scene's further satiric possibilities emerge only if it is read in juxtaposition to the embarrassment of Faulkner's biographers over the novelist's "fictions" about his supposed participation in World War I.[9] If the connection between Kenneth Rattner's fictive heroism and Faulkner's fictional war heroism seems too tenuous, Legwater's digging clearly revises the final story line of *The Hamlet,* in which the sewing-machine salesman Ratliffe is duped into buying a Frenchman's worthless property by Flem Snopes's nocturnal digging and seeding of silver coins on the grounds. In Gifford's disdain for Legwater, McCarthy's narrator displays full awareness of the absurdity of the attempt to recover accurately even the most recent past within a narrative, whether fictional or historical, that is based on lies.

Outer Dark: Parodic Families

Despite his first novel's satiric repudiation of history, McCarthy's second novel, *Outer Dark,* represents a more serious attempt to narrate the past, whose sole representative in *The Orchard Keeper* is Arthur Ownby. Reminiscent of and in many respects an extended revision of the fictional possibilities of Ownby's retreat into the Harrykin wilderness, *Outer Dark* also retreats into a historically remote rural Tennessee. Its landscape is a wilderness largely untouched by humanity or the forces of modernization. In the isolation of the wilderness surrounding the Chicken River, the tenuous family bonds between Culla and Rinthy Holme disintegrate at the novel's opening. It is not their incest that drives the brother and sister apart but Culla's inability to recognize his own sin in the form of his child, whom he abandons the day of its birth deep within the wilderness surrounding their isolated cabin. This abandonment impels first Rinthy to travel out from her home in search of her child taken by a peddler, then Culla to search for his sister, though only Rinthy will remain true to the original goal that motivates their separate errands into the Tennessee wilderness.

As in McCarthy's first novel, most of *Outer Dark* shows its characters in social isolation, steadily moving away from the urban South to its border or periphery, as Culla, Holme, and the tinker travel separately across a largely uninhabited Tennessee wilderness. As a result of their wandering, of course, Culla and Rinthy become isolated from the community. At several points later in the novel, two families hold out the hope of reintegrating Rinthy within the larger community. One family welcomes her in their home, offers her a bed whose headboard faces next to that of the bed of the husband and wife, and gives her a ride to town.[10] Rinthy, however, in order to wander in search of the tinker and her child, refuses their hospitality and the offer of marriage made by their comically lecherous son. Later a farmer and his wife seem to rescue Rinthy at her neediest point, but a meal that begins as a symbolic portrayal of harmonious familial hospitality soon disintegrates into an impassioned quarrel, with the wife hurling cooking implements at the husband, who in turn destroys his wife's newly churned butter (*OK,* 106–108).

A further ironic exception to the isolation of Culla, Rinthy, and the tinker is the gang of outlaws, depicted as an almost archetypal family, with its members bound together tightly. The bearded outlaw functions as father and leader, Harmon as oldest son, and the nameless mentally retarded mute as dependent baby. In the early scene when the band first encounters Culla, the bearded outlaw enacts the role of father and host, genially inviting Culla to share their fire, offering chunks of a burned and suspiciously "nameless" meat, then relieving him of his boots, to provide for the footwear "needs" of the bearded outlaw and his dependents (*OK,* 171–72). Given Culla's attempt to abandon his son, the outlaw's explanation for his theft functions as a moral indictment of his auditor: "I believe in takin care of my own" (*OK,* 181). In light of the outlaw's frequent murders, "takin care" takes on an eerie double meaning. Furthermore, only we and the narrative voice are aware that Culla earlier had stolen these same boots from a squire who was killed the next morning by the outlaws after he went in search of Culla. In the novel's climactic scene, the bearded leader will enact another ghastly parody of paternalism. As a patriarchal father, "providing" for the infantile needs of the mute and punishing Culla for his incest, the bearded outlaw slashes the throat of Culla's own child and offers up its blood to slake the mute's depraved thirst. As both meal and a sacrificial offering, Culla's child thus suffers the punishment for Culla and Rinthy's incest. Furthermore, the outlaw's murder of Culla's child actively achieves the death that Culla himself has sought near the novel's opening when he abandons the child in the woods.

Culla, the bearded outlaw, and the tinker—the three primary male characters of *Outer Dark*—act as paternalistic doubles of one another. The outlaw is representative of patriarchal judge and providing father, Culla is an emblem of the absent or denying father, and the tinker acts as a substitute father who finds and provides for the "chap" by furnishing it with a nursemaid, a substitute mother. When considered as a meditation on the cultural role of fatherhood, *Outer Dark* abundantly supplies paternal replacements, however unsatisfactory, for the missing father Kenneth Rattner in *The Orchard Keeper.* The fathers of the novel also insert McCarthy's early fiction into a genealogy of the imagination in Southern fiction—a genealogy that points our attention back to Faulkner's fiction.

Faulkner's Influence on
The Orchard Keeper and *Outer Dark*

McCarthy's first two novels acknowledge the inevitability of Faulkner's influence with an openness and detachment unavailable to those novelists such as Flannery O'Connor who immediately succeed Faulkner. Many striking qualities of *The Orchard Keeper* and *Outer Dark*—an obsession with violence, an exploration of often-perverse sexuality, an intimate knowledge of the complexities of class relations in the South, the sprawling lyrical style, and the inventiveness of imagery in the prose—seem to imitate or allude directly to Faulkner's fiction. McCarthy's early fiction also appears to take up Faulkner's exploration of Southern culture through the image of the patriarchal family.

In their studies of Faulkner's fiction, John Irwin and Eric Sundquist demonstrate how Faulkner's characters and plots function as adaptations of the structures within Freud's family romance or Oedipal complex.[11] Typically, a contemporary Southerner fulfills the function of son—as do Ike McCaslin, Colonel Sartoris Snopes, and Quentin Compson—with a conflicted relation of rebellion and obedience to a patriarchal father or grandfather such as Carothers McCaslin, Abner Snopes, Mr. Compson, or Thomas Sutpen, Compson's more satisfactory replacement as father figure (Irwin, 72). To Irwin and Sundquist, Faulkner's fiction often takes the classic Oedipal form of a complex of relations between grandfather, father, and son or takes the form of forbidden sexual relations between the races as a metaphoric representation of the slave system and the other racial sins of the Southern past. In *Doubling and Incest/Repetition and Revenge,* Irwin argues that "for Faulkner, doubling and incest are both images of the self-enclosed—the inability of the ego to break out of the circle of the self and of the individual to break out of the ring of the family—and as such, both appear in his novels as symbols of the state of the South after the Civil War, symbols of a region turned in upon itself" (Irwin, 59).

***Outer Dark:* Alienation and Isolation, the Exile and the Outcast.**   At first glance, Irwin's analysis of Faulkner would seem directly applicable to the prominent theme of fatherhood in McCarthy's early fiction. Thus at the beginning of *Outer Dark* the birth of Culla and Rinthy's child, the result of their incest, appears to closely reiterate Faulkner's use of incest in *The Sound and the Fury* as a device for the psychological exploration of Cassie and Quentin Compson. Through

Quentin's neurosis and suicide, Faulkner suggests the neurosis of the modern South. The wanderings of Culla and Rinthy Holme throughout *Outer Dark* are prompted by their initial incest and by Culla's attempt to deal with guilt by abandoning the child—a form of denial of the sin of his forbidden sexual attraction toward his sister. In fact, the tinker finds the child only because his suspicions are raised, first by Culla's repudiation of the pornographic drawings offered him, then by Culla's almost hysterical insistence that the tinker immediately depart the cabin grounds. Culla and Rinthy's lonely and isolated wandering throughout the remainder of the novel represents two opposing forms of alienation: alienation created by Culla's repression of his sin and guilt and by Rinthy's acceptance of hers.

The isolation of Culla and Rinthy is mirrored in the larger, more self-aware form of alienation adopted by the tinker, another of the novel's social exiles. Selling goods derided as cheap by storekeepers and putative clients such as Culla, the tinker experiences himself as an existential, rebellious "outcast." The difference is that the tinker repudiates the self-imposed or introjected guilt that accompanies Rinthy and Culla's isolation and alienation; he externalizes his guilt, blaming society for it and regarding himself as innocent victim. When Rinthy finally locates the tinker, offering to pay for her child, the tinker reveals that he has stolen the child as a punishment—a "repayment"—to society for treating him as an outcast:

> I give a lifetime wanderin in a country where I was despised. Can you give that? I give forty years strapped in front of a cart like a mule till I couldn't stand straight to be hanged. I've not got soul one in this world save a old halfcrazy sister that nobody never would have like they never would have me. I been rocked and shot at and whipped and kicked and dogbit from one end of this state to the other and you cain't pay that back. You ain't got nothin to pay it with. Them accounts is in blood and they ain't nothin in this world to pay em out with. (*OD*, 192–93)

Matthew 23:13, the biblical verse to which the title of the novel alludes, supplies a context by which to apply the title *Outer Dark* to the tinker and to the novel's main characters. The verse itself functions as an ending gloss to the enigmatic parable of the wedding of the king's son (Matthew 22:1–14)—a wedding used by Christ to emblematically contrast the joys of the kingdom of heaven to the despair of those outside that kingdom. While all the wedding guests—good and evil—appear well-dressed at the celebration of the marriage of the king's son, one guest appears "not dressed in wedding clothes" (Matthew 22:11). The king's punishment is that the man is to be bound "hand and foot, and cast into the outer darkness; in that place there shall be weeping and gnashing of teeth. For many are called, but few are chosen" (Matthew 22:13-14).

The verse has enigmatic application to much of the novel's ostensibly realistic details and poetic images. If in the parable the wedding guest's lack of respect is symbolically represented in his clothes, throughout the novel the raggedness of the clothing of Culla, Rinthy, and the tinker is continually reinforced in descriptive details. Near the novel's opening, Culla dreams of himself as part of a "beggared" multitude dressed in "rags," all asking a prophet for clemency; this passage segues into the description of the arriving tinker, dressed in "one ragged blue coat" (*OD*, 5–6). Immediately after their first murder, the outlaws dig up coffins to rob corpses for their clothes; entering a town, Culla encounters the coffins on display, one trailing "in stained pennants some rags of leached and tattered and absolutely colorless satin" (*OD*, 86). As we read the novel, the outlaws continually exchange clothes with those whom they murder (*OD*, 95, 170).

The biblical verse's description of the guest's punishment—to be cast in "outer darkness"—also reinforces the almost countless images of darkness that pervade the novel's imagery. In the novel's first four pages, the initial image is of the "shadow" (repeated three times in the first sentence alone) of the outlaws, who reach the river precisely at the point of "full dark" (*OD*, 3). The first sentence of the novel's next section begins with Culla's dream, from which he awakes in "quiet darkness," awaked by Rinthy "from dark to dark . . . under a black sun and into a night more dolorous." The events within the dream occur at the "cusp of eclipse," with the sun first about to "darken," then "blacken." Then, we are told, "the sun buckled and dark fell like a shout," never to "return" (*OD*, 5–6). The novel's two-word title, *Outer Dark*, is thus emblematic of the psychological alienation of Culla, Rinthy, the tinker, and the outlaws, beginning at the novel's opening and extending to the novel's end.

Fatherhood and the Father.   Yet the weak metaphoric fathers in *Outer Dark*—split into the diverse forms of Culla, the bearded outlaw, and the tinker—suggest that in McCarthy's early fiction Faulkner's Southern patriarchy has largely disappeared, not only from the sight of

McCarthy's protagonists but from the world of the fiction. McCarthy's protagonists may be sons, but they are largely depicted as autonomous—the sons of dead or absent fathers, or in Culla's case, a father who repudiates his own fatherhood. Kenneth Rattner in *The Orchard Keeper,* the father of John Wesley, has the most central role of all fathers in McCarthy's fiction, but even he is relegated to the opening chapter and one more brief appearance before the scene of his death. The two main characters of *Outer Dark,* Culla and Rinthy Holme, not only seem to lack parents but never seem to refer to or even remember them. Lester Ballard, the protagonist of *Child of God,* is the son of a suicide, with no family save that inscribed in the title, while in *Suttree* the title character repudiates and has been repudiated by his father. The father of the kid of *Blood Meridian* dies on the second page of the novel, and in *The Crossing* Billy Parham's father is murdered early in the novel, before Billy's return from his first journey into Mexico. *All the Pretty Horses* opens with the divorce of John Grady Cole's parents and his disinheritance, through his mother's sale of his grandfather's ranch, while his father is dying, either of lung cancer or of respiratory illness contracted in a wartime prison camp. From the early Southern novels to those set in the Southwest, McCarthy's fiction enacts the death, absence, or denial of the father.

McCarthy largely abandons the structuring metaphors of the family romance and miscegenation by which Faulkner's fiction had defined the South and its past. The contrast between McCarthy's first two novels, *The Orchard Keeper* and *Outer Dark,* and Faulkner's corpus reveals how McCarthy's early fiction reconstructs Southern literature and culture. Faulkner's imaginative achievements in *Absalom, Absalom!, Go Down, Moses,* and *The Hamlet* confront representatives of a New South— Quentin Compson, Ike McCaslin, Ratliffe—with the patriarchal cultural achievements and the sins of slavery, incest, and miscegenation of the Old South. Like the Agrarians at the beginning of the twentieth century in *I'll Take My Stand,* Faulkner's fiction defined the South as an agrarian society whose roots could be found in the economic, social, and religious systems of antebellum chattel slavery. In Faulkner, the archetypal Southerner for the antebellum period was the Cotton Belt planter; for the modern period, the archetypal Southerner was the aristocratic landowner who rents his inherited patrimony to tenant farmers during and following the period of Reconstruction.

Faulkner's fiction maps historically the record and influence of this agrarian culture of the Southern flatlands in *The Bear* and *Absalom, Absa-*

lom!, tracing it from its antebellum height, through its collapse after the Civil War, and to its reconstitution into the hierarchical system of share-cropping agriculture described in "Barn Burning" and the early sections of *The Hamlet*. Ike McCaslin's repudiation of his patrimony rejects this sharecropping system because of its antebellum roots in the chattel slav-ery of the plantation. The remainder of the Snopes trilogy, tracing the histories of the Snopes fathers, Abner and Flem, and their children, completes Faulkner's depiction of the emergence and dominance of an urban New South. In these novels, through Flem Snopes's move to town and new position as banker, Faulkner chronicles the dominance of the early twentieth-century small trading towns and mercantile classes (Flem) who eventually replace the agrarian system of sharecropping (Abner and his landlords).

In contrast to McCarthy's other fiction, *Outer Dark* seems a crucial exception, containing in Culla the only extended characterization of a Faulknerian father in McCarthy's fiction. Nevertheless, as we have seen, at the novel's beginning and end, Culla paradoxically defines his own fatherhood when he denies his bastard child and repudiates his own sta-tus as father. At this point, considering the implications of another pos-sible biblical allusion in the novel's title helps us explicate Culla's denial. While light and dark imagery pervades both New and Old Testaments, no book is so replete with the imagery as the First Epistle of John, the epistle whose main theme, not coincidentally, is to explicate the rela-tionship between God and believer as that of father and child. The first two chapters in particular are obsessed with distinguishing the true light or knowledge from the false light or darkness that blinds—a crucial image, given the novel's concluding trope of Culla returning from a swamp that "dead-ends" into a swamp—"a faintly smoking garden of the dead"—only to meet a "blind man" whom he watches "out of sight," wondering why someone has not warned him away (*OD*, 242). That Culla says nothing is indicative of his own inner darkness.

More directly relevant to Culla's denial of his own fatherhood is I John 2:23: "Whoever denies the Son does not have the Father; the one who confesses the Son has the Father also." For at the conclusion of the novel, despite the prompting of the also nameless outlaw leader—"What's his name? the man said"—Culla repudiates his child, his sin, and his responsibilities as lover and father by refusing to name his child, claiming, "I don't know" (*OD*, 235–36). The outlaw's response to Culla is significant. "They say people in hell ain't got names," he says. "But they had to be called somethin to get sent there" (*OD*, 236). Then he slashes the child's throat in front of Culla. Culla's lie thus links him to the arch-liar or anti-Christ, against whom the apostle warns his readers in the previous verse as the one "who denies the Father and the Son." Perhaps speaking for the third generation of Southern novelists, McCarthy's critique of the Southern father suggests that the prior generations of the Southern patriarch—whether the patriarch as writer or the Southern "founding fathers" of history—have denied their responsibility to their imaginative or cultural progeny.

The weak, dead, absent or denying fathers of McCarthy's fiction point toward an imaginative repudiation of the central importance of patriarchal father and family in Southern culture and the South's heroic myth of its history figured in the revered patriarch—Robert E. Lee or Colonel Sartoris—of the Confederate Lost Cause. We might conclude, as does Jason Humphries, that to the new generations of Southern writers and critics the South is no longer defined largely by reference to the "fathers" of the Civil War named in *The Fathers,* Allen Tate's only novel. The patriarchal antebellum slaveholders and Confederates have been replaced by a new set of terms, figures, and historical events, including the civil rights demonstrations and race riots of the 1960s.[12] Or perhaps more crucially, the meaning of Southern history—the Lost Cause—has been revised as another historical lie, as deluded as Culla's own lie or as Mrs. Rattner's fictional lie to John Wesley, which creates Kenneth Rattner, the heroic and pious husband and father.

The Question of the Faulknerian Style.

Other reviewers besides Prescott note many resemblances between McCarthy's first two novels and Faulkner's fiction, although most emphasize their stylistic similarities. Patrick Cuttrell complains of passages in *Outer Dark* "on which the shadow of Faulkner lies very dark—proving once again what a disastrous model for lesser men that writer is. Mr. McCarthy has got from him the interminable shapeless sentence and the trail of very literary epithets which look impressive."[13] More penetrating is Robert Coles's review of the novel in the *New Yorker.* Coles contrasts McCarthy's tinker to Faulkner's peddler Ratliffe and compares Rinthy to Lena Grove of *Light in August* (Coles, 135, 136). In reference to McCarthy's style, however, Coles notes only the necessity of the reader's close attention to both novels and concludes that McCarthy's style ranges from a variety of levels, from Faulknerian to the concise idioms of mountain speech (Coles, 134).

Overemphasizing Faulknerian similarities—the extended periods, the use of biblical allusions, recondite vocabulary, frequent italics—often prevented reviewers from recognizing not only the uniqueness of the style but the repudiation of Faulkner's imaginative constructions of Southern history and culture in McCarthy's early fiction. McCarthy's narrative style itself differentiates his first two novels from Faulkner's historical fiction in a variety of ways. As Chapter 6 discusses McCarthy's style in a broader context, here I focus on one example of how McCarthy's style—while capable of using Faulknerian registers—remains idiosyncratic, if anything more supple than Faulkner's rhetoric of the Southern voice. One characteristic idiosyncrasy of Faulkner's style, of course, is his flamboyant use of voiced italics, used in *Absalom, Absalom!* to render directly character consciousness—sometimes Quentin's but more usually the consciousness of the more historical characters such as Rosa, Sutpen, or Bon. *The Orchard Keeper* opens in the Appalachias of the depression and concludes in the late 1940s, ranging backwards through Arthur Ownby's italicized memories to his early adulthood during Reconstruction. While the use of italicized flashbacks at first might be seen as a narrative device invoking the Faulknerian tradition, the memories in *The Orchard Keeper,* however historical, are always connected directly to Arthur Ownby and always forbidden direct access to characters or memories of the antebellum South. Similar italicized passages in *Outer Dark* are no longer attached directly to a character's historical memory but always narrate actions by the outlaws outside the consciousness of the main characters Culla and Rinthy.

If a modernist analogue is desired for the use of italics in either novel, it would be perhaps Hemingway's *In Our Time* (and Hemingway himself here borrows from his early mentor Gertrude Stein). In Hemingway's work, disconnected short tales are joined together, historically if loosely, by the italicized passages from Nick Adams's war journal. These passages function as interludes within the margins between stories. McCarthy's italics are less narrowly Faulknerian; they are in fact more generally invocations of the modernist narrative techniques of Joyce, Aiken, Woolf, Eliot, Pound, and others.

Although McCarthy's South in *The Orchard Keeper* and *Outer Dark* is, if anything, more violent and desperate than Faulkner's, it is not defined by slavery or the Civil War. In Faulkner's fiction, it is the crucial historical events from these periods whose repression and return to memory structure the conflicted psyche of such Faulkner heroes as Colonel Sartoris Snopes, Quentin Compson, and Ike McCaslin. While McCarthy's second novel, *Outer Dark,* is a conventional historical novel in form, it completely skirts the antebellum South, the Confederacy, and Reconstruction. Instead, it begins and ends within a relatively brief historical period that is impossible to date authoritatively but seems placed in the late nineteenth century during or immediately following Reconstruction. McCarthy excises the antebellum South and slavery from the vision of his first two novels, though he refuses to restrict his vision solely to the contemporary or near-contemporary South of Flannery O'Connor and Eudora Welty's satiric realism. As do O'Connor's short fiction and her novel *Wise Blood,* most of McCarthy's early fiction (with the exception of *Outer Dark*) takes place against the background of the urbanized New South whose emergence is satirized through Faulkner's Compsons and Snopeses. Similarly, his fiction assumes the presence of the earlier small-town agricultural South of Ike McCaslin's adulthood and Quentin Compson's adolescence—a cultural landscape also assumed in most Southern fiction after Faulkner. McCarthy's early fiction may preserve individual elements of these three prior generations of twentieth-century Southern literature, but the elements preserved are recombined into a radically altered sense of the appropriate subject matter, material, form, and style of contemporary Southern fiction.

Race and Class in McCarthy's Appalachian South

Another crucial departure from Faulkner points to the reconstruction of Southern fiction in McCarthy's early work. Faulkner continually uses miscegenation as a symbol to investigate the influence of chattel slavery on Southern race relations. In McCarthy's Appalachian South, the history of slavery and race relations does not function centrally as in Faulkner, though fractured memorials of the cultural remains of the old slave system do rise briefly to the texts' surface. The Hobies, the family who run the illegal still that supplies Syldar with his whiskey, are descendants of a local leader of the Ku Klux Klan who was responsible for harrying African Americans from the community of Red Branch (*OK,* 144). At the opening of the novel, an old black church is the scene for Syldar's sexual escapade with a young girl. The only glimpse of slavery and the question of race in McCarthy's next novel, *Outer Dark,* is seen through a crippled black liveryman working for a country squire who verbally abuses those whom he considers his inferiors—both the vagrant Culla and his liveryman (*OD,* 47–49). Of McCarthy's Appalachian novels only *Suttree* foregrounds, through Ab Jones, the question of race relations, whereas *The Stonemason,* a more recent drama, explores the question of race more fully through the African-American family whose relationships are the focus of the play.

Two conclusions might be drawn about this restriction of slavery and race relations to the margins of McCarthy's fiction. First, this restriction allows McCarthy's fiction imaginative room to escape the power of Faulkner's tradition and its vision of Southern culture. This relative inattention to race in McCarthy's novels also has the more positive function of drawing attention to the autonomy of the Appalachian South from the Delta South. As Cleanth Brooks established in his early, book-length study of Faulkner's fiction, the Delta was the basis for Faulkner's Yoknapatawpha County, whose yeoman farmers, planters, and slaves form an imaginative microcosm of the larger South.[14] As historians and political scientists who have studied the South have shown, historically and culturally, African Americans and the agricultural and economic system of chattel slavery played a prominent role more in the cotton, tobacco, or sugarcane growing areas of the tidewater or coastal plain and Mississippi Delta areas of the South than was the case in the mountainous Appalachian South.

Acknowledging its divergences from the larger South, Neal R. Peirce calls this Appalachian South "the outback," judging it to be "one of the most physically and culturally isolated regions of the United States."[15] Discussing the uniqueness of the political structure of Appalachia and Republican East Tennessee in a state that was, after Reconstruction, exclusively Democratic-controlled, V. O. Key, Jr., notes that "Even before The War a sense of separatism set off East Tennesseeans from their fellow citizens to the west. . . . Slavery was both unprofitable and unpleasing to the people of the mountains of East Tennessee. The plantation system never flourished in the hills and the small farmer who tilled his own land could take no stock in the theory of slavery as a divinely ordained institution."[16] Nevertheless, as suggested in the racist Hobie of *The Orchard Keeper,* the squire of *Outer Dark,* the menacing "White-Caps" of *Child of God,* and the police beatings of Ab Jones in *Suttree,* this relative absence of African-American characters does not necessarily suggest an absence of racial prejudice on the part of the Appalachian South, but it does point to the forces that structure this region in a cultural pattern distinct from the larger South. Indeed, McCarthy's portrayal of the Appalachian South raises important questions about the rationale for the monolithic dominance of the "plantation" image associated with the South as an undivided culture—a unitary image uncritically reflected in Southern literature, in the mass media (an image fixed apparently indelibly in *Gone with the Wind*), and in popular cultural productions that deal with the South.

The problem of class in Appalachia is not ignored, for the characters scrutinized most carefully in *The Orchard Keeper* and in *Outer Dark* represent a level of poverty made bearable only by the characters' unawareness of any alternatives. If to the middle and upper classes such characters seem ignorantly dependent on a way of life that offers them only a bare subsistence, that way of life more positively can be seen to represent an independence from modern lifestyles based on consumption and excess. Nor can the novels, perhaps with the exception of the characterization of Arthur Ownby in *The Orchard Keeper,* be criticized as romantic in their depiction of lifestyles or characters. The characters' impoverishment and deprivation are painted in details given no more or less emphasis than their routine actions, their spare speech, or the landscape. At several points in the narrative of their journeys, Culla and Rinthy's pinching hunger is vividly depicted; more significantly, their brief recognition and then inattention to that hunger suggest that to such characters hunger is only another of the burdens of their lifestyle.

In contrast to characters such as these—people who represent the rural, ancient lifestyle of the hills—are two classes of characters with a lifestyle made possible not only by cultural differences but also by their regional location. These are the farmers or small tradesmen of the valley villages and farms, such as Mr. Eller who owns the Red Branch general store in *The Orchard Keeper* and the rural farmers in *Outer Dark* who briefly offer Rinthy shelter and a ride to town. Such characters of the Appalachian lowlands have accommodated to or been absorbed by a cash-exchange economy and play the role of middleman to the upper classes, represented by Sheriff Gifford in *The Orchard Keeper* or the squire and the auctioneer in *Outer Dark*. Such propertied characters, reminiscent of the Snopeses in Faulkner or the farmers and townsmen of O'Connor's fiction, represent not only a relative wealth and power in comparison to the other classes but also an ideology alien to that of the other characters. The squire's lecture to Culla that he has "earned" all his wealth by the labor of his own two hands—"What I got I earned"—is given the lie both by the mute testimony of his black farrier and by his automatic equation of Culla's poverty with his shiftlessness.

The squire's uncritical consumption of the Horatio Alger myth of rising in class by pulling on one's bootstraps is pointedly shown to contribute to his own death. Angrily riding out in search of Culla, who flees after stealing the squire's new boots, he encounters not the "shiftless" Culla but the outlaws who represent the very bottom of social class. More centrally, they represent man's potential for the "outer dark" or ultimate evil. The narration dispassionately, almost clinically, notes how one outlaw "severs" the squire's spine with a tool that the outlaws earlier had stolen from the squire's own barn, just as Culla had stolen the squire's boots (*OD*, 35, 49–50). The multiple ironies of the squire's death might seem incidental or accidental were it not that a similar character named Clark, a grotesquely fat auctioneer and general store owner, apparently is hanged on his own rope by the outlaws the evening after he hires Holme to dig graves for three vagrants hanged for grave-robbing (*OK*, 142–43, 146). The careful narrative description of the bearded outlaw's clothes reveals that the mysterious outlaws, not the hanged vagrants, were guilty of the graverobbing (*OK*, 87–88, 170). While the outlaws' murders are seen as issuing from an irrational evil, seen in the larger context of the chance connections to Culla, those murders often function as a type of revenge against the ideology of the propertied classes, who associate wealth with morality and ignore their own exploitation of the lower classes.

At the end of *The Orchard Keeper* Marion Syldar offers a more dramatic recognition of the gulf in class, region, and ideology between characters such as Arthur Ownby, John Wesley Rattner, and Culla Holme and those at the top of the social stratum such as Sheriff Gifford and the squire. In the course of Rattner's visit to him in prison, Syldar convinces the boy to avoid blood vengeance for Gifford's beating and imprisonment of Syldar. Earlier in the novel, Syldar has beaten Gifford in his own bed as revenge for Gifford's threatening the boy. Yet after the boy leaves the prison, Syldar reveals his innermost thoughts: "That's not true what I said. It was a damned lie ever word. He's a rogue and a outlaw hisself and you're welcome to shoot him, burn him down in his bed, any damn thing, because he's a traitor to boot and maybe a man steals from greed or murders in anger but he sells his own neighbors out for money and it's few lie that deep in the pit, that far beyond the pale" (*OK*, 214–15). The passage's concluding metaphoric images of the pit and the area "beyond the pale" evoke biblical associations with the betraying Judas and the hell-destined sinner, whereas within the novel's own imagery Sheriff Gifford is metonymically associated with the decayed corpse of Kenneth Rattner, John Wesley's father, which throughout the novel has lain rotting in its own pit. It is Rattner who, like the outlaws in *Outer Dark*, tries to murder Syldar for his automobile and is killed by him in turn. But through this lie, Syldar unknowingly atones for his earlier sin by saving Rattner's son, who flees Gifford and the mountains, only to return to Red Branch at the novel's conclusion as Syldar himself had returned at the novel's beginning.

The novel's depiction of class differences within the larger context of a traditional lifestyle at first may seem reminiscent of the Vanderbilt Agrarians. But a crucial distinction is that the Agrarians tended to represent agrarianism through its propertied classes. McCarthy's investigation of the Appalachian South is grounded instead in the very lowest echelon, the equivalent to Faulkner's Abner Snopes in "Barn Burning." A better analogy in fiction, particularly given the historical role of the Scotch-Irish in settling the Appalachians, would be to that of Sir Walter Scott's Waverley novels, in which the traditionalism of the Scottish Highlanders is viewed against the economic and social modernism of England, with the Lowland Scots, particularly the tradesmen, continually playing the role of middlemen.

Historical Consciousness in *The Orchard Keeper*

Faulkner's fiction often relies on *askesis,* a sudden revelation of historical insight to such Faulkner heroes as Quentin Compson or Ike McCaslin. But a historical awareness that takes the form of askesis is denied to virtually all McCarthy's main characters—Syldar, John Wesley Rattner, and Ownby of *The Orchard Keeper* or Culla of *Outer Dark.* The very title of *The Orchard Keeper* underlines the essential dramatic irony of the novel: only we, the dark narrative voice, and a few characters near the novel's conclusion are aware of the hidden historical connections between the three generations of protagonists. While sifting Kenneth Rattner's ashes, the storekeeper Eller, the coroner, and two county officials identify the corpse but decide to keep the secret to protect John Wesley and his mother from the consequences of that truth. Not even these characters, unlike us, know that John Wesley himself has unwittingly cremated his father's corpse when he and two other boys on a cold winter's day light a fire in a cave to warm up after trapping. With the exception of Ownby and Rinthy, McCarthy's characters seem to live largely unaware of even their own history, not to mention the larger narrative of Southern history.

The conclusions of *The Orchard Keeper* and *Child of God* trace the outlines of postmodern alienation in which the solitary consciousness—the narrator's and the reader's—reflects and operates on an externalized nature, man, and history. The world and history, both of nature and of society, are revealed as constructs of the individual's perspective. Through Ownby, Syldar, and Rattner, McCarthy suggests that a Southern history and culture defined by the Civil War and chattel slavery take a very different form in the border South, for the peripheral culture of the mountain underclass. To be sure, Appalachian history inscrutably operates below the surface of the fiction and the consciousness of its characters. Although *The Orchard Keeper* is embedded in a historical context, beginning in the mid-1930s with Syldar's killing of Kenneth Rattner in self-defense and ending in the late 1940s with "young" Rattner's return to Red Branch to visit his mother's grave, most of the action occurs in two years of the early 1940s. As we have seen, the crucial historical event of the main narrative action is ironic: John Wesley's inadvertent participation in the cremation of the remains of his father. In the novel's evocative and elegiac ending, Rattner returns to the village of Red Branch to visit his mother's grave in 1948, three years after her death (*OK,* 245). This nocturnal afterlude underscores the predominant theme of the novel: the cultural exile of contemporary Southerners from their own pasts and from Southern history. While this scene at the maternal grave has already been discussed briefly in terms of Rattner's repudiation of personal history, the ending also revises Southern literary history, most notably Thomas Wolfe's repudiation of the exile's return, "You can never go home again," in *Look Homeward, Angel* and Tate's elegy "To the Confederate Dead."

In Tate's poem a contemporary Southerner, looking at the war graves, mourns the disjunction between a heroic Confederate past and the banalities of the modern South. Although twentieth-century Southern literature is replete with such elegiac scenes, McCarthy's ending adds a new register of the anti-elegiac. Both John Wesley and the narrative voice seem to distance themselves from the novel's dead; this repudiation also seems directed more generally against the Southern past, at least its past as represented in the literature of the Southern renaissance. The final chapter of *The Orchard Keeper* begins with Rattner's return home, gazing from the yard at the falling leaves surrounding the dilapidated house: "Old dry leaves rattled frail and withered as old voices, trailed stiffly down, rocking like thinworn shells downward through seawater, or spun, curling ancient parchments on which no message at all appeared" (*OK,* 244). While the image of the decayed house evokes Rattner's mature distance from his childhood, the imagery of the leaves alludes to one of the most ancient of poetic images. From Tate's poem to

Shelley's "Ode to the West Wind" to Shakespeare's Sonnet 110 and back to Homer's *Iliad* (in which the souls of the dead summoned by Ulysses are compared to the autumn leaves), the elegiac, lyric, and epic traditions employ leaves as an image for the dead, death, and memories of the dead. Reflecting that "it was never his house anyway," Rattner repudiates his past, beginning with the house of his childhood and ending at his mother's gravestone (*OK,* 244).

Earlier, interrupting Rattner's move from his childhood home to the cemetery, the narrative voice had shifted to an ironic representation of the novel's dominant image—the progressive decay of his father's corpse in the pit: "The dead [are] sheathed in the earth's crust, . . . their bones brindled with mold and the celled marrow going to frail stone" (*OK,* 244–45). Rather than reasserting the elegy's essential consolation that the dead still live, the narrator announces a final disjunction between Southern present and past. At the cemetery, after patting his mother's stone, "as if perhaps to conjure up some image, evoke again some allegiance with a name, a place, hallucinated recollections in which faces merged inextricably, and yet true and fixed" (*OK,* 245), Rattner leaves the cemetery by "the western road." The narrator remarks obliquely in the novel's final sentences: "They are gone now. Fled, banished in death or exile, lost, undone. Over the land sun and wind still move to burn and sway the trees, the grasses. No avatar, no scion, no vestige of that people remains. On the lips of the strange race that now dwells there their names are myth, legend, dust" (*OK,* 246). Presumably, the passage's "they" directly refers to the separation that death makes between John Wesley and his dead mother. While the nature of "land sun and wind" is timeless in its operations on "the trees, the grasses," John Wesley is estranged, a member of the "strange race" of dwellers, a person who can only utter his mother's name, not summon her presence.

But the image of the end of a bloodline or legacy—"no avatar, no scion"—refers indirectly to the childless Arthur Ownby, the last of his line. Like Mrs. Rattner, he too has died, sane but alone in a prison for the criminally insane. His death, hidden in the margins of the text, marks an end not only to his bloodline but also to his ancient lifestyle of finding a marginal subsistence from the mountains. As befits a writer whose childhood was spent in the "border" country of Tennessee and Knoxville (where the flat farming country of the agrarian South abuts the hill country of the Appalachians), McCarthy's first two novels revise earlier Southern fiction in part by attending to the Southern periphery of the poor white mountain-dwelling populations. *The Orchard Keeper* directs our attention to this peripheral culture by exploring characters such as Arthur Ownby. Arthur's exclamation to the young Rattner, "I'm Brushy Bound," points to the essential pathos of his life, alluding both to his flight from the law into the wild Harrykin before his capture and to his expectation of his final destination: an incarceration and death at the state penitentiary at Brushy.

The final passage of *The Orchard Keeper* names Ownby as the last "avatar" of man operating within and as part of nature, for once he emerges from the isolated safety of the wilderness to trade roots at Eller's store he is caught by the law and imprisoned. In the inability of Rattner and his friends to trap muskrat, mink, or wildcat, the novel demonstrates the postmodern disconnection not only from the past but from nature, which humanity itself has depleted. The farming family of *Outer Dark* that offers Rinthy shelter, a bed, and rides to and from town reiterates this theme of the dying race. The narrator's final glimpse of the family paints its return home by wagon: "On their chairs in such black immobility these travelers could have been stone figures quarried from the architecture of an older time" (*OD*, 77). In contrast to Rinthy and Culla's constant motion and consequent exile and alienation is the static and historical "immobility" of this family. Yet the response of their son, when asked where he has gone in town (he rather lewdly has invited Rinthy to see a show with him), is ominous: "I ain't been nowheres" (*OK*, 77). Like Culla and Rinthy's aimless wanderings in the concluding scenes following their child's murder, the youth's narrative of his brief wandering has no final destination or meaning. At his first meeting with the outlaws, Culla will claim he "wasn't headed no place special" (*OD*, 172), a denial to which the bearded outlaw mysteriously alludes at their second meeting when he mumbles enigmatically, "From nowheres, nowhere bound" (*OD*, 233). Nor do the wanderings of either Rattner, father or son, have a final destination or meaning.

At least Ownby appears to know his destination, can envision his life as ending in a clearly defined destination. If the largely heroic portrait of Ownby in the first novel represents this Southern periphery in the most favorable light, McCarthy's representation of the hill South is darkened by the characters of *Outer Dark:* Rinthy's stubborn maternalism, Culla's sullen and obdurate guilt, the murderous joie de vivre of the outlaws. While on one hand such characters are representative of historical Southern Appalachia, their status as exiles makes them historical prefigurations of Rattner and postmodern humanity. The aimless wandering of such characters typifies the postmodern distrust of history as fixed or meaningful. To Vereen Bell, the purposeless wandering of McCarthy's characters and narratives reveals the absence of plot, in the sense of multifaceted story foreshadowing an implied ending or resolution. Bell argues that McCarthy's "modernist, elliptical narrative technique" suggests a nihilistic "antimetaphysical bias" that "binds us to the [novels'] phenomenal world."[17]

History, whether of the individual or of a culture such as the South, can indeed be narrated as only a wandering endless series with no limit other than death. We can observe a teleology in history if we wish, but we cannot control it. From the perspective of a current observer like John Wesley Rattner, history and the past are not a list of events and their causes; rather, historical names are "myth, legend, dust," implying an absolute separation between the consciousness of the present survivors and the otherness of the dead acts of history. Unlike Culla and Rinthy, John Wesley Rattner is a figure for the contemporary artist who is of "the strange race" now dwelling in the New South. And while the final sentences of the concluding passage of *The Orchard Keeper* reinforce Rattner's sense of disconnection from a dead history, the preceding sentences seem to optimistically point forward into a more promising future for Rattner: "The sun broke through the final shelf of clouds and bathed for a moment the dripping trees with blood, tinted the stones a diaphanous wash of color. . . . He passed through the gap in the fence, past the torn iron palings and out to the western road, . . . the darkening headlands drawing off the day, heraldic, pennoned in flame, the fleeing minions scattering their shadows in the wake of the sun" (*OK,* 246). The sun's "wake" seems to banish the ghosts of the past—the "feeling minions"—and our last glimpse of Rattner catches him no longer pensive with memory but, in Whitmanesque fashion, stepping out of the graveyard to set forth on the open Western road. Viewed in the context of the literature of the Southern renaissance, McCarthy's narratives might be seen not as nihilistic but as examples of a contemporary renewal of Southern fiction.

Nor are Rattner and his contemporaries the only generation cut off from their cultural past. The last sentence's "strange race" that "dwells there" has a sliding reference that includes the more belated generation of the narrative voice and the text's implied readers, originally of the generation of the 1960s but now constituting a still later generation. All generations of readers and McCarthy's narrator are separated from a history that belongs not to them but to the past. To be cast into a timeless "outer dark" is not merely the plight of the contemporary Southern writer or that of Culla Holme and the lost blind man at the conclusion of *Outer Dark*: it is the historical fate of the contemporary, whether Southerner or not. Like John Wesley Rattner and Culla Holme, each individual experiences life as a social and historical outcast. McCarthy's first two novels, published in the latter half of the 1960s, thus redefine the New South by means of the overlapping Southern border or peripheral culture of the Appalachias and reconstruct along contemporary lines the tradition of Southern literature that was established in the work of the two generations of modern Southern writers before McCarthy.

Chapter Three

Postmodern Outcasts and Alienation: *Child of God* and *Suttree*

If *The Orchard Keeper* and *Outer Dark* reconstruct early twentieth-century Southern literature, McCarthy's next two novels, *Child of God* and *Suttree,* use the techniques of modern fiction to explore several cases of contemporary alienation. First orphan, then necrophile, murderer, and fugitive, the notorious Lester Ballard of *Child of God* (1973) is the first of a series of characters who revitalize the "underground man" of Dostoevsky, Richard Wright, and Ralph Ellison. In McCarthy's next novel, *Suttree* (1979), he explores a mismatched pair of antiheroes, Gene Harrogate and Cornelius Suttree, in order to examine alienation within a more contemporary, urban Americana. The novel unblinkingly scrutinizes this pair, their environs of the Knoxville slum of McAnally Flats, and their "company of thieves, derelicts, miscreants, pariahs, poltroons, spalpeens, curmudgeons, clotpolls, murderers, gamblers, bawds, whores, trulls, brigands, topers, tosspots, sots and archsots, lobcocks, smellsmocks, runagates, rakes, and other assorted and felonious debauchees."[1]

Set within a contemporary, post–World War II milieu, *Suttree* and *Child of God* merge Southern literature with modernism's dominant imagery and thematics of social and psychological disconnection. In its twin themes of alienation and death, in its provocative style, in its superimposition of the imagery of the underground man on a modernist wasteland, *Suttree* is a post-Southern equivalent to Ellison's *Invisible Man,* Eliot's *The Waste Land,* and Joyce's *Ulysses.*

The Underground Man

One measure of McCarthy's growing mastery of his craft is his ability to exact from readers not only a fascination with but a grudging sympathy for Lester Ballard, the antihero of *Child of God.* And this sympathy is achieved despite—or is in part made possible by—the narrator's objectivity, affording us only limited access to Lester's mind. Our first glimpse of Lester occurs at the novel's beginning, with the emergence of

a "small, unclean, unshaven" man from the barn door of a farm property
that is being auctioned off in default of county taxes.[2] We learn a few
pages later that the property had belonged to Lester's father, who years
previously had hanged himself in the same barn. A rope, perhaps the
very rope used by his father, hangs behind Lester from the loft as he
emerges (*CG,* 4, 7, 21). In one of the few passages in which the narrative
voice comments directly on Lester for our guidance, the narrator interjects obliquely, "A child of God much like yourself perhaps" (*CG,* 4). At
first reading, this comment signifies little, a seeming appeal to the
democratic egalitarianism at the center of American political rhetoric
and to the equally commonplace Christian doctrine of the fundamental
equality of all souls. Nevertheless, as the novel and Lester's character
inexorably unfold, this phrase attracts further significations so that to
interpret its ambiguities is to interpret the ambiguities of Lester's character, the novel's title, and the novel itself. How can a man like Lester—
murderer and necrophile—be a "child of God"? Is the narrator's beginning comment "much like yourself" meant at face value, asserting that
Lester shares a fundamental humanity with his Tennessee community
and with the community of the novel's readers? Might the title be an
ironic assertion of the opposing view? Or is the comment meant to
imply that, inasmuch as Lester shares our humanity, we all share at least
a potential for his otherwise inexplicable perversity?

In answer to these implicit questions, McCarthy's narrator points to
the chronicle of Lester's deeds conveyed in spare, often poetic prose,
leavened with strikingly little moral or other forms of direct narrative
comment. But in a manner reminiscent of Faulkner's folksy first-person
commentator Ratliff in *The Hamlet,* the narration is periodically interrupted with interpretive and moralistic comments by various members
of Lester's rural village community of Sevier, Tennessee. All of these
rural commentators repudiate Lester. Early in the novel, after telling the
story of Lester's hitting a younger boy, one comments, "I never liked
Lester Ballard from that day. I never liked him much before that. He
never done nothing to me" (*CG,* 18). Although the speaker points to the
fight as a cause of his dislike for Lester and as an early sign of why the
Sevier community was justified in repudiating him, we note that his and
the community's judgment of Lester seems to arbitrarily *precede* the
actions cited to justify his social exile. Like his village contemporaries,
our desire as readers initially is to distance ourselves from Lester and
Lester's deeds by coming to a final, authoritative view of him, his
actions, and his motives, categorically naming and dismissing him as

murderer or necrophile. Yet the title's ambiguity, the authorial voice's moral reticence, and the narrative's matter-of-fact scrutiny of the details of Lester's life frustrate our desire for such an easily achieved interpretive distance. McCarthy's title places his readers in a quandary: to deny Lester's humanity—his status as a "child of God"—jeopardizes not only our egalitarian ideology but our notions of our own humanity.

Although sharing Lester's social and psychological alienation from the respectable community, Cornelius Suttree and Gene Harrogate are positioned more complexly within the more contemporary urban environment of Knoxville. Of the two outcasts in *Suttree,* Harrogate is apparently the simpler character, a largely comic revision of two sets of characters in McCarthy's earlier fiction—naive rural adolescents such as John Wesley Rattner and Rinthy Holme, and exiled criminals such as Arthur Ownby, Marion Syldar, Culla Holme, and Lester Ballard. From our first vision of Harrogate, the comic perspective predominates. Sent to the workhouse for having intercourse with watermelons (and the description of his evening "conjugal" visits is one of the more comic passages in recent American fiction), Harrogate is nicknamed "watermelon man" by his fellow prisoners and dubbed "moonlight melonmounter" by the narrative voice (*S,* 48–49). Reflecting Suttree's consciousness, the narrative voice assesses Harrogate in a direct moral statement rarely encountered in McCarthy's fiction: "He was not lovable. This adenoidal leptosome that crouched above his bed like a wizened bird, his razorous shoulderblades jutting in the thin cloth of his striped shirt. Sly, rat-faced, a convicted pervert of a botanical bent. Who would do worse when in the world again. Bet on it. But something in him so transparent, something vulnerable. As he looked back at Suttree with his almost witless equanimity his naked face was suddenly taken away in darkness" (*S,* 54). Perhaps representative of or coinciding with Suttree's point of view, the passage indicates three various views of Harrogate: the negative ("sly," "rat-faced"), which stresses his perversion and cunning; the positive ("vulnerable," "witless equanimity"), which emphasizes his childish qualities of unflagging and native optimism and his enjoyment of life; and the tragic ("taken away in darkness"), which points to his dark ending near the narrative's close. If Lester Ballard in *Child of God* is a tragicomic exile, Gene Harrogate is his inverted double, a predominantly comic figure who begins in a clownish perversion and ends in darkness.

Like Harrogate, an alien from respectable Knoxville society, Suttree nevertheless is a member of a defined community—that of the society of outcasts in the McAnally Flats slum that is the novel's primary setting.

As most critics conclude, Cornelius Suttree—known variously as Suttree, Sut, Youngblood, Bud, and Buddy—is McCarthy's most complex character, certainly to this point in his oeuvre and perhaps including his later works. Vereen Bell asserts that "Cornelius Suttree is McCarthy's first informed witness and resisting victim of his fear and knowledge. Suttree is in fact a new character in McCarthy's work because he brings a new order of experience to McCarthy's now more complex but still recognizable fictional world. . . . He is mature, educated, and literate" (Bell 1988, 72). As the novel proceeds, we learn a variety of external, background details that round out Suttree's characterization: that he has been imprisoned for inadvertently sleeping in his friends' car while they robbed a drugstore (*S*, 321); that he has been to college (47); that he has repudiated his father's bourgeois existence to live in McAnally Flats (13–14); that he sleeps in a houseboat he bought upon release from prison (15); that his almost suicidal drinking sprees are in communion with his ne'er-do-well friends (23); that he is a twin whose other identical brother had died inexplicably at birth (14, 17–18).

Like Dostoevsky's underground man and Ellison's invisible man, Suttree's alienation on the houseboat is knowing and purposeful. Following a bitter conversation with his alcoholic uncle early in the novel, Suttree seeks out his drinking fellows among the underclass: "In this tall room, the cracked plaster sootstreaked with the shapes of laths beneath, this barrenness, this fellowship of the doomed. Where life pulsed obscenely fecund" (*S*, 23). This passage, crucial for its insight into the motives compelling Suttree's choice of life, can be read as a summary, even a quotation of Suttree's thoughts. Or it can be read as the more distanced perspective of the novel's narrator. In one of the few articles that directly address McCarthy's narrative discourse, Andrew Bartlett points to a distance, termed "voyeuristic," between Ballard's perspective and that of the narrative discourse; the term suggests the alienation I have found representative of the underground characters of both novels.[3] Yet the consciousness of Suttree is more widely represented in the narrative as free indirect discourse, making him a more pronounced focal character than is Ballard.[4] To be sure, as this passage suggests, the subtle shifts in focus between Suttree's alienated point of view and that of the objectivist narration are difficult, often impossible to detect authoritatively. Whatever the passage's point of view, in the "fellowship of the doomed" of McAnally Flats, Suttree finds a paradoxical affirmation of life lacking in his former, respectable existence as upper-class scion, undergraduate, and father.

Lester Ballard, Gene Harrogate, and Cornelius Suttree thus can be viewed as variants of a single character type. Though the differences between their crimes are significant, they are all criminals. All three characters live on the margins of society: Suttree in his houseboat or, when drunk or ill, in flophouses; Lester in an abandoned house and, after he inadvertently burns it down, in caves; the "city rat" Harrogate in an earthen hollow beneath the bridge over the Tennessee River. If Ballard and Harrogate are orphaned, left dependent on their own devices in the face of the world's indifference, Suttree lives as if he has no family. Before the novel's opening, Suttree has repudiated his wealthy and socially respectable father, partly in response to his father's contempt for his lower-class wife and her family (*S*, 13–14, 19). While in the workhouse, Suttree repudiates his mother (*S*, 61–62); when he attends his son's funeral, soon after his release, we learn that he has abandoned his wife and child before the narrative begins (*S*, 151, 158).

All three characters have internalized this isolation from family and society, existing in a state of alienation and anomie. At an early point in *Child of God,* Lester Ballard attends a church service, coming in late, only to be ignored by congregation and minister despite his loud "snuffles" (*CG*, 31–32). Throughout the later narrative, Ballard strives to rejoin the society that he feels has wronged and exiled him; attempts to strike back against it as when he attempts to stop the auction of his property; and seeks through his necrophilia and grotesque collection of corpses to form a community, of sorts, underground. Near the novel's conclusion, having escaped back to his cave after being threatened with lynching by the relatives of his victims, Ballard asserts his own affiliation with society, nonchalantly turning himself in at the hospital counter and remarking, "I'm supposed to be here" (*CG*, 192). Yet only in his death does Ballard rejoin human society, provisionally. Dissected first at a medical school, "At the end of three months when the class was closed Ballard was scraped from the table into a plastic bag and taken with others of his kind to a cemetery outside the city and there interred" (*CG*, 194). Although he is buried with "other of his kind," the novel's conclusion is ambiguous: Does his burial symbolize his reintegration into the community, or is he buried separately in a pauper's cemetery shared only by other outcasts like himself, all wards of the state?

Although his society treats him as an alien and exile, Harrogate alone of the underground characters refuses to internalize society's view of himself, at least until the novel's end. Near the novel's beginning, Harrogate is shot in the midst of his conjugal visits to a nearby melon field by a farmer who terms him "Lecher. Unnatural." Yet when he sees Harrogate's youthfulness and agony, the farmer wishes he could "call back that skeltering lead" and "keeps saying for him to hush, kneeling there, not touching him," later bringing him ice cream in the hospital (*S,* 35, 42). Cognizant of Harrogate's difference from his fellow men, Suttree seeks to dissuade the youth at the workhouse from pursuing plans for escape, saying, "You look wrong. You will always look wrong"—an assertion that Harrogate denies. Lester Ballard, Suttree, and Harrogate share broad characteristics that categorize them as variations of the underground man.

Symbolic Landscapes of Social Alienation

If many reviewers and critics find the characters in McCarthy's fiction either unsympathetic or horrific (in Lester Ballard's case), the landscapes and the descriptive prose usually evoke unreserved admiration. Indeed, McCarthy may own the most accomplished eye and vocabulary for natural description in contemporary American fiction. If the landscapes of these novels perform a mimetic function, they also supply images that highlight, reinforce, and counterpoint the novels' characterizations and ideological concerns. *Suttree* maintains the brooding tone of the earlier novels, and its interludes on the French Broad River and in Gatlinburg depict the Tennessee wilderness as impressively as the rural landscapes are depicted in *Outer Dark.* Yet *Suttree* supplements these rural landscapes with detailed symbolic canvases of the contemporary, often decayed urban South of Knoxville.

The Orchard Keeper, Outer Dark, and *Child of God* provide a meticulously painted landscape of the Tennessee forests, interspersed with small rural towns, settlements, and homes and overlaid with a series of dark, gothic imagery. One wintry forest scene in *Child of God* typifies the symbolic gothicism of McCarthy's rural landscapes. Crossing the mountain woods, Ballard encounters a "windfelled tulip poplar," its root holding "aloft . . . two stones the size of fieldwagons, great tablets on which was writ only a tale of vanished seas with ancient shells in cameo and fishes etched in lime" (*CG,* 128). Reaching a road "shrouded" by knee-deep snow and "unmarked by any track at all," Ballard walks through the landscape in complete isolation. Earlier, the narration had commented obliquely, "At one time in the world there were woods that no one owned and these were like them" (*CG,* 127). The surrounding landscape portrays Ballard as a throwback representative of Rousseau's natural man. Like the stones held in the tree roots, he predates civilization and socialized man.

In *The American Adam* R.W. B. Lewis has traced the American mode of the pastoral, in which an Edenic wilderness is substituted for the bucolic, and an innocent Adam substituted for the shepherd or Virgilian bucolic farmer. The American Adam operates as a variation of the pathetic fallacy, transferring the inferred innocence of the wilderness to the representative American identity.[5] Within its setting of primitive wilderness, *Child of God* reverses Lewis's thesis. Unlike Thoreau at Walden Pond, Ballard's isolation in nature neither regenerates nor restores a lost innocence; it corrupts this contemporary inversion of the American Adam. Or is it that he reverts to an internalized state of nature? Despite the beauty of the winter landscape, it is no pastoral scene but a primal wilderness bereft of human order. In a parallel scene two chapters later, Ballard walks among giant fallen trees: "Disorder in the woods, trees down, new paths needed. Given charge Ballard would have made things more orderly in the woods and in men's souls" (*CG,* 136). His unerring aim with the rifle, his unthinking violence—the shots at the dumpkeeper's daughter and the boy in the truck appear spontaneous—are fascistic, stemming from a drive to impose a willed order on those persons who thwart his desire. Yet it is his own chaotic life that Ballard wills to order through a violence projected on others.

Ballard, Harrogate, and the Cave.   Reinforcing the novels' characterization of the underground man are the descriptions of the homes in *Child of God* and *Suttree.* Lester's two habitations, the abandoned house and the cave, not only provide a necessary realistic setting but iconically represent his isolation. In keeping with its larger breadth, *Suttree* provides a series of symbolic habitations, all poised between the novel's two antipodal symbolic landscapes, the river and the slum.

Ballard inhabits two caves: one after he burns down the abandoned house that serves him as shelter in the first half of the novel, and another an old sinkhole in which he hides as a criminal. "In the bowels of the mountain," over a mile from where he sleeps in the first cave's opening, is a "tall and bell-shaped cavern" with walls "slavered over . . . with wet and bloodred mud." There he assembles a second grotesque family of corpses "on ledges or pallets of stone where dead people lay like saints" (*CG,* 135). Both mud and corpses depict his attraction to violence, his misanthropy, his ambivalent craving for companionship. After murdering a young woman, wounding her boyfriend with his rifle, and then fleeing to the sinkhole, Lester treats these "rancid moldcrept" corpses as personal possessions, dragging each miles through a cold rain. The next day he suffers frostbite, "gibbering, a sound not quite crying that echoed from the walls of the grotto like the mutterings of a band of sympathetic apes" (*CG,* 159). Particularly revelatory is Ballard's last night in the "underground" of the sinkhole: there for the first time he cries. That night after hearing his father's whistle in the noise of the underground stream, Lester dreams of a strange ride in the forest in which he is "riding to his death." Noting that "each leaf he passed he'd never pass again," the perspective reverses, now with the leaves riding "over his face like veils" (*CG,* 170–1).

Immediately preceding the chapter that recounts Lester's attack on Greer, the man who bought the Ballard house at auction, Lester's dream clarifies that this attack is a form of suicide; his inarticulate wish is to join his true family composed of his dead father and collection of corpses. Given this death wish, the birth imagery that depicts his final emergence from the cave is particularly ironic. Trapped in a cavern with only a thin hole in its roof, he wishes "for some brute midwife to spald him from his rocky keep" (*CG,* 189) and emerges headfirst, covered "all over with red mud" (*CG,* 192). His fate at novel's end repeats that of the more sympathetic primitive Arthur Ownby in *The Orchard Keeper.* In this form of blood-covered newborn, Ballard immediately turns himself in to the hospital and enters the new life of his own living death, interred inside a cage in "a ward for the criminally insane" at the state hospital at Knoxville (*CG,* 193).

With comic touches largely muted in the preceding novel, *Suttree* uses the cave motif to reinforce this motif of the underground man. Isolated in caves or in viaducts in the earth are a series of characters: Gene Harrogate, the Native American fisherman Michael, and the ragpicker. Harrogate's largely comic attempts to set up house in the viaduct— scavenging crates, trash cans, a mattress, and construction lanterns and assembling them in the earth under the bridge over First Creek—suggest that his characterization is a comic revision of Ballard in the preceding novel. Especially comic is Suttree's reaction to "the cityrat" Harrogate's parodic guided tour of his new "home":

> He ushered in his guest expansively. How you like it Sut?
> Suttree looked around, shaking his head.
> What I like about it is they's plenty of room. Don't you?
> You better get rid of those parking meters, Suttree said. (*S,* 117)

Throughout the novel Harrogate consistently displays a naïveté, ego-centrism, and optimism incongruous with an underground man, though various oblique suggestions foreshadow his bitter ending. A parodic double of the "rags to riches" hero of Benjamin Franklin and Horatio Alger, Harrogate obsessively occupies himself in a series of naively clever schemes that require his emergence into the Knoxville daylight. Hearing of the city's one-dollar bounty for rabid bats, he attempts various means to poison them with bait, ingenuously settling on launching poisoned bait into the air with a slingshot. With "a light heart and deep rejoicing for the fortune of it made the load less heavy," he arrives at the hospital with a sackful of bats; denied his bounty by a doctor, he nonetheless cheerily confesses to his scheme, content with the dollar and quarter paid him to reveal the details of his scheme (*S,* 217–18).

His next scheme is to dig through underground Knoxville in search of a bank vault; eventually resorting to explosives, he inadvertently dynamites a concrete-protected cistern and only after the passage of several days is rescued, "covered with dried sewage," by a concerned Suttree. Harrogate's sexuality, home, and escapades in his "underground" economy all express his alienation. Yet the novel's relocation of the underground from rural wilderness to urban Knoxville is a significant departure from the earlier novel: "Suttree pressed on, down the curious undersides of the city, through black and slaverous cavities where foul liquors seeped. He had not known how hollow the city was" (*S,* 276). Suttree and Harrogate's alienation is not unique but a representation, if exaggerated, of the psychological isolation of contemporary man above-ground. Unaware of the symbolic implications of his plight, covered with sewage and in torment, Harrogate echoes the rich man Dives in Hades: "I'd give ten dollars for a glass of icewater. . . . Cash money" (*S,* 277). Like Lazarus comforted by Abraham, Harrogate is succored by Suttree and reemerges from his symbolic burial in the underground wasteland.

Yet Suttree's aid is temporary and ineffectual. Harrogate again will emulate the rags-to-riches myth, running an entrepreneurial route of "two hunerd and eight-six" public phones, which he robs with a hook inserted through the coin returns (*S,* 419). Ignoring Suttree's warnings of his certain capture and incarceration in the penitentiary, Harrogate initially evades capture by a detective. Yet for the first time in the novel, he has no plans for his future, looking "frail and wasted with defeat." Refusing Suttree's advice to sneak onto a train to elude a law unfaltering in its pursuit, he reveals his theft was intended to make himself an outlaw, "I knew that, . . . but I went and done it anyways" (*S*, 437). In an almost suicidal gesture reminiscent of Ballard's surrender, his subsequent attempt at armed robbery is an act of desperation: "He was caught at his first robbery. White lights crossed like warring swords the little grocery store and back, his small figure tortured there cringing and blinking as if he were being burnt" (*S*, 439). Soon Harrogate is on a train ride to the same penitentiary at Brushy Mountain where *The Orchard Keeper*'s Arthur Ownby, after his capture, believes he will die.

In still another allusion linking Harrogate's psychology to Ballard's, our last vision of the city rat reiterates Ballard's introspection before his surrender, when he encounters a young boy, "his nose puttied against the glass," staring out the window of a schoolbus: "There was nothing out there to see but he was looking anyway." Recognizing the scene, Ballard searches his memory, eventually to identify himself with the image: "it came to him that the boy looked like himself" (*CG*, 191). Haunted by the image and identifying himself with "the nothing out there," Ballard turns himself in. (Is this "nothing out there" glimpsed by the child and Ballard an ironic allusion to Wallace Stevens's snowman, who, "nothing himself, beholds / Nothing that is not there"?) Harrogate's final train journey through the winter landscape, with "the long wail of the engine hanging over the country like a thing damned of all deliverance," implies a hitherto uncharacteristic introspection and psychic death similar to Ballard's: "The city rat could see his pinched face watching him back from the cold glass, out there racing among the wires and the bitter trees, and he closed his eyes" (*S*, 439). With "closed eyes" against his former optimistic illusions, Harrogate experiences psychic death. The image of his former self as freed youth in the train window is detached from the doubled self of the embittered, imprisoned contemporary man whose identity is belatedly recognized on the train and formed in the despair that follows the underground explosion. Harrogate's tragic knowledge of himself comes too late for redemption. Such is the case for almost all of the doomed of McAnally Flats save Suttree himself, whose redemption in the novel's final scene is ambiguous and provisional at best.

The Abandoned House.   In *Child of God* the decayed, abandoned house in which Ballard temporarily resides is emblematic of his temporary provisional state, half connected to his socialized self, half to his more primitive, alienated identity. Section 2 of the novel begins with his molestation of the first female corpse, which he discovers in an idling car, asphyxiated by carbon monoxide poisoning. For her he buys a wardrobe and with her he sets up house, temporarily. When two young boys verge on discovering his grotesque parody of housekeeping, his attempts at concealing her in the attic result in a black-comic resurrection and in a consummation of his social estrangement. He first builds a fire that symbolizes a refuge against the harsh cold of the wilderness and the harsher economic environment. Tying the corpse to a length of rope, he climbs up the ladder pulling the corpse, which "began to bump slowly up the ladder. Halfway up she paused, dangling. Then she began to rise again" (*CG,* 95). The narrative point of view, placing Ballard out of frame in order to focus exclusively on the image of the corpse's "climb" up the ladder, parodies the Christian myths of resurrection and annunciation.

As a Southerner positioned outside of a traditional community, the necrophile Ballard reveals his desire not only for integration within community and family but for a postmodern version of immortality. Hence his fastidious preservation of all corpses, male and female alike, despite his sexual violation of the latter only. By fetching the girl's corpse alternately next to the fire or into the attic, Ballard either defrosts the corpse for conjugal companionship or freezes it to preserve its "afterlife." Yet by building up the fire, he burns down his house, his marginally socialized existence, and his faith. In the "advent of this sad gray light" of the next morning, in parodic emulation of Mary Magdalen at the tomb, he searches for his beloved's remains in the ashes, only to fail—"He found not so much as a bone. It was as if she'd never been." In a failed communion, he eats sandwiches, squatting "in a warm place among the ashes eating them, black fingerprints on pale bread, eyes dark and huge and vacant" (*CG,* 107). Later, when the dumpkeeper tells him of one Parton who is burned along with his house, Ballard mourns the loss of his "first love" in a deadpan remark turned into grotesque dramatic irony: "Did they ever find any of him?" (*CG,* 112). If the townspeople of Sevier seek to "find" their dead from Ballard in order to afford them a Christian burial underground in anticipation of their resurrection, Ballard parodically acts out his wish for a resurrection in this, his only life. After the house burns, Ballard's inhabitation of caves is still another repetition of the resurrection, here a form of self-entombment or life-in-death that mirrors the death-in-life of his corpses.

In *Suttree* various images of the decayed or parodic house—Daddy Watson's abandoned railroad car, the decayed ruins of a family estate and Suttree's parish school, the houseboats of Suttree and the Reese

family—furnish an anachronistic sense of the historic remains of an earlier mode of life on which contemporary urban America is superim-
posed. Watson, an old railroader, still dresses himself in "striped engi-
neer's cap" and railroad watch, residing in an old abandoned caboose in
the rail yard. The rapid pace of social change in America's technological
modernization has made an anachronism not only of his trade but his
very identity. While Suttree retars his boat, Watson comically asks him
for help—"I got a leak in my caboose roof"—an innocent reference that
inadvertently connotes his psychological problem of becoming stuck in
time, as his repeated glances at his "enormous railroader's timepiece"
suggest (S, 87). The day after a night's debauch, Suttree takes the bus to
the ruins of his old parochial school on Magnolia Avenue. Entering to
the "gnashing of weeds" in the lot and staring at "scrawled obscenities"
on the blackboard of this "derelict school for lechers," he notices and
ignores an ancient priest in the doorway, a "catatonic shaman" who,
after Suttree abandons the house, stands "in the baywindow watching
like a paper priest in a pulpit or a prophet sealed in glass" (S, 304–305).

Such diminished icons of the personal or Knoxville's past amount to
what Andrew Bartlett terms a "discourse of archaeology" in McCarthy's
fiction—a discourse that "positions itself at a distance from any authoritative pretensions to transcending suffering or mortality by attachment
to allegorical theology or to conventional traditions of (fictional)
decency" (Bartlett, 9). To retain faith is to live inauthentically in the
past, ultimately to become mad like Daddy Watson, whom Suttree last
glimpses in an asylum in "a striped railroader's hat . . . holding a huge
watch in his hand" (S, 434). Earlier in the novel, Suttree falls asleep,
drunk, in a church amidst memories of the sacred ceremonies of his
childhood worship and of the priests drinking coffee and talking shop in
the Market Lunch. Waking to a priest's admonishment, Suttree
declares, "It's not God's house" (S, 254–55). Knoxville and the postmodern Suttree have abandoned the faith of their past, preserved only in
the ruined "remains" of the city's architecture and his memories.

The Houseboat and the River.   While the image of the ruined
house is used throughout American literature, it functions in Southern
literature—for example, in *Absalom, Absalom!*—to remind the reader of
the Civil War's destruction of slavery, the plantation system, and its aristocracy.[6] Nevertheless, in McCarthy's fiction this image is unhistorical,
theological, contemporary, and suggestive of his redirection of Southern

fiction toward a modern, even postmodern, narrative. In *Suttree* another powerful symbolic register (beyond that of house and cave) opposes the river to the shore of Knoxville's McAnally Flats. Again, this image has its analogue in Southern fiction, in *Huckleberry Finn*'s opposition of river to shore, but McCarthy follows Twain's lead in transcending a purely sectional affiliation for this symbolic register of the narrative. McCarthy's river and shore echo the literary history of these images preceding and following Twain: they function both as realistic regional detail and as universal symbols of postmodern contemporary existence.

In Eliot's *The Waste Land* the river Thames operates as one of the primary images conveying the poem's theme of the sterility of life in the modern world. The poem's depiction of the river is replete with images of mud, sewage, and decay; the only life forms are the rats who feed off the carrion and waste on the riverbanks. In *Bleak House* Dickens had made similar symbolic use of the Thames through the image of the mud below and fog above stretching from the river to London. In *Our Mutual Friend* he would develop further the symbolic implications of the river and its inhabitants, evoking an ideology of social decay and psychological death. Lizzy Hexam's vulturelike father rows the river in search of dead bodies to rob and turn in for rewards while the comic hero Boffin is a dustman who turns his dustheaps of London's waste into wealth. Suttree and his neighbor, the alcoholic dumpkeeper, are modern versions of Dickens's Hexam and Boffin.

In *Suttree,* as an early descriptive passage suggests, the Tennessee River operates as a central symbol analogous to the Thames: "He turned heavily on the cot and put one eye to a space in the rough board wall. The river flowing past out there. Cloaca Maxima. Death by drowning, the ticking of a dead man's watch" (*S,* 13). "Death by drowning" alludes directly to the title of the section of *The Waste Land* in which the Thames and the associated figures of the drowned sailor and hanged man denote the decayed state of the West. John Harmon is the drowned man of *Our Mutual Friend,* a depressed bourgeois hero who fakes his drowning in the Thames to test the character of his betrothed, Bella Wilfer. Suttree's first tour of the river ends with the memorable image of the recovery by grappling hook of an anonymous drowned suicide who had jumped from the bridge. Suttree, who has just completed his route of freeing fish from the hooks of his trotline, must watch a ghastly mimicry of his own fishing: "One of the workers was kneeling over the corpse trying to pry the grapnel loose. The crowd was watching him and he was sweating and working at the hook" (*S,* 9).

So Suttree is the analogue of this symbolic figure, the drowned man. While he views his life in the houseboat on the river as a repudiation of his father, it is also a living suicide analogous to Ballard in his cave. Paradoxically, the river is also the novel's primary symbol of life—the life in nature and the lust for life represented by the heart. Suttree makes his living, in the economic and social sense, on the river's fish, though he refuses to eat them. Following his encounter with the drowned man, Suttree rests in his houseboat: "He crossed the cabin and stretched himself out on the cot. Closing his eyes. A faint breeze from the window stirring his hair. The shantyboat trembled slightly in the river and one of the steel drums beneath the floor expanded in the heat with a melancholy bong. Eyes resting. This hushed and mazy Sunday. The heart beneath the breastbone pumping. The blood on its appointed rounds" (S, 13). As symbol of life's fecundity, of the will to live, the river functions as an antipode to the image of the McAnally slum that stretches along its banks. As in Dickens and Eliot, the river serves also as sewer and trash receptacle for the city's waste; a recurrent image is that of the condoms deposited on its shore, floating in its water, and at one point left dangling by receding waters in the trees on its bank. The symbol is ambiguous, at the same time connoting the sterility of loveless desire, lifeless waste, and the imperatives of the drives for love and reproduction. Another avatar for Suttree, along with Daddy Watson and the ragman, is old Maggeson, who occupies himself "plying the trade he has devised for himself," poling a skiff on the river and "wielding a longhandled hook" to retrieve these discarded remnants of desire (S, 65).

Thematically significant is still another scene in which the river functions as temporary cemetery. The river, it suggests, operates as primary representation of Suttree's psyche, in which the two forces of life and death coexist in unresolved conflict. Suttree's sleep after the seduction of a young woman is interrupted by the appearance of his friend Leonard, catamite and burglar, who requests the use of Suttree's boat to bury his father, dead for several months but left unburied so that his mother could continue to receive his Social Security payments. Protesting the interruption, the girl demands that Suttree drive her home: the symbolic choice is between Eros, embodied in the girl, and Thanatos, represented by Leonard and his father. Suttree chooses to aid in the comic burial, Leonard wrapping chains fastened with dime-store locks around the corpse, which is wound in a bedsheet "like a dead klansman" and which lies in the boat, "one leg already reaching over the side into the river as if the old man couldn't wait" (S, 251).

Less comic is the ragman's conversation with Suttree, two chapters later, confessing his death wish: "Here's one that's sick of living" (*S,* 257). Near the novel's end, Suttree finds the ragpicker's corpse, "eyes shut and his mouth set and his hands lay clenched at either side. He looked as if he had forced himself to death" (*S,* 422). Yet the novel's most horrific river burial and one of the most memorable scenes in McCarthy's fiction is the living entombment of another of Suttree's young lovers, Wanda Reese, inside the cliffs looming over the river bank: "The wall of slate above the camp had toppled in the darkness, whole jagged ledges crashing down, great plates of stone separating along the seams with dry shrieks and collapsing with a roar upon the ground below, the dull boom of it echoing across the river and back again. . . . In a raw pool of lightning an image of baroque pieta, the woman gibbering and kneeling in the rain clutching at sheared limbs and rags of meat among the slabs of rock" (*S,* 362). The chapter's final image is of Suttree again on the river, this time floating back to Knoxville, "with no plans for going back the way he'd come" (*S,* 363). The river operates as agent of death and as metaphor for Suttree's life— a one-way lifestream that cannot be repeated or reversed.

Urban Knoxville: "Unreal City" as Underworld.   McAnally Flats, the primary setting of the novel, superimposes the two figurative landscapes of underworld and wasteland. The three-page italicized prolegomenon introduces the novel as an absurdist drama, with Suttree functioning as protagonist and McAnally Flats—"a world within the world"—as stage: "This city constructed on no known paradigm, a mongrel architecture reading back through the works of man in a brief delineation of the aberrant disordered and mad. A carnival of shapes upreared on the river plain that has dried up the sap of earth for miles about" (*S,* 3–4). The drama is an allegory with Suttree in the role of Everyman in that Suttree's midnight walks in McAnally are transformed figuratively into our own walks: "Dear friend, now in these soot-blacked brick or cobbled corridors . . . no soul shall walk save you" (*S,* 3). While the beginning "Dear Friend" apostrophizes Suttree, it also addresses its readers, assigning us our role of audience; the narrative voice performs the role of playwright. McAnally transforms from mimetic landscape into the metaphoric vehicle for the Shakespearean trope of the world as stage: "The rest indeed is silence. It has begun to rain. . . . A curtain is rising on the western world. A fine rain of soot, dead beetles, anonymous small bones. The audience sits webbed in dust.

Within the gutted sockets of the interlocutor's skull a spider sleeps and
the jointed ruins of the hanged fool dangle from the flies, bone pendu-
lum in motley. Fourfooted shapes go to and fro over the boards. Ruder
forms survive" (*S*, 5).

Opposed to the death of the human is another form of play—that of
animal life: it is the "ruder forms" that "survive," while the world of the
human and its representations does not. A fully realized representation
of a historicized city and its inhabitants, most of *Suttree* is intensely
mimetic, save for these carnivalesque dream visions and another form of
vision reflected in the ending. Yet the introduction and these visionary
passages suggest that mimetic realism is hardly the text's sole or even
authoritative mode of representation. Furthermore, the prolegomenon
suggests that Suttree's dilemma is our own: how to live authentically
within the absurdist world in which he finds himself. If "ruder forms
survive," may also the human survive? If so, how then to live?

Two Views of the Underground Man

Coinciding with this dramatic backdrop of the theater of the absurd are
copious images of the clown and carnival. At various times Ballard, Suttree, and Harrogate are all portrayed as characters whose clownish acts
and dress accrue further significations of absurdity to the novels. Pivotal
to both the literature of the underground man and to the absurdist theater of Beckett is the self-consciousness of life's and one's own absurdity.
This theater of the absurd operates as comic vision linking life to death,
though in McCarthy's postmodern narratives, unlike Beckett's, this
absurdist vision is by no means the only vision proffered or authorized
by the narrative. Again, only Suttree exhibits a full recognition of his
own and life's absurdity; Suttree is the most complexly realized character largely by means of his self-conscious choice of alienation, nihilism,
and exile, whereas the pathos of Ballard and Harrogate lies in the condition that only we and the narrator are fully aware of their absurdity.

Gene Harrogate and Lester Ballard as Comic Antiheroes.   The
clown motif represents the progressive fragmentation of Lester's psyche.
Living in his cave after his murder of the dumpkeeper's daughter, "he'd
long been wearing the underclothes of his female victims but now he
took to appearing in their outerwear as well. A gothic doll in illfit
clothes, its carmine mouth floating detached and bright in the white
landscape" (*CG*, 140). Fleeing from his second and final murder, Lester

is termed a "crazed mountain troll clutching up a pair of bloodstained breeches by one hand and calling out in a high mad gibbering" (*CG,* 152). In flight from a posse a few days later, his hair is compared to that of a rag-doll, "hung from his thin skull in lank wet strings" (*CG,* 154). Finally, in the abortive attempt to murder Greer, he is dressed "in frightwig and skirts," the wig "fashioned whole from a dried human scalp" (*CG,* 172–73). While his crossdressing suggests his introjection of and identification with his female victims, his bloodied "carmine mouth" is a ghoulish mimicry or distortion of the clown image.

In *Suttree* Harrogate is similarly depicted. Suttree is aghast at and bemused by Harrogate's appearance, fresh from his release from the workhouse: his shirt "fashioned from an enormous pair of striped drawers, his neck stuck through the ripped seam of his crotch, his arms hanging from the capacious legholes like sticks"; his pants "a pair of outsize pastrycook's trousers with cuffs that reverted back nearly to his knees"; and his "enormous sneakers." After furnishing Harrogate with other clothing, Suttree concludes that Harrogate "looked less like a clown and more like a refugee" (*S,* 114). Two opposing scenes later in the novel emphasize the inappropriateness of Suttree's clothing to sketch his own psychological state. In the first, Suttree inexplicably leaves his impoverished Knoxville existence for the country, apparently to fish. Lost wandering in the mountains for days, at the end of his ordeal he encounters a crossbow hunter whom he mistakes for an hallucination. A glimpse of himself shocks Suttree into normalcy: "He looked down at himself, at the rags of crokersack, the spats of knitting that had been his socks, at the twill trousers black with woodash, the bulbed green knees of them hanging" (*S,* 288–89). In the second scene near the novel's end, Suttree is costumed as pimp by Joyce (his prostitute lover), wearing alligator shoes, camelhair overcoat, "beltless gabardine slacks with little zippers at the sides and a winecolored shirt with a crafty placket" (*S,* 400). Suttree's clothing, chosen at the extremes of poverty or luxury, suggests his alienated psychological state, his lack of self-definition.

A series of carnival images further sketch the main characters' psychological isolation and the novels' absurdist sensibilities. *Child of God* opens with the image of a truckload of musicians, who "came like a caravan of carnival folk up through the swales of broomstraw . . . , the musicians on chairs in the truckbed teetering and tuning their instruments, the fat man with guitar grinning and gesturing to others in a car behind" (*CG,* 3). In contrast to their clownishness is the serious situation of auctioning Lester's family home. Terming the musicians as "fools," he threatens to shoot neither the musicians nor the county residents at the auction but the auctioneer (*CG,* 4). Symptomatic of Lester's progressing alienation is a later account of his shooting prowess at the county fair. Thrown out of one contest for cheating, he is himself cheated by the barker at the shooting gallery. Ballard responds by shooting again, winning two giant teddy bears and a tiger, which he then "loaded up" to carry to the fireworks exhibit.

These carnival toys suggest the pathos and menace of Ballard. By the light of the fireworks, in the midst of "a sea of country people. . .you could see among the faces a young girl with candyapple on her lips and her eyes wide." The girl is described in the sensual terms of Lester's desire, as a "womanchild from beyond the years, rapt below the sulphur glow and pitchlight of some medieval fun fair." Her repudiation of Lester reflects society's repudiation: "in the flood of this breaking brimstone galaxy, she saw the man with the bear watching her and she edged closer to the girl by her side" (*CG,* 65). The next, brief chapter describes Lester at home, closing with the image of the toys as they "watch from the walls, their plastic eyes shining in the firelight and their red flannel tongues out" (*CG,* 67). Here the absurdist imagery of plastic eye and tongue reflects as in a carnival mirror the eyes and red lips of the girl who is the object of Lester's desire.

Continually thwarted in his desire for love and social integration, Lester resorts to a series of substitutes, ultimately to the language of his gun, as his earlier threats against the auctioneer had hinted. Lester will cling to the carnival toys as substitute for family and society until his final capture, even while he uses corpses as substitutes for the unrequited desire aimed at the girl in the carnival scene. Vereen Bell writes that "the truly horrifying aspect of his ghoulish family is that it is less like an underground city of the dead than it is like a monstrous dollhouse where the corpses, along with his stuffed bears and tiger, become facsimile people" (Bell 1988, 61). Mark Winchell reads the same imagery, noting that Ballard "plays house" with his toys and corpses and concluding that "the point is not that there is no distinction between normality and abnormality but that in assaulting that distinction, mockery of the normal becomes a special kind of perversion."[7] In their understandable emphasis on the horror of his perversion, his obsessive misreading of the woman as object, as merely body, Bell and Winchell err only in failing to note the pathos in his substitutions of stuffed animal and corpse—objects of an unrequited, inhuman desire—for a reciprocated human love. Lester's inhuman desires are a simulacrum of love.

Though he cannot articulate his desire, his pathologies demonstrate that his unconscious knows what it is that he misses. His error is in perceiving not merely the female but the whole world as objective spectacle, with himself its collector.

Employed in a manner so reminiscent of the imagery in *Child of God,* the carnival imagery in *Suttree* often seems an amplified revision of the earlier novel. But in *Suttree's* introduction and in a series of hallucinatory dream visions scattered throughout the narrative, the imagery expands to evoke Beckett's absurdist theater and Shakespeare's metonymic equation of the stage and world. Several passages suggest Suttree's desire to retreat from adulthood to a more innocent, childlike state in which the world itself is a grand performance for one's amusement. The first such image occurs when Suttree hears of his child's death. Unable to remember his son's face, "all he could remember was the tiny hand in his as they went to the carnival fair and a fleeting image of elf's eyes wonderstruck at the wide world in its wheeling. Where a ferriswheel swung in the night and painted girls were dancing and skyrockets went aloft and broke to shed a harlequin light above the fairgrounds and the upturned faces" (*S,* 150). The passage's echoes of Nietzsche's Zarusthustrian circus and the Romantic apotheosis of childhood innocence, mediated by Emerson to American romanticism, elicits two ideological readings—of the world as absurd performance and the world as sublime spectacle. But McCarthy complicates Suttree's guilt, through his almost insane insistence on digging his son's grave. In his grief he reverts back to childhood, likening his own "dread" preceding his son's funeral to his fear of his "father in the aftermath of some child's transgression" (*S,* 152). The very theatricality of Suttree's reaction to his son's death suggests that the dread and fear provoked by his son's death are overdetermined, expressive more of his own selfishness and his own dread: "Death is what the living carry with them. A state of dread, like some uncanny foretaste of a bitter memory" (*S,* 153).

In a similar passage, during a lover's vacation at an idyllic resort setting with Joyce, his prostitute lover, Suttree feels her breast against him and "wondered if she were ever a child at a fair dazed by the constellations of light and the hurdygurdy music of the merrygoround and the raucous calls of the barkers. Who saw in all that shoddy world a vision that child's grace knows and never the sweat and the bad teeth and the nameless stains in the sawdust, . . . and the vacant look of solitaries who go among these garish holdings seeking a thing they could not name" (*S,* 408–409). His own question cynically mirrors and distorts the child's innocent wonder; the passage suggests that he withdraws in bad faith, spurning her as jaded prostitute though he continually has benefited from the money earned by her trade. It is his own death that Suttree dreads in his son's death and in Joyce's love; it is his own childish wonder at the world's "harlequin light," not that of his son or Joyce, that he craves to reexperience.

Suttree as Absurdist Antihero.   A series of dream visions in the novel further develops this carnival image as a primal scene of the consciousness that rather arbitrarily assigns forms and meanings to the arbitrary dance of the phenomena that make up the world. The first such vision is an apparent hallucination that Suttree experiences in the hospital while he is treated for a skull fracture suffered in a bar brawl. The narrative point of view is indeterminate, apparently representing the collective voice of Suttree's friends and acquaintances who participated in the fight: "We saw you took down to the brainsurgeon's keep, deep in the cellar, under the street. Where the saws sang in stoven skulls" (*S,* 188). Suddenly, the point of view shifts from exterior, realistic representation to an internalized dream vision that can only be Suttree's: "Out there in the blue moonlight a gray shecorpse being loaded into a truck. It pulled away into the night. Horned minstrels, small dancing dogs in harlequin garb hobbled after" (*S,* 188). From this vision of a corpse escorted by harlequins, the perspective abruptly shifts, suddenly panning to an omniscient, wide-angle perspective of Knoxville as bleak underworld: "The night is cold and colder, a fog moves with menace in the streets. Malefic stirrings underfoot, a foul breath rising visibly from the pierced sewerlids. . . . Out there in the winter streets a few ashen anthroparians scuttling yet through the falling soot. Above them the shape of the city a colossal horde of retorts and alembics ranged against a starless sky" (*S,* 188). The allusions to fog, night, and "anthroparians" are reminiscent of the bleak, fog-obscured beginning of Dickens's *Bleak House,* which envisions London similarly as a Hades-like underworld. The passage ends uncannily, with a hortatory, prophetic address to the unconscious protagonist: "Uneasy sleeper you will live to see the city of your birth pulled down to the last stone" (*S,* 188). Yet it is not Knoxville itself that is deconstructed at the novel's ending but McAnally Flats, the novel's objective correlative for Suttree's psyche.

Might this prophetic voice here and in similar passages constitute the response of Suttree's superego to the imaginary dream representations of his unconscious? Vereen Bell's early essay on *Suttree* reads the novel's conflict in terms of "the negotiations between the ego and the contrary world" but assigns passages with such "intensity of consciousness" to the perspective of the novelist or "the novel itself."[8] Whatever the identity of this voice, these carnivalesque dream visions point to a more primal, disordered form of perception that has its existence beyond or underneath the more civilized or rational epistemic perception of the world. The dense poetic imagery of the passage suggests that this perception verges upon that of the romantic imagination; the "uneasy sleeper" may refer not only to the hallucinating Suttree but perhaps to the sleeping faculty of his imagination or unconscious—a faculty whose rich verbal imagery rivals that of the novel's narrative perception. As I shall demonstrate in the next two chapters, it is this problem of the epistemic perception of the world that will increasingly absorb McCarthy's Southwestern fiction.

Thus in *Suttree* we often are uncertain of the boundary between realistic representation, hallucination, imaginary vision, and dream; the image of the carnival encompasses and merges all four states. Half-starved in the Tennessee wilderness, a day before he encounters the hunter with crossbow, Suttree envisions an encounter with "a troupe of squalid merrymakers"—trolls, gnomes, "chimeras and cacodemoni skewered up on boarspears"—from whom issue "sounds of carnival." His response is "a half grin of wry doubt" representing the state of his perception, trapped in the boundaries between rational apprehension and fantastic imagination (*S*, 287–88). The hermeneutics of deciphering these entangled layers of psychological and textual representations becomes most problematic precisely at the two later climactic points of the text: the complex series of dream visions, memories, and prophetic visions Suttree encounters, first in response to imbibing a drug mixed by the "black witch known as Mother She," next in the throes of a fever that almost kills him and from which he emerges at the novel's end. As we shall see, his conversations with the black speakeasy owner Ab Jones and the visionary ending of the novel suggest that such a sense of detached absurdity is one that Suttree must resist in order to authentically act and define his existence in the world.

Death and Rebirth in *Suttree*

Nihilism and Death.   Suttree's dread of death and the stratagems he uses to evade or deflect his fear are representations, however extreme, of our own fear. And he must verge on a physical death and experience several forms of psychological death before the novel will close. Through his double, Suttree also is confronted with the problem of his identity. But does the novel's ending represent a resolution, even a provisional one, of his dilemma of his identity and existence? If so, is that resolution a satisfactory one?

Every critic of *Suttree*, following the lead of Vereen Bell in his long chapter in *The Achievement of Cormac McCarthy*, has recognized that Suttree's problems stem from his fear of death. Bell calls attention to a passage in the novel's prolegomenon that directly poses the problem:

> The night is quiet. Like a camp before battle. The city beset by a thing unknown and will it come from forest or sea? The murengers have walled the pale, the gates are shut, but lo the thing's inside and can you guess his shape? Where he's kept or what's the counter of his face? Is he a weaver, bloody shuttle shot through a timewarp, a carder of souls from the world's nap? Or a hunter with hounds or do bone horses draw his deadcart through the streets and does he call his trade to each? (*S*, 4–5)

The imagery of the passage—the thing inside, the hunter and hounds, the horse and cart—recurs through the text on both literal and metaphoric levels. For instance, a coal seller by the name of General and his horse Golgotha open the chapter after Suttree's return from Lynchburg (162); the image of the hunter and hounds is echoed in the novel's conclusion (471). Bell reads the opening passage of "the thing inside" by associating Suttree's consciousness with the walled city; despite his best defenses, death "has breached even the walls of consciousness, infecting his will to be" (Bell 1988, 69). His consciousness of death produces in Suttree what Bell in an earlier essay had termed an existential, "ambiguous nihilism" and John Lewis Longley, Jr., "a metaphysics of death."[9]

Frank Shelton expands Bell's existential reading, finding the novel's center in its opposition between life and suicide, comparing its resolution to Camus's meditation on suicide in "The Myth of Sisyphus."[10] And in a fine essay, Thomas D. Young, Jr., supplies a Freudian gloss on Bell's more existential reading, commenting that "the city as aberrant accretion . . . aberrant because it rises from the need to check the very impulses that gave it being—is replicated in Suttree's unwelcome intellectuality."[11] Young finds Suttree's consciousness to be symptomatic of the inhibitions in Freud's *Civilization and Its Discontents*—inhibitions that enable civilization by censoring free expression of the instinctual drives, thereby also giving rise to neurosis.

The very sensibility that enables Suttree to critique his father's bour-geois ideology and ally himself with those in McAnally who are figura-tively "outside" the city leaves him open to neurotic and suicidal behav-ior: his dysfunctional love affairs, his paranoid fear of hospitals, his alcoholic binges and brawling. Such behavior seems a method of court-ing rather than evading his own death. In particular, while his drinking binges may anaesthetize his ego against its awareness of the death-in-life surrounding him, they also result in a series of metaphoric deaths. In one drunken brawl, Suttree is struck by a floor buffer that fractures his skull and paradoxically brings on the very visionary death state he is attempting to evade. In another scene, late in the novel, Suttree and his friend Blind Richard sit drinking at Ab Jones's place, the tabletop formed of a headstone. Challenged by Suttree to read the name under-neath, Richard discovers that the name is the same as their brawling friend William Callahan (*S,* 371). The next morning, Reese, the father of Suttree's dead lover Wanda, appears ghostlike at Suttree's houseboat to divide shares, while one chapter later Callahan is shot and dies in Sut-tree's arms (372, 376).

The very sensitivity of Suttree's imaginative perception, lacking in most other McCarthy characters, may betray us into excessive sympathy. The end of the prolegomenon depicting the "unknown" besieger of McAnally warns us and Suttree: "Dear friend he is not to be dwelt upon for it is by just suchwise that he's invited in." Suttree's obsession with evading death constitutes a form of its embrace. As grotesque as Lester's perversions are Suttree's death visions, which end in the common image of the embrace and sexual intercourse with a hag redolent of death. During his deathlike fever, Suttree dreams of intercourse with "a gross dancer" with "yellow puckered belly," lips "hiding little rows of rubber teeth" (*S,* 449). Lester Ballard and Suttree share this obsession with Death, only Lester's embrace is literal while Suttree's is self-conscious, metaphysical, and imaginative. Surrounded by the deaths of his family and comrades, haunted by his own death visions, and indulging in suici-dal behavior, Suttree somehow seems to emerge from his dilemma, choosing life at the novel's close.

The Twin: Suttree and AntiSuttree. While Bell's existential and Young's Freudian readings help us attend to the organizing theme of death in the novel, Suttree's embrace of death is a symptom, not the cause, of illness. Suttree is an instance of the divided consciousness of modernity. This divided consciousness, whether neurotic or nihilistic, is represented powerfully throughout in the form of the ghostly double or "antiSuttree." As we early discover in the conversation with his uncle, Suttree's knowledge of the arbitrariness of his existence stems from an awareness of himself as the surviving twin, his identical twin having died inexplicably at birth (S, 14, 17–18). This "antiSuttree" haunts him continually: outside Lynchburg "some doublegoer, some othersuttree eluded him in these woods" (S, 287). Noting a series of passages in which this twin motif occurs, Thomas Young reads this opposition between Suttree and his twin in terms of the opposition between consciousness and the universe of death, expressing his "preoccupation with time and mortality" (Young, 75–76, 79). Yet this antiSuttree has a further signification than this thematic association with death or nihilism. Curiously, the ending suggests that it is only by merging his identity with that of this other self that Suttree can emerge from his death in life.

The novel's persistent imagery of the double indicates that Suttree's dilemma stems from a fragmentation of his psyche, a split between two principles of self that must somehow be merged or reincorporated. Rather than Young's orthodox Freudian analysis, a Lacanian reading might further illuminate Suttree's double consciousness. The first principle of the self is the primary Suttree of the novel, trapped within the construct of his family—the forbidding father who worships society's structures of power in the courts and business, writing him that "there is nothing occurring in the streets"; his lower-class mother whom he sees as attempting to infantilize him in her tears at their prison meeting; his dead twin; his fantasies of the dead grandfather who threatens to take him into the grave. This Suttree corresponds to the Lacanian I or speaking self.[12] This Suttree speaks through his rebellions—his alcoholism, his vocation of fishing, his residence on the houseboat—against the father's social law and inhibitions that he sees as constraining or repressing the expression of what he feels to be his authentic self.

We have already noted the primary structure of Suttree's familial relationships, which take the form of Suttree's rebellion against and repudiation of his family. Curiously, in his relationships with women, Suttree mimics the very behavior of the father he has repudiated. The father, he tells his uncle, treats his mother as social inferior or maid; Suttree similarly betrays his own sense of superiority to his mother, inferior in her open expression of grief at the workhouse. His refusal of the prostitute Joyce's love appears another rebellion, in that he cynically smiles at their parody of bourgeois love and courtship. The night after moving with Joyce to a new apartment, Suttree introspectively denies himself and the relationship, "staring into space, detached, a displaced soul musing on the hiatus between himself and the Suttree moving through these strange quarters." Later, gazing out the window, he offers a "mute toast" with "a gesture indifferent and almost cynical" to an impoverished old man across the street (*S,* 402). The distance between himself and the antiSuttree also distances himself from his feelings for Joyce, dooming their relationship. Furthermore, in a social sense, Suttree rejects her as inferior, in mimicry of the structure of his father's view of his mother. Finally, his relationship with Wanda Reese again is one of social inequality; characteristically, at several points he tries to end the relationship by removing himself from the family camp and from her (*S,* 355). Although his grief after her death is genuine, after watching—but not joining in—the demonstrative grief of her mother, he leaves immediately for Knoxville (*S,* 362–63).

The twin or antiSuttree corresponds to the more primal or primitive self of the Lacanian *moi,* the inarticulate imaginary self that is composed first out of the incorporation of the fragmented images of the outside world. In the Lacanian mirror stage, the infant consolidates the formerly fragmented sense of self into a single Gestalt symbolized by the whole human figure reflected in the mirror.[13] Thereafter, this agency of the self is composed of a series of unconscious relations in which it desires the recognition of the Other; human relations are structured by the forms by which this self seeks the desired recognition of itself as a whole. Thus in his alcoholic and fevered visions, Suttree's unconscious takes the form of his dead twin, the "othersuttree."

Suttree's Rebirth.   In the encounters with his double, the primary, conscious Suttree is confronted by his unconscious, fragmented self. In the death visions it is this primitive, imaginary self that speaks in dreamlike, fantastic images to the primary, conscious Suttree. A critical problem in reading the novel is the formative principle or logic of the conclusion, which implicitly allows Suttree to avoid Lester's or Harrogate's fate. Critics disagree both on whether to read this conclusion as a rebirth or merely as an ending. In part, the interpretive problem is that, in comparison with the copious material delineating his dilemma, the resolution—if it is resolution—is given only a minimum of space, represented primarily by a few hallucinatory dream states elusive in imagery and implication. In the novel's indefinite conclusion, Suttree runs away from Knoxville and his past. The affirmation in the final scene—what he runs toward—is unspecified, though hauntingly powerful. I would suggest that only through reincorporating this unconscious self can Suttree "resolve" the dilemma of his life.

However abstract or vague is the process of Suttree's rebirth in the visionary scenes of the concluding chapters, it can be broken down into rough stages. Three almost simultaneous stages take shape: first, his acceptance of his own death (not merely the intellectual acceptance of death as a universal process but a visionary experience of death); second, the reintegration of his identity into a single form; third, his implicit affirmation of the Other, the validity or worth of the lives of the doomed with whom he has lived for the past years in McAnally. In his death visions Suttree confronts his friends and relatives in death (S, 452), is suffered entrance to the death world by a Charon in the guise of a turtle-hunter he met as a child (S, 455), and experiences a parodic self-judgment, accused of murdering first "Tweetiepie" and then his great-uncle by "lycanthropy" (S, 454–58).

Suttree's psychic rebirth is symbolized by one of the final dream visions, in which he witnesses the rebirth of an Atlantean continent rising from the sea floor:

> As we watched there reared out of the smoking brine a city of old bone coughed up from the sea's floor, pale attic bone delicate as shell and half melting . . . , and across the whole a frieze of archer and warrior and marblebreasted maid all listing west and moving slowly their stone limbs. As these figures began to cool and take on life Suttree among the watchers said that this time there are witnesses, for life does not come slowly. It rises in one massive mutation and all is changed utterly and forever. We have witnessed this thing today which prefigures for all time the way in which historic orders proceed. (S, 459)

Here Suttree's dream self or unconscious perceives his surroundings not just as redolent of death but in a universal historic process defined by the flux between death, life, and rebirth.

Suttree eventually experiences a psychic reintegration that amounts to a rebirth. Given unacquiesced last rites by a priest who explains his survival with "God must have been watching over you," Suttree rejoins, "You would not believe what watches. . . . Nothing ever stops moving" (S, 461). Here he reiterates the conception of life as flux encapsulated in the Atlantean vision above. But this principle is also directed at the self. In a parodic postmodern creed of the self, Suttree affirms to the priest, "There is one Suttree and one Suttree only" (S, 461). There are many

Suttrees—the "othersuttree" of the unconscious, the Suttree in the visions who "watches" or regards himself, the Suttree of the fragmentary childhood memories—yet all are here collapsed into one dynamic principle of the living Suttree. Furthermore, this integration of the self makes possible a reintegration of Suttree into society—or perhaps the causal relationship is the reverse. In the midst of his fever, Suttree tells the nurse, "I know all souls are one and all souls are lonely" (*S,* 459). The statement comments not only on his own alienation but on what he has learned of those who surround him, during the disintegration of his own community through the deaths of Callahan and Ab Jones, the emigration of J-Bone and other friends, and the imprisonment of Harrogate. Suttree is at his most sympathetic in the almost nurturing role he plays to Harrogate as substitute son. Ab Jones, the elderly black bar owner and rebel, correspondingly fulfills the function of father to Suttree. Ab Jones recognizes Suttree as a man of good faith toward himself and others of McAnally, telling him, "You got a good heart, Youngblood. Look out for you own" (*S,* 203). After the disappearance of his community, Suttree takes Jones's advice by leaving McAnally Flats, looking out for himself in a way that Harrogate, who earlier refused to flee, has not.

The Water of Life versus the River.

By fleeing McAnally Flats, Suttree reintegrates himself and achieves at least a provisional affirmation of life—his own and the life surrounding him. The imagery of the conclusion of *Suttree* suggests such an affirmation. Leaving the rubble of McAnally, which is being razed to make room for a new highway, Suttree emerges on the highway and watches a construction crew. A young boy first dips water to the working crew, then, seeing Suttree at the roadside, crosses the ditch and offers "the dipper up all bright and dripping." Two hermetic symbols of Suttree's self and social integration close the novel: he sees himself "twinned" in the boy's eyes; next a car stops for him without his beckoning. The novel concludes with the image of death's hounds that "sniff" where Suttree recently has stood and with the injunction, "I have seen them in a dream, slaverous and wild and their eyes crazed with ravening for souls in this world. Fly them" (*S,* 470–71). The closing sentence represents two resolutions—one relatively clear and the other problematic. First, the narrator's use of the first person "I" is symptomatic. Who is this I? Apparently, the voice is the same as that of the prolegomenon, with its warning against dwelling upon the "thing outside." While this "I" might be associated with an omniscient narrative observer, it may instead represent the reflective consciousness of Suttree, locating its own moral voice or working through its submergence in the dream visions of the unconscious. And in one sense, this advice may contradict Suttree's own experience: while his departure from McAnally is a flight or escape from death, it has only been by confronting death in the form of his own unconscious that Suttree is able to thus affirm and presumably reorient his life.

Despite *Child of God*'s and *Suttree*'s shared theme of the underground man and a series of common images and scenes, it is not only Suttree's more acute consciousness but his ability to sustain social connections that make possible a kind of provisional redemption near the novel's end—connections that Lester in *Child of God* is denied, or denies himself. In terms of this social dimension, Suttree's resolution of his dilemma is especially problematic. We can only infer that his flight is constructive, reintegrative, and life-affirming. At the same time, however, Suttree's flight from Knoxville seems merely to repeat his repudiations of or flights from family, Joyce, and the Reeses. Indeed, in the opening of his next novel, *Blood Meridian,* McCarthy has his protagonist escape Tennessee for the violence of the West, thereby revising both the conclusion of *Suttree* and John Wesley Rattner's departure from Red Branch in *The Orchard Keeper.* Nevertheless, in that Suttree flies not only away from death but presumably toward life, he thereby can evade Harrogate's or Lester Ballard's fate and follows Ab Jones's advice to "look out." Presumably he has concluded his "look-out," finding his heart and a new Suttree, and is now searching for a new community. But the ending with Suttree on the road makes such a reading only a possibility, not a definitive solution to Suttree's dilemma.

Chapter Four

Rewriting the Southwest: *Blood Meridian* as a Revisionary Western

In the previous two chapters, Cormac McCarthy's early fiction from *The Orchard Keeper* to *Suttree* is read as a merging of the tradition of Southern literature with characteristic features of literary modernism and postmodernism. McCarthy's 1985 novel *Blood Meridian or the Evening Redness in the West* represents a crucial shift in his imagination—a shift away from the "Southern" orientation of his first five Tennessee novels and toward the Southwest. A historical novel of the American West, *Blood Meridian* imagines the human dimensions of the conquest by the North American empire of the Southwest territories and the Native American tribes inhabiting them. Sharing the setting of this 1985 novel but covering more contemporary periods of Southwestern history, the first two novels of the Border Trilogy (initiated by the 1991 publication of *All the Pretty Horses*) examine cultural conflict in the modern Southwest. Thus the last phase of McCarthy's novel-writing career mirrors the shape of American history from the westward continental expansion in the nineteenth century to the urbanization of the contemporary American West.[1]

"Lighting Out for the Territory"

Blood Meridian's migration to a Western setting and its investigation of the violence of nineteenth-century Western expansion are not unanticipated in McCarthy's earlier fiction. The conclusion of *The Orchard Keeper* anticipates this movement west through John Wesley Rattner's departure from the enclosed cemetery "out to the western road." Having turned his back on his home, his past, and the Southern Appalachias, Rattner implicitly sets out on the road to make a new beginning for himself. Viewed in this context, the concluding passage of *Suttree* seemingly would represent another escape to the West. Suttree departs

Knoxville hitchhiking (though his direction is unspecified) along the highway whose construction has required the razing of his adopted home of McAnally Flats. In McCarthy's early fiction the movement away or westward from the geographical South is associated with psychological rebirth or renewal. Those characters unable to escape the cultural confines of their environs—Arthur Ownby in *The Orchard Keeper,* Lester Ballard in *Child of God,* Culla Holme in *Outer Dark,* and Gene Harrogate in *Suttree*—end up trapped in literal or psychological death.

Yet the opening of *Blood Meridian* questions earlier positive associations between westward migration and self-renewal. In its very first period—"See the child"—the novel introduces its unnamed protagonist, the 14-year-old son of an alcoholic, widowed schoolteacher.[2] His flight westward is sketched for the next few pages—from Memphis to St. Louis to New Orleans and finally to Galveston and Nacogdoches. Debarking the boat in Galveston, "only now is the child finally divested of all that he has been. His origins are become remote as is his destiny" (*BM,* 4–5). Once arrived in the West, "the child" loses his childhood and is transformed into a character who will be known henceforth as "the kid." It is the positioning of this journey in the narrative that constitutes it as a revision of such journeys in McCarthy's earlier fiction. Although Rinthy's early departure from her home in search of her child in *Outer Dark* might appear to anticipate the kid's journey, her and Culla's paths are elliptical, ending geographically where they began. If McCarthy's early novels achieve closure through a series of successful or abortive escapes, *Blood Meridian* opens with a westward escape whose consequences are envisioned in the remainder of the novel until its conclusion, two years after the extinction of the buffalo, a symbol of the historic closure of the Western frontier (*BM,* 316–17). Closing the narrative proper, of course, is the kid's death, the conclusion of his life's journey westward.

The Kid's Wilderness Escape: Self-Purification or Purgatory?

While the novel revises McCarthy's earlier fiction, the account of the kid's childhood in the opening pages also rewrites the American romance. Like Huckleberry Finn or Ike McCaslin of *The Bear,* the kid undertakes the American masculine romance of "lighting out for the territory"—an embarkation in which the Western wilderness represents a new origin for the self "divested" of Huck's "sivilization."[3] For example, the choice of "divested" in the passage quoted earlier revises Faulkner's "relinquished" in *The Bear,* a term used to describe Ike

McCaslin's symbolic renunciation of his inherited property and the curse of plantation slavery, and also "dispossessed," which refers to the dual dispossession of the African slaves and Native Americans from the land. Ike maintains that by holding the right of property to be superior to the natural rights of man or nature, Western man is "dispossessed" from an Edenic state within the self, a state whose analogue is the bear, symbol of pure wilderness and a pure primitive self.[4] What is "divested" from these American male heroes are the husks of their past—familial, cultural, geographic—that surround and confine the innermost self.[5] Purged of the historical past, this self is reborn in the Western wilderness, apparently purified; the kid's eyes, for instance, are depicted as "oddly innocent" despite the omnipresent violence he experiences from the very beginning of his journey (*BM,* 4). Leo Marx has argued that this association between wilderness and purification defines American fiction from the nineteenth century to the modernism of James and Faulkner.[6] More recently, examining the development of the authority of the American writer from the American Renaissance to modernity, Jerome Loving contends that "the central experience in American literature in the nineteenth century (if not also in the twentieth) is essentially the puritanical desire for the prelapsarian—that second chance of coming into experience anew."[7]

Like Lester Ballard, the kid in *Blood Meridian* nevertheless is always denied such authentic rebirth, though several of his experiences parody or mock these rebirths at the heart of the canonical novels in the early American tradition. In one such episode, the kid is reborn into his new identity as Indian fighter, his Eastern identity eradicated after a Comanche attack in which all save one of his companions are killed: "With darkness one soul rose wondrously from among the new slain dead and stole away in the moonlight. . . . He went forth stained and stinking like some reeking issue of the incarnate dam of war herself" (*BM,* 55). Meeting with a troop of Mexican cavalrymen, he is granted a drink of water, then told by the leader, "When the lambs is lost in the mountain" they "is cry. Sometime come the mother. Sometime the wolf" (*BM,* 65). While sharing the naïveté of his predecessors Ike McCaslin and Huck, the kid is denied the ethical growth that follows their wilderness rebirths.

In his recent study of postmodernism, John McGowan parallels this retreat by American fictional characters into a purified self to the flight of American writers toward an "autonomy" inside the sanctity of nonrepresentational art. Both forms of escape, he argues, are analogues of international modernism's flight away from Western commercial society.[8] Despite the precariousness of their position "outside" Western civilization, Huck's "good heart" and Ike's renunciation constitute such an attempt to critique a monolithic Western culture by an escape within the autonomous self. In a postmodern rewriting of the tradition, McCarthy's *Blood Meridian* further critiques this attempt to flee into the "territory" of art or into the heart in order to achieve a critique of society. The novel does so by complicating the "nature" of the kid's "heart," of the wilderness, and of man's authority over nature and other men. With the kid newly arrived in Texas, the Western portion of the narrative is introduced by a fictional koan posed to the kid and to readers: "Not again in all the world's turning will there be terrains so wild and barbarous to try whether the stuff of creation may be shaped to man's will or whether his own heart is not another kind of clay" (*BM,* 5). Apparently, the narrative will inquire first into the relation between nature and man—specifically the extent of man's autonomy and authority over nature—and then into man's ethos to judge whether the "heart" signifies a moral principle inherent in the self (like Huck's "good" heart) or whether it denotes merely a biological function.

Border Violence.　In another act of self-revision, the geographical movement of McCarthy's fiction to the Southwest in *Blood Meridian* redefines the definition of "border" in his earlier fiction from a hill–valley or North–South border to one tilted along a Northeasterly to Southwesterly plane. By tracing the violent lives of the kid, the judge, and their various historic or fictional cohorts in the Glanton gang of scalphunters, *Blood Meridian* intensifies McCarthy's early interest in the violence which accompanies the clash of cultures along geographical and cultural borders. *The Orchard Keeper, Outer Dark,* and *Child of God* had examined violent conflict between the more settled "Southern" society of the villages and cities of Tennessee and the culture represented by the "Appalachian" characters such as Arthur Ownby, Culla Holme and the mysterious gang of outlaws who are his antagonists, Lester Ballard, and the Reese family. All genealogically descend from Arthur Ownby of *The Orchard Keeper,* who on one hand is fiercely independent, individualistic, true to his own code yet also quick to violence, suspicious of the literal or cultural intrusions of the outside, modern world. The road leading into Red Branch connects it both to the modern world of Knoxville and Atlanta and to Arthur's wilderness home in the hills, defining a border between hill and valley, Appalachian and Southern culture, past and modernity.

Frederic Church: Frontier, Sunset, and the American Apocalypse.   This westward escape or liberation of the enclosed self and the problem of intercultural border violence caused by such escapes are encapsulated symbolically in the image specified in the novel's full title, *Blood Meridian or the Evening Redness in the West.* The novel's dominant image is the bloody Western sunset from which the novel's title is derived—an image inherited from many Easterners' reaction to the Western sunset and employed in American fiction first, to my knowledge, in Fenimore Cooper's *The Prairie.* In that novel the bloody sunset is linked first to the dying Leatherstocking (whose violence is considered a "pure" kind), then associated with the family of Ishmael Bush, the original settlers of the American prairie. The family's violence introduces original sin to that prairie in the form of the murder of kin. In McCarthy, this bloody sunset is associated first with the kid as he departs Nacogdoches traveling again westward after his first meeting with the judge: "the evening sun declines before him beyond an endless swale and dark falls here like a thunderclap and a cold wind sets the weeds to gnashing" (*BM,* 15). The central function of this imagery of the declining sun is strengthened by repetition a few pages later as the kid enters Bexar on the Texas frontier: "the sun was just down and to the west lay reefs of bloodred clouds" (*BM,* 21).

The image of "bloodred clouds," reiterated in a series of similar passages, probably alludes to the great American romantic painter Frederic Church, several of whose greatest paintings, like the celebrated 1860 *Twilight in the Wilderness,* focus on the same image of blood-red clouds at evening stretched over a darkened American wilderness. This 1860 painting is an apocalyptic revision of earlier canvases such as the 1856 *Twilight (Sunset), Sunset* and the 1850 *Twilight, "Short arbiter 'twixt day and night.'"* In the latter work, whose title alludes to Satan's return to Paradise in Book 9 of *Paradise Lost,* Church had dramatized the evening sunlight extending over the Vermont wilderness. In these landscape paintings, as Franklin Kelly suggests, Church moves away from a pastoral vision and toward a heightened allegorical presentation combining mimetic (indeed, almost photographic) details with an allegorical tension between dark and light.[9] His manipulation of light transforms the realistic into the apocalyptic: the extended blood-red sky and darkened

landscape of Church's 1860 painting point toward the American apocalypse impending in the events preceding the outbreak of Civil War
(Kelly, 59). McCarthy's sunset is transformed into a similar apocalyptic
scene by the attachment of a further detail, both realistic and allegorical: out of these clouds "rose little desert nighthawks like fugitives from
some great fire at the earth's end" (*BM*, 21). This reference to fire
mimetically reinforces the color and heat of the desert sun in the landscape yet supplies a further allegorical context—that of the earth's holocaust, which will presage the end of earthly time in the Christian apocalypse.

In *Blood Meridian* the sky's "bloodred" color also signifies the blood
and violence accompanying the kid's passage west. Heading into this
red sunset first after abandoning his father in Tennessee (the account of
that journey "marks" the passage of McCarthy's narrative imagination
from South to West), the kid is inducted into the Western culture of violence through three brawls, described in uncommonly brutal detail. In
one, he and a ne'er-do-well named Toadvine set fire to a hotel door,
kicking unconscious the man inside, while in another the kid jams the
shards of a bottle end into a barman's eye (*BM*, 9, 25). In both brawls,
the kid's violence is largely motiveless, blinding the barman for refusing
him a drink after finishing his own self-appointed task of sweeping the
bar's floor. Ironically, the kid's maiming of the bartender makes him
"eligible" for recruitment into the company of filibusterers led by a Captain White, who attempts to lure the kid into enrolling with the
promise of a homestead in Mexican territory at the end of the fighting
(*BM*, 34). As White's troop heads west into the desert, the rising sun,
with a "deeper run of color like blood seeping up in sudden reaches flar-
ing planewise," is characterized as "squat and pulsing and malevolent
behind them" (*BM*, 45).

In White's company, the kid receives a bloody tutelage into Indian
warfare and, jailed in Sonora for filibustering, eventually signs up with
John Joel Glanton and his band of scalphunters. With Glanton's gang,
immediately before the kid's first battle with the Apache, the sun at
evening is compared to a "holocaust" above "crumpled butcherpaper
mountains" lying in "sharp shadowfold"; by chucking his horse forward,
Glanton "passed and so passed into the problematical destruction of
darkness" (*BM*, 105). Although many similar passages could be analyzed, the narrative's predominant image clearly and unflinchingly
establishes a poetics of Western violence associated with the apocalyptic
decline of the sun over the Western landscape (*BM*, 132–33, 139,

281–82, 293–94). In this context, the *blood meridian* of the title is used as an extremity, peak, or climax; the period covered by the events of the novel is chosen as the historical position when the bloodshed of the West is at its peak. McCarthy's first "western" thus concurs with the earlier tradition of Fenimore Cooper's historical romances and the later western in acknowledging the extraordinary brutality of this historical period in Western expansionism. But as opposed to Cooper's "good" killer Natty Bumppo or the hero represented in John Wayne's cowboy gunfighters or Clint Eastwood's more naturalistic revision of Wayne's gunfighters, in *Blood Meridian* all characters have "hearts of clay" and are led to their eventual doom by the fallen vision of the group's two leaders, Judge Holden and John Joel Glanton.

The Revisionary Western and Historical Romance

As these references to Wayne and Eastwood imply, *Blood Meridian* might usefully be regarded as what I would term a "revisionary western," a postmodern form of the historical romance. As a fictional mode, the historical romance implies a special or extraordinary relation between fictional and historical elements, combined in a larger imaginative narrative. The revisionary western applies this combination of fictional and historical elements from the historical romance but also selects, revises, and reassimilates materials from the indigenous western—the genre that began in the 1880s in the dime novel and, with the invention of the motion picture, gained influence, popularity, and respectability, eventually becoming known as "the Hollywood western." The revisionary western revises the earlier tradition of the western in a postmodern fashion, reusing and parodying elements of the genre and of the historical record in order to critique the historical myth of our traditional narratives of the West.

A Historical Romance of Manifest Destiny.   The first third of the novel, detailing the kid's recruitment into White's filibusterers and then into the Glanton gang of scalphunters, aptly illustrates McCarthy's integration of fact and fiction into the larger narrative of a historical romance. The episode with Captain White and his company of filibusterers is almost entirely fictional. To be sure, the historical period immediately preceding and subsequent to the Mexican War teemed with political rhetoric and plots to extend the American empire by war, intrigue, or filibuster. A fictional character, White superbly represents these attempts to acquire territory for the American empire in the Western territories. Mimicking speeches and editorials by Stephen Douglass, John O'Sullivan, William Swain, and other expansionists,[10] his speech to the kid interprets the Treaty of Guadelupe Hidalgo as a betrayal of the American volunteers fighting in the Mexican War and dismisses the Mexican possessors of the Southwestern territories as "barbarians" and "mongrels" unfit for republican government (*BM,* 33-34).

As analyzed by historians such as Alan Weinberg, the rhetoric of Manifest Destiny justified territorial acquisition by combining racism with an appropriated version of the Puritan notion of predestination. The ideology of Manifest Destiny held that one race, the Anglo-Saxon, combined with the political form of republican government, comprised an elect nation that held the true title to the American landscape; justification for the individual and the communal enterprise of expansion and settlement lay in the subjugation of nature, both within man and without.[11] The "foreordained" geographical limits of the United States were commonly held to extend from the Atlantic to Pacific, although the nation's North and South "predestined" perimeters were debated before, during, and after the Mexican War. Desires for territorial acquisition competed with Northern fears of the extension of slavery (along with low-wage black workers) into the territories and with Southern fears of contaminating Anglo settlers in Mexican territory with "colored" or "mixed" blood.[12] This expansionist ideology was modernized in the Golden Age western, which tended to divide territorial antagonists into allegorical groups of "good" white and "bad" black hats (or white and red skin).

White's rhetoric, however, is exposed by subsequent events as the raving of a lunatic. Another prominent feature of the rhetoric of Manifest Destiny used the military successes of the new American nation—the Revolution, the Mexican War—as indicative first of Anglo-Saxon racial superiority and second of the nation's divine mandate to spread over and possess the North American continent. White justifies his invasion by arguing that the Mexican government's inability to protect its citizens against the Apache signifies its inferiority and cowardice. Yet in his very first engagement he loses his entire company to the Comanche, then is beheaded by a Mexican trooper who lays claim to his gun and horse and pickles his head. Judged even on the terms of his own rhetoric, White's defeat in battle contradicts his assurance in his racial and national superiority. While in a Mexican stockade, the kid comments on White's beheading: "By rights they ought to pickle mine. For ever takin up with such a fool" (*BM,* 70). Though the distinctions between the kid and McCarthy's narrator are many, here the kid appears to speak in part for the narrator. While the kid judges White in practical terms, not necessarily in contradiction of White's rhetoric, the narration here implies as foolish his equation of military victory with a divine principle behind history, particularly the assumption that such victories (and a sense of superiority based on a peculiar mixture of racial Darwinism and religious rhetoric) would automatically ensure victory in future engagements. As we shall see, in the subsequent parts of the novel Judge Holden will take White's place as a far more powerful and persuasive rhetorical proponent of a similar ideology.

The Glanton Gang and Border History.   The episode of Captain White and his filibusterers is a complete work of fiction in which the literary imagination supplements the historical record. In the historical romance it is necessary merely that such characters or incidents pass the test of verisimilitude. Hawthorne's romances use the supernatural and self-deconstructive narrative commentary to question the very foundations of our knowledge of the verisimilar in history and historical narrative. To many readers' surprise, Glanton, many members of his troop, and many of their actions are not at all exaggerated but based on historical records. To be sure, as in all historical romance, the narrative is a complicated mixture of documented fact and imaginative vision. For readers interested in McCarthy's use of the history, John Sepich in *Notes on "Blood Meridian"* meticulously traces the historical documentation on which the novel's events and characters are based. Here, to illustrate the tension between history and romance in *Blood Meridian,* I will briefly point to two diametrically opposed incidents: the Yuma massacre near the close of the narrative and a point midway in the novel in which the kid becomes separated from Glanton's troop. In the Yuma episode, McCarthy bases the manner of death of Glanton and other members of his troop on eyewitness testimony, depositions, and newspaper accounts. Sepich's study traces even the narrative's descriptions of the Yuma chiefs to historical sources. According to Sepich, the escapes from the massacre by the kid, Tobin, the judge, Toadvine, and David Brown are again based on historical detail, for several in Glanton's historical troop had escaped the massacre by virtue of having been assigned to a polecutting detail.[13]

In an imaginary episode earlier in the novel, however, after having been assigned the task of killing two wounded members of Glanton's

troop, the kid is separated from Glanton's troop as they are chased by
the Mexican cavalry commander Elias. From the vantage point of a
mesa a few days later, the kid watches below an engagement between
Elias's and Glanton's men: "He saw from that high rimland the collision
of armies remote and silent upon the plain below. The dark little horses
circled and the landscape shifted in the paling light and the mountains
beyond brooded in darkening silhouette. The distant horsemen rode and
parried and a faint drift of smoke passed over them and they moved on
up the deepening shade of the valley floor leaving behind them the
shapes of mortal men who had lost their lives in that place" (*BM,* 213).

The historical record shows that Glanton's men actually met but
never militarily engaged Elias (Sepich, 50); the incident instead functions to distance the kid and ourselves from the action below, which first
is perceived as a painting in motion because we share the kid's detached
perspective on the events. Yet this esthetic apprehension of the events is
darkened—literally by the fallen men and more figuratively by the
awareness of the pathetic fallacy of the "brooding" mountains, which
suggest, perhaps, the novel's own brooding engagement with history.
There is, in this and many other scenes, a pervasive sense of distance
between the narrative voice and events—a distance that creates a continual sense of an irony heightened by the knowledge that aspects of the
novel are in fact "historical," not imaginary. In a recent study of the
American historical romance, Emily Miller Budick writes, "What distinguishes the historical from the fictive imagination is that historical consciousness trains its subjectivity on a world that is, at whatever remove,
decidedly not its own creation and not a replication of itself. In historical
romance the reality of the past is verifiable through agencies outside the
single perceiving self."[14]

The mountains in McCarthy's depiction of the battle seem representative of this paradox of history to the contemporary observer—a history from which we seem removed. Or restated, the problem is not the
existence of history per se, for few would deny that the past—or a
past—occurred. Yet the revisionary western as historical romance must
struggle with the discursive tension between fictional and historical narrative. In her attempt to use historical fiction as indicative of a "verifiable" past outside of the observing consciousness, Budick may miss the
point of Hayden White's *Metahistory* (1973), or in order to retreat to a
more stable definition of history, she may ignore the problem of representing history through narrative and language. Since Carlyle's *French
Revolution* (1837), if not earlier, we have been aware of the problematic

status of narrative in historical discourse, hence modern and academic history's flight away from historical explanation by what White terms "emplotment" (or narrative) toward formal argument. But White notes that no history can entirely evade narrative emplotment.[15] The problem lies in the very mediation of history through discourse, thereby relying on a narrative whose truth is always in doubt. We nonetheless must attempt to determine through historical interpretation a past that in turn seems to determine, limit, or brood over us.

Yet the engagement between Glanton and Elias here represented in McCarthy's novel is entirely unverifiable and therefore fictive and unhistorical. We might correct Budick's account of the function of the historical romance by proposing instead that in the historical romance, history's claims to interpretive authority are challenged by the absence of such a broodingly transcendental witness as the *Blood Meridian*'s mountain or its authoritative narrator. As Hawthorne's example in *The Scarlet Letter* suggests, historical romance replicates yet parodies the interpretive truth claims of historical narrative.

Adopting a view radically opposed to Budick's analysis of the historical romance, Fredric Jameson notes that Sir Walter Scott's development of the genre represents a principle of narrative and social "freedom from that reality principle" of an "oppressive" realistic novel of the present.[16] This definition largely follows the lead of Richard Chase's seminal analysis in *The American Novel and Its Tradition* (1957), arguing that after Scott, the novel in the American tradition has been typically associated with the romance. Chase extends this claim to argue that the romance dominates pre–Civil War fiction; influences Twain, James, and Faulkner; and attempts to delineate an authentic self "outside" the social vision of the European novel of manners.[17] While Jameson focuses on the implications of the second term—the romance—in Scott's historical romance, his remarks largely elide the implications of the first term, its historical dimension. Although an element of escape or escapism is indeed central to the mode, as we have seen in discussing the significance of the kid's journey west, we need to ask, What, then, is the function of its historical dimension? Jane Tompkins's examination of Fenimore Cooper's historical romance in *Sensational Designs* (1985) suggests that the historical novel in the vein of Scott and Fenimore Cooper sketches the cultural dimensions of historical change.[18] We should balance Jameson's analysis of the mode's escapism with this opposed counterfunction. If the realistic novel in the nineteenth century is driven by the conflict between social norms and human desire, in the historical romance individuals often act as representations of cultural conflict, particularly conflicts between cultures. In Walter Scott the conflict is among the English and the lowland and highland Scots, and in Cooper among the colonials, English, French, Delaware, and Huron (or between the Pawnee and Sioux in *The Prairie)*.

The Frontier as Border Zone. As a historical romance, *Blood Meridian* begins its revisionary project in its selection of narrative materials to tell a story (not The Story) of the Southwest, avoiding the well-covered ranching era after the Civil War to focus on the largely ignored era of Manifest Destiny. To apply Jane Tompkins's definition of the historical romance to *Blood Meridian*, we might ask what culture is represented and what cultural work is performed by the kid, Glanton, his scalphunters, and Judge Holden. In answer we might resort to still another theorist, this time one of the American frontier. In *Letters from an American Farmer* (1782), Crèvecoeur, before Turner and de Tocqueville, was perhaps the earliest critic of the American frontier, defining it as the outermost band of the geographic extension of Euro-American society, rather than the dividing line between civilization and wilderness of Turner's or William Byrd's frontier. In his twelfth letter Crèvecoeur defines frontier society as a unique cultural formulation: multicultural, violent, and predominantly masculine. And this violence was most extreme at the far frontier, the farthest point of Anglo settlement, where all cultural restrictions were dissipated and Anglo and Native American cultures regressed into a violence that seemed primordial. Describing the Glanton troop, McCarthy writes, "They wandered the borderland for weeks seeking some sign of the Apache. . . . Above all else they appeared wholly at venture, primal, provisional, devoid of order. Like being provoked out of the absolute rock and set nameless and at no remove from their own loomings to wander ravenous and doomed and mute as gorgons shambling the brutal wastes of Gondwanaland in a time before nomenclature was and each was all" (*BM*, 172). Throughout the novel, the kid and Glanton's gang trace the nineteenth-century Southwestern frontier at its farthest, most violent extent south and westward.

In terms similar to Crèvecoeur's, two contemporary critics of the frontier, Howard Lamar and Leonard Thompson, redefine Turner's conception of frontier as a line dividing civilization from open or uncultivated land: "We regard a frontier not as a boundary or line, but as a territory or zone of interpenetration between two previously distinct societies. Usually, one of the societies is indigenous to the region, or at least has occupied it for many generations; the other is intrusive. The frontier 'opens' in a given zone when the first representatives of an intrusive society arrive; it 'closes' when a single political authority has established hegemony over the zone."[19] The Southwestern frontier during Manifest Destiny was just such a border zone of collision, a zone in which three cultures struggle for territorial and cultural hegemony: the American Anglo, Native American, and Hispanic.

The Glanton gang of scalphunters, McCarthy's choice of subject matter in *Blood Meridian,* are antiheroic borderers who can wield their "trade" profitably only in the frontier, at the margins of American society and of the geographical nation. Glanton and his men very much are reminiscent of the murderous gang in *Outer Dark* and the "White Caps" in *Child of God* who roam the Tennessee countryside preying on innocents. Glanton himself, we are reminded, is wanted in "civilized" Texas and must skirt its borders or be hanged; Toadvine, a member of the gang who befriends the kid, is wanted, captured, and hanged by the California authorities (*BM,* 172, 285). Safely removed to the landscape of the Western frontier, such gangs often are romanticized both in American history and in the cinematic western. In his postmodern version of the historical romance, McCarthy avoids Fenimore Cooper's error in romanticizing his borderers' brutality and violence against the innocent—a brutality rendered in full naturalistic detail throughout the novel, most notably in the massacres of the peaceful Tiguas and various Mexican villagers or in the judge and Vandiemenlander's use of newborn puppies for target practice (*BM,* 173–74, 180–81, 192–93).

Glanton's Frontier Violence: The Cultural Work of Manifest Destiny.

To apply to the novel Lamar and Thompson's thesis of the frontier as a border zone in which cultures strive for hegemony, Glanton and his gang (along with Captain White) would appear to represent the Anglo-American empire's drive toward hegemony. The violence of Glanton and his troop is thus a form of the "cultural work" that Tompkins locates in the historical romance. But McCarthy complicates such a reading with the extreme individualism of the Glanton troop, whose allegiances are pledged only to their murderous trade. Life at the border zone involves a series of violent clashes between and within cultures, yet McCarthy's novel reminds us that all such historical and ethnic clashes are experienced dramatically by individuals rather than by the groups formed by historical perspective.

The ideological allegiances of Glanton and his gang are far less clear than those of White. Glanton makes no political speeches such as the one delivered to the kid by White. While Glanton's scalphunting performs the dirty work preparing for the eventual hegemony of the Anglo-American empire as it expanded into the Southwest (the Apaches, of course, were the last tribe "subdued" in the period after the Civil War), he is hired by the Sonoran governor. His willingness to kill, scalp, and redeem Hispanic scalps to the Sonoran authorities when Apache scalps prove difficult to harvest well may signify the same conviction that White displays—a conviction of the superiority of his nation and race. The novel openly acknowledges the overtly racist ideology spurring Glanton's choice of trade; he refers to non-Anglos as "niggers" whose contaminated blood cancels their right to life. At his death he utters the insult for the last time to the Yuma chief who beheads him; indeed, by this time readers are inclined to cheer the Yuma on (*BM*, 255, 275). Yet Glanton's greed and propensity for unrestrained violence explain his scalphunting just as satisfactorily as his racism or ideology; scalphunting is just a means of financing his journey to his ultimate destination of the California goldmines (*BM*, 232–33). Far from a patriot or even nationalist, after betraying and massacring the Yuma, Glanton turns his gang against his own countrymen at the Yuma ford, robbing them as they migrate across the Colorado River (*BM*, 262).

Given Glanton's racism, a superb dramatic irony of the novel is that Glanton's band of scalphunters—which includes several Delaware Indians, a Hispanic, and an African American—are as polyglot as the crew of Melville's *Pequod*. As in *Moby-Dick* (1851), death unites all, although McCarthy's killers are viewed far less romantically than Melville's whalehunters. In his "Knights and Squires" chapter, Melville compares the *Pequod*'s democratically and racially egalitarian crew to medieval knights of chivalry. The allegiance by his troop to Glanton's code of killing makes all members of equal standing, whatever their race. An early incident underlines this membership whose only requisite qualification is the ability to kill. In the gang are two Jacksons, "one black, one white, both forenamed John" and each with enmity for the other. Warned away from the campfire by his Anglo double, the African American beheads his counterpart with a bowie knife; Glanton's only response is to walk away from the corpse's campfire. Only an injury making them unable to fight or desertion cancels membership in the troop; hence Glanton sends out the Delawares to kill Grannyrat, the Mexican War veteran who deserts the band.

Hegemony as Conclusion of Frontier Stage.   The question of the Southwestern frontier—whether Mexico, the United States, or Native American tribes would achieve hegemony over the frontier territories in Northern Mexico—is answered only in part by the fate of Captain White. Later, in the Glanton troop's escape to California, the question of territorial hegemony is posed again, though the novel elides consideration of the struggle over California statehood or, for that matter, of the Indian Wars succeeding the Civil War. Nevertheless, by the novel's end, the American empire has achieved hegemony over the Indian territories and California and extends geographically from east to west, abandoning claims to such Northern Mexican territory as Sonora, which is historically in dispute and coveted by White at the novel's beginning. If Glanton does the work of Manifest Destiny and mirrors many of the racial (and racist) views driving the extension of the American empire, he is no ideologue: he regards his personal war against the Apache largely as a matter of business.

The Judge: The Ethos of Manifest Destiny

Far more successful than White or Glanton as representative of the ideology of the historical period of Manifest Destiny is Judge Holden. He is the novel's most educated and experienced observer, its most fascinating and complex character. From the beginning of the narrative his name, his motives, and even his very existence are inexplicable, often verging on the diabolical. The latter is suggested by the ex-priest Tobin's interpolated tale dealing with how the judge became a member of the gang. Chased by Apaches, with all their powder gone, the gang encounter the judge in the middle of the desert: "then about the meridian of the day we come upon the judge on his rock there in that wilderness by his single self. . . . And there he set. No horse. Just him and his legs crossed, smilin as we rode up. Like he'd been expecting us" (*BM,* 124). The nearly supernatural nature of his appearance is accentuated by the prescience of his actions: apprised of the gang's plight, he locates and collects bat guano, then sends the gang riding around the mountain to lure away the Apaches while he burns alder for charcoal. Finally, leading the gang and the pursuing Apaches up a dormant volcano, he collects sulfur crystals in the volcano's flume, mixes all ingredients, and creates a fine gunpowder, with which the troop massacres its pursuers, who believe the troop helpless. Marveling at the judge's intellectual gifts and his mastery of the arts of dancing and fiddling, yet terming the judge "a sooty-souled rascal," Tobin introduces the tale to the kid as illustrative of his proverb, "There's little equity in the Lord's gifts" (*BM*, 122). But at the conclusion of his tale, he refuses to answer the kid's question, "What's he a judge of?" The ex-priest's implication of a diabolic agency behind the judge's gifts and his sudden appearance is strengthened by the judge's sudden appearance at the end of the novel when he murders the kid.

The judge's name suggests his interpretive function within the narrative: in the Southwestern border zone, devoid of law, the judge personifies the law of the narrative's events. His is the voice who supplies an apologetics and rational ideology for the gang's violence, murders, and massacres. His ideology amounts to a metaphysics of a will to knowledge, combining a nihilistic affirmation of the self with a philosophical justification of war. To the judge, no law has the authority to restrain man's original will: man instead must impose his will on the natural world and other men—first through his knowledge of nature (the Emersonian Not-Me) and finally through violence as the ultimate extension of the individual's will on the opposition of nature and other men. In several of the interludes between the novel's main acts of violence, the judge, an amateur biologist and zoologist, collects specimens, then sketches a record of them in his journal, to the amazement of the largely illiterate troop. The judge explains to them,

> Whatever in creation exists without my knowledge exists without my consent. . . . These anonymous creatures . . . may seem little or nothing in the world. Yet the smallest crumb can devour us. Any smallest thing beneath yon rock out of men's knowing. Only nature can enslave man and only when the existence of each last entity is routed out and made to stand naked before him will he be properly suzerain of the earth. . . . This is my claim, he said. And yet everywhere upon it are pockets of autonomous life. Autonomous. In order for it to be mine nothing must be permitted to occur upon it save by my dispensation. (*BM*, 198–99)

The Judge as Rational Egotist.   "Dispensation," the last word of the passage, is a key term in evangelical Protestant theology, referring to the different covenants regulating the relations between Jehovah and man.[20] In the American Western wilderness, surrounded by an illusion of empty space, the judge combines the Judeo-Christian sense of nature as servant to man with the Enlightenment's restriction of the mind's faculties to Reason, motivated by the consequent power over nature provided by rational knowledge and science. In his speech, man arrogates to himself the divine absolute authority over the creation. Or as a supreme egoist, he no doubt refers to himself. The judge speaks and acts not merely as a diabolical agency, as in Tobin's interpretation, but as a nineteenth-century version of Blake's Urizen, a representation of the unrestricted will to power of the transcendental Reason.[21]

With the moral universe shrunk to reflect merely the will's desire for absolute sovereignty over the external (whether man or nature), the judge is spokesman for as extreme and paranoid an individualism as Melville's Ahab. Claiming he would "strike the sun" if it dared insult him, Ahab counters Starbuck's arguments against pursuing revenge by appealing to natural, moral, and ultimately divine limits on man's actions in nature. Echoing Ahab's claim, using the frontier language of the homesteader and miner, the judge upholds not merely the right of property but a more radical philosophy of the reason's right to an unlimited conquest of nature. Severed from moral, ethical, or legal limitations on his will, man must be free to exert his own absolute authority. In response to Tobin's demur that "no man" can know all of nature, the judge responds, "The man who believes that the secrets of the world are forever hidden lives in mystery and fear. Superstition will drag him down. The rain will erode the deeds of his life. But that man who sets himself the task of singling out the threat of order from the tapestry will by the decision alone have taken charge of the world and it is only by such taking charge that he will effect a way to dictate the terms of his own fate" (*BM,* 199). His speech clarifies his position as representative of the marriage of power and reason in the modernity of the West.

Vereen Bell writes that "what the judge says and he and his confederates act out eventually seems like an only slightly demented revival of Enlightenment philosophy, and the judge's intellectual imperialism may be read finally as an instance of what happens if Enlightenment doctrine is pressed to its logical conclusion" (Bell 1988, 124). He is thus the "judge," not merely of the American West but of Western rationality. The narrative's final sentence (before the epilogue) suggests both the judge's absolute triumph over Southwestern history and his corresponding ecstatic response: "He never sleeps. He says he will never die. He dances in light and in shadow and he is a great favorite. He never sleeps, the judge. He is dancing, dancing. He says that he will never die" (*BM,* 335).

The Violence of Western History: The Conquest of Nature and Cultural Conflict.

The judge thus represents an impulse or drive toward conquest that is not inherently irrational but inherent in reason itself—a drive that the historical period itself reveals. Unlike Glanton's troop, and rather than representing the pioneer of Crève-coeur's analysis who has descended toward a "primitive" state of hunter-gatherer, the judge represents a will, implicit in the Western mind and the historical impetus behind the American Western expansion, to wield an absolute power over nature. Such an analysis is paralleled in one of the more influential recent historians of the American West. Studying the development of the American empire in *Rivers of Empire* (1985), Donald Worster argues that the American West should be viewed as a "hydraulic empire" based on an environmental reshaping through irri-gation—a reshaping that in the contemporary West is tantamount to terraforming. In its dependence on wide-scale irrigation, the American West is an empire that parallels the engineering and social achievements of Egyptian and Mayan empires. All three are empires in which social and economic power flows to those who control nature by controlling the water flow. Those who have controlled the Western waters have been the true conquerors or power elite of the West.[22] The central ques-tion posed at a key point of Worster's narrative in *Rivers of Empire* (and one reiterated in his collected essays, *Under Western Skies)* is whether the environmental, economic, and social costs of the rapid Western expan-sion were justifiable or whether a more reasoned development of both the Western territory and its waters—one adjusting society to the West's aridity—would have been saner (Worster, 54–60, 70–73). Worster associates a "sane" development with a recognition of "natural" limitations, associating the present Western hydraulic society with insanity. Nevertheless, the judge and the history of the Southwest repu-diate such an ethos, with man as ideally a co-equal, dependent on, or at least respectful of, natural and environmental limitations.

In the last decade a number of writers, including such historians as Daniel Worster and Patricia Limerick and such novelists as Wallace Stegner and Leslie Silko, have questioned the histories of the American West, substituting new narratives for the old. At the same time, recent studies in literary criticism—for instance, Jane Tompkins's *West of Every-thing* (1994) and Richard Slotkin's *Gunfighter Nation* (1992)—have focused attention on the literary and popular western. Paralleling these revisionist histories is the recent revival, in both fiction and film, of the once-dead genre of the western. Whatever compels this redirection of our cultural gaze toward the western, in *Blood Meridian*'s theme of con-quest McCarthy anticipates this revival of interest in revising Western history and literature.

In the preface of her revisionary history of the American West, *The Legacy of Conquest* (1987), Patricia Limerick announces her desire to contradict or redress the imbalances or oversights of the "old" Western historians.[23] The theme of conquest, from which Limerick coins her title and to which Worster's "empire" alludes, provides a metaphoric template of the deep structure for their narration of Western history. Limerick acknowledges the centrality of the concept in her narrative when she writes,

> Conquest forms the historical bedrock of the whole nation, and the American West is a preeminent case study in conquest and its consequences. Conquest was a literal, territorial form of economic growth. Westward expansion was the most concrete, down-to-earth demonstration of the economic habit on which the entire nation became dependent. If it is difficult for Americans to imagine that an economy might be stable and also healthy, many of the forces that fostered that attitude can be traced to the Western side of American history. (Limerick, 27)

Western history, to Limerick, is the capitalistic cycle of boom and bust writ large, throughout time and geography. Her history thus operates as a historical, social, economic, and environmental critique of the ideology of Manifest Destiny.

The Judge's Philosophy of Conquest: War, History, and the Will.   If the judge operates in the narrative as a symbolic spokesperson for Reason's struggle for supreme knowledge of and authority over nature, he also articulates an ideology of conquest that defends unlimited war as the supreme arbiter of the conflict between unrestricted wills—national, cultural, or individual. Hence his or Glanton's refusal to intervene in disagreements between individuals of the gang. "War was always here," the judge argues to David Brown in a key passage. "The ultimate trade awaiting its ultimate practitioner" (*BM,* 248). Carrying one step further Johan Huizenga's identification of man with play in *Homo Ludens* (1944), he argues that war is the ultimate game, with an ultimate wager. It is a symbolic game of divination, a kind of martial Calvinism: "War is the truest form of divination. It is the testing of one's will and the will of another within that larger will which because it binds them is therefore forced to select" (*BM,* 249)—select, that is, between the opposed wills of the antagonists.

Unclear in the judge's argument is the ontological nature of this "larger will." Does he appeal, as did the Puritans and the proponents of

Manifest Destiny, to the providential will of the Judeo-Christian God? Or is his argument Hegelian, discerning a larger will behind historical conflicts—conflicts that are resolved in the teleology of the Spirit driving history or the mind's apprehension of that history? Approaching the judge as a philosopher may be misleading, for our first glimpse of him demonstrates that he often speaks in jest, as an idle intellectual game testing the powers of his own rhetoric. The kid first encounters him in a tent meeting in which the judge interrupts the sermon by accusing the speaker of unnatural "congress" with a goat. After the ensuing riot, when questioned about his knowledge, he baldly admits he has never met or even heard of the evangelist he has falsely accused. Nevertheless he concludes his argument about war by asserting that "war is the ultimate game because war is at last a forcing of the unity of existence. War is god" (*BM*, 249). The passage suggests that his philosophy inverts Hegel's, replacing the unity of Spirit closing Hegelian history with a unitary culture willed and achieved through the exercise of power.

Thus the judge's ideology of war resembles a philosophy of history, a historical ideology. Responding to the scalphunter Irving's proverbial objection that "might does not make right," he responds, "Moral law is an invention of mankind for the disenfranchisement of the powerful in favor of the weak. Historical law subverts it at every turn. . . . The willingness of the principals [in war] to forgo further argument as the triviality which it in fact is and to petition directly the chambers of the historical absolute clearly indicates of how little moment are the opinions and of what great moment the divergences thereof. For the argument is indeed trivial, but not so the separate wills thereby made manifest" (*BM*, 250). Appealing like Hegel to history, the judge replaces the spirit driving history by a unitary will. But his philosophy is more Nietzschean than Hegelian, amounting to a précis of Nietzsche's *Towards a Genealogy of Morals* (1887), especially its devastating critique of Western ethics through an analysis of the relations between master and slave.

Of course readers may deny McCarthy's emblematic association of the judge with the history of the American West or may reject his portrait of the judge as exaggerated or excessively allegoric. Based on these passages, many critics identify the narrative's own perspective or ideology with that of the judge—an understandable impression given that the judge's considerable powers of rhetoric are rivalled only by the narrative voice. Certainly no other character (all oppressively taciturn) is given sufficient moral, ethical, or intellectual stature to oppose him rhetorically, nor does the narrative voice intrude into the narration to undertake a moral or philosophic critique. The temptation to equate judge and narrative perspective further is reinforced by the memorable image of the judge's dance of victory at the narrative's close. Undeniably, the judge is triumphant, if analyzed in the Nietzschean terms of the power relations throughout the novel. Yet if the judge functions as representative of a triumphant ideological and cultural force, to effectively restrain the judge would be to rewrite the narrative of the historical conquest of the West, to write a fantasy (such as Worster's wish that the natural limits of the West were realized), not a historical romance of the West. And some characters do act in resistance, however ineffectual, to the judge's will and philosophy.

Critiques of the Judge.   An implicit repudiation of Judge Holden is supplied primarily by three characters: the kid, Tobin, and David Brown. Of these characters, the kid most effectively represents the judge's antagonist, though until the point of the Yuma massacre their antagonism is largely repressed. The judge's primary interlocutor during his address on war, Brown responds weakly, as he does on several other occasions, with "You're crazy Holden" (*BM*, 249). As we have seen, Tobin advances his theory of the judge as diabolic agent in his story of the gunpowder; during the judge's war lecture, Tobin declines to dispute but also refuses to "secondsay" the judge's "notions" (*BM*, 251). After the Yuma massacre, Tobin allies with the kid against the judge and is shot by the latter. As is the case throughout the novel, the kid acts as a silent witness of the judge—a silence that might be taken to be complicit. Yet the judge does not interpret that silence as complicity.

The kid functions as the naive observing perspective of the novel, as does Lester Ballard in *Child of God*, from whose viewpoint we observe most of the action. Perhaps McCarthy selects the kid as observer because of his inability to generalize on those events, either from an ethical, political, or other ideological perspective. Or perhaps his position as observer is explained by his resemblance to Samuel Chamberlain, whose memoir, *My Confession* (1956), supplied McCarthy with many details of Glanton and his gang and virtually all our information about the historical judge. Again, John Sepich traces this enmity between the kid and the judge to its historical source in Chamberlain, who rode with the Glanton gang and professed a continual antipathy toward the judge. Though many other members of the Glanton gang can be located in other historical records, Chamberlain is the only source verifying the judge's historical existence. In *Blood Meridian* the judge's hostility toward the kid—a hostility that extends from the events after the Yuma massacre to the novel's end—thus might be explained by the reference to Chamberlain as an historical analogue to the kid (Sepich, 14, 20).

Yet in McCarthy's novel, the events ensuing after the massacre reveal the antagonists and lay the groundwork for the judge's murder of the kid. The judge's hostility to the kid at first appears merely spiteful or egotistical. Toadvine and the kid flee the attack upriver, pursued by the Yuma, who hang back after one is killed by the kid's pistol shot. A day later at a waterhole, they first encounter Tobin; then the next day they see the judge followed by an imbecile under the judge's charge, both naked. The appearance of the pair is described in terms almost preternatural: "They neared through the desert dawn like beings of a mode little more than tangential to the world at large, . . . [l]ike things whose very portent renders them ambiguous. Like things so charged with meaning that their forms are dimmed" (*BM*, 281–82). Responding to the judge's offer to barter with those at the waterhole, Toadvine exchanges his hat for the judge's $125 in gold and is then offered dried meat that has "bedraped" the judge (the meat's source ominously unspecified). The kid and Tobin, on the other hand, refuse to break bread with the judge and repudiate his offer of $500 for the kid's pistol. The four at the waterhole thus divide into two opposed pairs, with Tobin urging the kid to commit cold-blooded murder: "Do him. . . . You'll get no second chance lad. Do it. He is naked. He is unarmed. . . . Do it for the love of God. Do it or I swear your life is forfeit" (*BM*, 285). Without comment, the kid refuses to fire or trade, leaving the waterhole.

Subsequent events prove Tobin's advice to be sound. On the next day, after the kid and Tobin encounter David Brown headed toward the river, the judge, now rather suspiciously dressed in Toadvine and Brown's clothes, fires with Brown's rifle on Tobin and the kid. Curiously, though the kid twice more has opportunities to kill the judge, he again refuses, allowing the judge to again pass unharmed under his gunsights (*BM*, 288, 298). Yet rather than professing gratitude, the judge calls out to the kid: "No assassin. . . . And no partisan either. There's a flawed place in the fabric of your heart. . . . You alone were mutinous. You alone reserved in your soul some corner of clemency for the heathen" (*BM*, 299). These charges, reiterated at three points in the novel, may be dismissed as insanity or casuistry. Nevertheless, they help clarify the narrative's function as a meditation on historical and intercultural violence.

According to the judge, the kid's refusal to sell the pistol is an ethical position. While the kid has shown no reluctance to shed blood in the engagements with the Apache, he has demonstrated his good intentions at several points, aiding Brown in drawing an arrow through his leg, although Tobin warns him, "Fool. . . . Don't you know he'd of took you with him?" (*BM,* 163). Given the charge of killing two of the wounded, the "Mexican" and a Kentuckian named Shelby, the kid leaves them to the "mercies" of the pursuing Elias and the Apache. Finally, even after Holden has shot Tobin, the kid repudiates the use of violence to settle their quarrel with the judge. The judge interprets such acts as symbolic not of the kid's affiliation with but as his repudiation of the gang through his disavowal of its violence (none of the troop help Brown, and one of the Delawares fighting with the group unhesitatingly brains one of his wounded tribesman with a boulder). Encountering the kid jailed in San Diego because of the judge's false charge of his responsibility for the Yuma massacre and the murders of Toadvine and Brown, the judge again charges, "You came forward, he said, to take part in a work. But you were a witness against yourself. You sat in judgement on your own deeds. You put your own allowances before the judgements of history and you broke with the body of which you were pledged a part. . . . If war is not holy man is nothing but antic clay" (*BM,* 307).

Here at the jail and in their final conversation, the judge reiterates a position that at first seems contradictory. As we recall, he has defended war as the ultimate arbiter, unifying opposed wills through the death of the loser. His philosophy poses as an ultimate individualism. In his defense of war to Brown, the judge thus uses the hypothetical analogy between war and two men at cards wagering with their lives. On the contrary, he also maintains that war is a collective enterprise, represented in the novel by the Glanton gang. Before their first engagement with the Apache, the scalphunters are described as follows: "They rode like men invested with a purpose whose origins were antecedent to them, like blood legatees of an order both imperative and remote. Although each man among them was discrete unto himself, conjoined they made a thing that had not been before and in that communal soul were wastes hardly reckonable" (*BM,* 152). The troop can be viewed as representative of a communal will in two respects—either in light of the judge's thesis of the transcendental sanctity of war as the telos of history or as a living representative of the cultural imperative of using violence to possess the continent. For the kid to restrict the group's common ethos of murder by his own individual consciousness is a betrayal of history, the gang, and their "communal soul." Or at least the judge regards it so; the perspective of the readers and narrative may instead coincide with that of the kid. The only two critics to discuss this issue present two alternative readings of the kid's murder and the judge's arguments. Sepich applies a reading of a Faustian compact between the kid, Glanton, and Holden to conclude that Holden's charges are "reliable"; the kid's murder concludes his failure to repudiate his diabolic contract (Sepich, 125–28). Bell, on the other hand, dismisses both the judge's charges against the kid and his speech on war as a rationalized insanity (Bell 1988, 119). Both critics are in part correct: the kid unconsciously does represent a partial repudiation of the gang, while Holden speaks for himself and history but not for the narrative perspective. We should note that the narrator uses a rare moral term, "waste," in describing the journey of the troop's "communal soul." Analogous to the desert in which they ride is the deserted vacuum in their souls.

The Novel's Problematic Ending.

The conversation between the two antagonists in the Fort Griffin bar years later provides an appropriate narrative frame with which to review the judge's agonistic philosophy and his charges against the kid. Recognizing the judge, who is sitting "alone as if he were some other sort of man entire and he seemed little changed or none in all these years," the kid turns away in repudiation of their former companionship in the gang—a companionship to which the judge soon refers by calling the kid, "The last of the true" (*BM*, 327). When the kid dismisses their encounter as meaningless chance, the judge's response characteristically is to appeal to "the history of all" as an orchestrated "event, a ceremony," and finally a ritual that "includes the letting of blood," foreshadowing his intent to murder the kid. The judge ends the conversation by identifying himself as a true, the kid as a false dancer: "As war becomes dishonored and its nobility called into question, those honorable men who recognize the sanctity of blood will become excluded from the dance. . . . And yet there will be one there always who is a true dancer"—namely, the judge himself (*BM*, 331). Thus a few hours later he murders the kid in the jakes behind the bar and dances his dance of triumph.

As he has articulated earlier in his agonistic philosophy, the judge resorts to violence rather than what he terms the "trivialities" of ethical argumentation to resolve any conflict involving ownership or philosophy. The kid and judge thus can be said to embody two opposed historical perspectives. The judge represents an affirmation of war and the possession of the Southwest through violence. The kid's "good heart," which the judge refers to as "a witness against yourself," suggests an ethical repudiation of the judge's and the gang's violence, although as member of the gang's culture the kid participates in and benefits from that violence. In their final confrontation, surely most readers' sympathies are engaged by the kid, not the judge. The final irony of the novel's ending is that while traveling to Fort Griffin, the kid has killed, admittedly in self-defense, a young tough (reminiscent in fact of the kid himself at the narrative's beginning). After an argument in which the youth denies that the kid's scapular (formerly Toadvine's) is formed out of human scalps, he had attempted to bushwhack the kid in the night. Might not this youth's denial of the bloody origin of the scapular represent a cultural and historical desire to repress the legacy of conquest in the history of the West? A portion of the rhetoric of Manifest Destiny—the sense of an "exceptional" national identity, of national mission to enlighten the darkened world—remains crucial to the national self-image. Of course, as Thomas Hietala points out, in the twentieth century this rhetoric of mission must now repress consciousness of the historical manner and means of the era of territorial expansion, as well as the racism that was the psychological and social concomitant of that expansion (Hietala, 256–57).

The Metaphysics of Historical Violence

Like revisionary historians such as Limerick and Worster who more broadly scrutinize the dynamics of social and economic power in the development of the region, McCarthy's novel dramatizes the theme of conquest primarily through its unrelenting violence. Yet even if McCarthy shares Limerick and Worster's concerns with examining the process of empire-building, are these concerns sufficient proof of a revisionary critique? Or are they merely another uncritical extension of the judge's tradition of American violence often reflected uncritically in the western? If the classic western offered a simplified allegorical history of a violent struggle between black and white hats, a hermeneutics for McCarthy's new western is more complicated in that lawlessness is remarkable more for its resemblances to law and authority, not its dissimilarities. Our "new" westerns deconstruct both law and lawlessness as anarchic projections of the masculine will on the cultural and natural chaos of the West.

Degeneration through American Violence: Glanton, Toadvine, Tobin. *Blood Meridian* scrutinizes American violence, analyzing its function in the national ideology, history, and identity. Such violence has been the theme of the American historical novel, for Cooper, for Twain (the Twain of *Huck Finn* at least), for Crane (in *The Red Badge of Courage* [1895]), for Hemingway, for Faulkner, and for Mailer, if I may enfold McCarthy's fiction momentarily into the male tradition of novelistic violence to which he affiliates himself by both his choice of subject matter and his style. In this novel, the dynamics of cultural exchange are primarily controlled not by language but by violence.

An incident just before Glanton's troop heads for California illustrates this discourse of a community of violence which heightens in intensity as we continue through the narrative. After the kid rejoins the band, "federated with invisible wires of vigilance" and advancing "with a single resonance" (*BM*, 226), they meet up with Mangas Colorados's Apaches outside the Tucson presidio. As both parties tense under an "unratified" truce, Glanton's horse bites and severs a vein of the horse of an Apache chieftain: "when Glanton spun to look at his men he found them frozen in deadlock with the savages, they and their arms wired into a construction taut and fragile as those puzzles wherein the placement of each piece is predicated upon every other and they in turn so that none can move for bringing down the structure entire." When the Apache pony sprays blood by tossing its head, "Horseblood or any blood a tremor ran that perilous architecture" (*BM*, 229). In the discourse of violence, a primitive and finally uncontrollable dynamic exchange of violence causes individuals to lose their former cultural and social identity, forming a new communal ethos of violence represented by the Glanton gang, or their cultural antitheses of the Comanche and Apache raiders.

If the preceding passage illustrates the difficulty of restraining violence in a community founded on violence, it might be compared with several of the battle scenes, which, from an esthetic point of view, probably comprise the best writing in the novel. Perhaps most memorable is the first such scene in which the identity of Captain White's company (as well as the kid's individual identity) is dismembered, militarily, literally, and figuratively by the attacking Comanche. This dismemberment, as well as the Comanche mode of warfare, is dramatized in a flamboyantly long period:

> Now driving in a wild frieze of headlong horses with eyes walled and teeth cropped and naked riders with clusters of arrows clenched in their

jaws and their shields winking in the dust and up the far side of the ruined ranks in a piping of boneflutes and dropping down off the sides of their mounts with one heel hung in the withers strap and their short bows flexing beneath the outstretched necks of the ponies until they had circled the company and cut their ranks in two and then rising up again like funhouse figures, some with nightmare faces painted on their breasts, riding down the unhorsed Saxons and spearing and clubbing them and leaping from their mounts with knives and running about on the ground with a peculiar bandylegged trot like creatures driven to alien forms of locomotion and stripping the clothes from the dead and seizing them up by the hair and passing their blades about the skulls of the living and the dead alike and snatching aloft the bloody wigs and hacking and chopping at the naked bodies, ripping off limbs, heads, gutting the strange white torsos and holding up great handfuls of viscera, genitals, some of the savages so slathered with gore they might have rolled in it like dogs. . . . And everywhere the dying groaned and gibbered and horses lay screaming. (*BM,* 54)

The narrative voice's reliance on the conjunctive "and"—a stylistic feature on which Twain's Huck had relied—careens both the onlooking kid and ourselves at a breakneck pace through the mind-numbing violence of the attack, which in reality lasts only a few moments. Yet the internal repetition of the present participle in the modifiers strung on the end of the period (a hallmark of the Faulknerian style) renders a violence that is contradictorily static, timeless, esthetic.

Our imagination recoils at the acts of violence signified in the passage, perhaps then against the novel itself. Most disturbing is the mesmerizing spell, even the esthetic appeal, of the style; the language seems inappropriately stylized, "violently" opposed to the sense of the passage. Some readers justifiably might charge that the style of McCarthy's novel creates a pornography—or is it a sadography?—of violence.[24] This charge has been waged (often legitimately) against Sam Peckinpah, Clint Eastwood, and the entire genre of the Hollywood western, not to mention most popular "action" films, the modern heirs of the Hollywood western. In fact, the use of the present participle in McCarthy's Comanche charge is reminiscent of the long slow-motion massacre scene that concludes *The Wild Bunch,* a scene imitated in the endings of *Bonnie and Clyde, Butch Cassidy and the Sundance Kid,* and now myriad other action movies.

The function and significance of narrative violence, whether in film or the novel, should be interpreted on a case by case basis, within the context of the rhetorical function of that violence within the work as a whole. Violence merely may pander to the audience's conscious or unconscious aggression, as is often the case in American film. Such violence is often used ritualistically, to purge evil through a narrative scapegoat, as René Girard argues in *Violence and the Sacred* (1977). In such symbolic forms of violence, the audience is asked to identify with the violence by vicarious participation. Certainly many victims of the novel's violence operate as scapegoats for the perpetrators of violence; yet neither we nor the narrative perspective identifies with the murder or sees the violence as purgative of human evil. Or violence may be used more artistically to dramatize the conflict in values between characters or conflicts in the social or historical forces that the characters represent. Such violence, particularly when aimed against the defenseless, might operate rhetorically to raise in the audience's consciousness the question of their own complicity in the very violence they witness, through identifying with the victim, not the perpetrators. Such consciousness is provoked in *Blood Meridian* in those scenes involving violence aimed against the defenseless or innocent: for instance, in the judge's shooting and scalping of the young Apache boy—an act that even the coarse Toadvine protests (*BM,* 164). Yet because of the narrative distance in the novel, most of the acts of violence involve no such identifications with either aggressor or victim.

The pervasive violence and the hyperesthetic quality of that violence in *Blood Meridian,* I suggest, does not exist merely for its own sake. The novel's violence is in fact "historical" in the fullest sense of the term; it is used so as to represent the dynamic ethnic, racial, and social tensions of this period of Western history. As we have seen, that violence, particularly as performed by Judge Holden's band of scalphunters, is not an ex nihilo creation of the imagination but based on historical men and deeds. This is not to say that we take no pleasure in this violence, for its linguistic "rendering" is neither unadorned nor unesthetic. This very esthetic pleasure may compel the reader to a guilty consciousness of his or her own esthetic consumption of narrated violence. And this guilty sense of participation may be McCarthy's point. The very disjunction between his poetic style and the "viciousness" of the violence his language represents, both in this passage and elsewhere, should lead us to question the characters who wield that violence, their motives, and the social and historical tensions they represent. Does averting our eyes from the violent acts of the national history banish those acts or absolve the present from the burden of the past?

Unless we associate the novel's ethos with Judge Holden's justifications of war, the narrative in fact justifies none of its recorded violence. Instead, in the manner of a repetition compulsion, the novel dwells obsessively on the excessive and unjustifiable violent depravity of Glanton's troop. The only justification supplied for their various massacres, beyond the scalp bounty to which the troop soon quit all pretense of claim, is their psychopathic racism aimed against all members of non-white races, particularly Native Americans and Mexicans. The McCarthy narrator's sole extended psychological investigation of the murderous Captain Glanton at a point immediately preceding his death is revealing: "He watched the fire and if he saw portents there it was much the same to him . . . for he was complete at every hour. Whether his history should run concomitant with men and nations, whether it should cease. He'd long forsworn all weighing of consequence and allowing as he did that men's destinies are given yet he usurped to contain within him all that he would ever be in the world. . . . He claimed agency and said so" (*BM,* 243).

Despite his own Calvinistic belief in predestination ("all men's destinies are given"), Glanton interprets murder as an assertion of his own, or his right to form, an individualistic identity ("to contain within him all"). In similar fashion, the geographical expansion to the Southwest that culminated in the Mexican War was defended as "Young America," a symbolic assertion of the American leap from childish colonial dependence to an assertive young cultural manhood of assertive individualism (Weinberg, 153; Merk, 25, 32).

Such a psychoanalytic interpretation of the scalphunters' violence parallels Richard Slotkin's analysis of the western in *Gunfighter Nation.* In the western, he argues, the historical imagination rewrites the fundamental history of westward national expansion in order to justify that history and turn to it for self-identification in the various guises of myth, legend, history, fiction, and film. As he argues in the first book of his study of the frontier myth, *Regeneration through Violence* (1973), European culture was refashioned in its dual encounter with the wilderness and with its warfare with the Native American tribes, so that the European became reborn into a new, American "savage" identity, adopting native styles of warfare, hunting, agriculture, architecture. Slotkin notes the contradiction that even as the European colonials adopted elements of native culture, they also adopted a racism that viewed Native Americans as "savage," denied their humanity, and waged a series of wars to dispossess them of their lands.[25] Richard Drinnon extends Slotkin's thesis by analyzing the function of racism in the psychosocial formation of the national identity: "Racism defined natives as nonpersons within the settlement culture and was in a real sense the enabling experience of the rising American empire: Indian-hating identified the dark others that white settlers were not and must not under any circumstances become."[26] Slotkin and Drinnon's detailed historic tracings of this violence and its function in the national psychosocial identity, as they are reflected in American literature, are flawed only by these scholars' difficulty in identifying a critical or antimythical element against "regeneration through violence" in the literary and popular traditions.

McCarthy's narrative of the kid's journey west, as Michael Herr's blurb on the Vintage edition perceptively suggests, is a fictional lesson in the historical "regeneration through violence" that Slotkin and Drinnon survey. After wandering through the desert, the kid is imprisoned in Chihuahua, only to join the Apache fighters led by the historic judge and Glanton, who use Apache-like guerrilla tactics against the Apache men, women, children, and hostages, as well as a series of Mexican villagers (BM, 155–59). Yet after the orgy of violence that extends from Mexico to the Colorado River ford, the kid apparently recoils against his blood-formed identity, only to die unable to articulate, even to act out or live on, his repudiation.

Why base a novel on the sordid history of Glanton's troop of Indian killers? The narrative's violence achieves not merely a revisionary western but something perhaps superior to revision—an attempt at a dramatic and ritualized reexperience of American history as it was lived. Or as we wish it were not lived. It insists that readers not only be reminded intellectually of the violence of the nation's history but, in the form of the novel's dramatic representation of the living present, experience firsthand the horror and fascination of that violence. Tragedy should have a cathartic effect, yet in McCarthy, the more clearly the violence is rendered, the more bathetic it becomes and the more obscure seems our modern moral distance or "perspective" on that violence, incarnated in the kid's unconscious repudiation of the gang. In order for that violence to be reexperienced, McCarthy's narrative, through the figure of the judge, seems to require a momentary imaginative suspension, a violent sublimation of our postmodern vantage point of moral superiority. Our postmodern detachment from our own history assumes a superior, "uninvolved" angle of vision that McCarthy suggests may be an illusion of our historical distance (or ignorance). Blood Meridian's attempt at the reenactment of history through fiction is all the more tragic in its failure—for it is finally only fiction—but as a dramatic fiction it may more successfully express the bloody tragedy of Western history than any historian.

McCarthy's novel forces its readers, through the kid's journey, to confront the history of violence and the unicultural rhetoric of the antebellum period of Manifest Destiny. His narrative insists that the national history was multicultural but its multiculturalism took the form of a violent confrontation between the cultures of the West—a violent confrontation fueled by racism and the West's drive to dominate nature. One means of dealing with the history of that violent confrontation is to defend it, like the judge; romanticize it, like the western; or repress it completely by forgetting the legacy of conquest. Yet the latter response is not necessarily to repudiate the judge or his deeds, for we live in a nation whose identity was shaped—geographically and culturally—by his violence. A better repudiation and a better task for the revisionary imagination is the laborious imaginary task of constructing a new multi-ethnic West and nation using a language that opposes itself to the expressive violence of the judge and Glanton.

Chapter Five

The Border Trilogy: Individualism, History, and Cultural Crossings

Why the Popular Reception?

If *Blood Meridian* marks a turn in McCarthy's fiction away from the thematic and regional concerns of Southern fiction and toward a Southwestern and historical fiction, *All the Pretty Horses* marks a similar turning point in the critical and popular reception of McCarthy's fiction. Its rapid rise to the top of the best-seller lists (with seven printings in the first two months of its release in May of 1992) and its overwhelmingly positive reviews placed McCarthy in the position of one of the nation's foremost novelists.[1] At the same time, from 1992 to 1993, Vintage reprinted his earlier fiction, which sold respectably for the first time.

Such a reversal in publishing fortunes might be ascribed to fate, luck, or to the vagaries or fads of publishing and popular taste. There is a close overlap in setting (the border region joining the Southwestern United States to Northern Mexico) and form (that of historical romance) connecting *Blood Meridian* to The Border Trilogy, whose first two installments are *All the Pretty Horses* and its 1994 sequel, *The Crossing*. Why, then, did the novels of the trilogy suddenly find a popular reception largely denied to *Blood Meridian?*

In an influential lecture on modernism, the philosopher Jürgen Habermas distinguishes between two forms of modernity—one a "consciousness of an epoch that relates itself to the past of antiquity," the other a more "radicalized" form of the modern that attempts to sever "itself from all specific historical ties" and to flee into "the novelty of the next style."[2] On the one hand is the mythic, historical, and classical modernism of T. S. Eliot, Pound, Joyce, and Woolf; on the other are movements such as Dadaism and other avant-gardist art. The primary project of the latter modernism is to sever the "new" art from past traditions of art, while to "make it new" is the more ambiguous credo of the former modernism. McCarthy's fiction preceding The Border Trilogy displays various characteristics that reflect another key project of modernism: to disconnect art from commercialism of society, particularly commercialized forms of mass culture, thereby creating a renewed elitist art.[3] An important explanation for the commercial "failure" of McCarthy's early fiction lies in the protagonists of the Southern fiction and *Blood Meridian,* antiheroes who block a popular audience's desire to identify with the protagonist. Furthermore, in their loosely episodic structure, these novels also frustrate readings that would trace the deepening psychological awareness of the protagonist, while the fiction also resists formalist critical readings attending to congruences between narrative structure and theme. McCarthy's recondite style mixing colloquial, archaic, and formal diction also contributes to the uncommercialism of his early fiction.

These uncommercial characteristics help explain the discrepancy between the often glowing reviews of McCarthy's fiction and the noticeably tepid market response to that fiction. Thus Richard Brodhead and Jane Tompkins would seem to overestimate the role of reviews in their analysis of the canonization of Hawthorne in contrast to the wider audience of popular romance. Certainly, the friendly reviews of McCarthy's early fiction would have us expect a wider audience.[4] A close analogy for McCarthy's early lack of a popular audience is the last half of Melville's career beginning with *Moby-Dick,* in which Melville anticipates the anticommercialism of the late James, Faulkner, and Joyce, overestimating a popular audience's patience for stylistic and formal experimentation. From *The Orchard Keeper* to *Blood Meridian,* McCarthy's fiction would attract the attention of a series of reviewers and critics whose reading practices were largely sympathetic to modernist, uncommercial art.

In the novels of The Border Trilogy, however, McCarthy opens his fiction to the commercial, combining the form of the western with a self-consciously postmodern fiction. What McCarthy's most sensitive early critics—Edwin Arnold, Leo Daugherty, and Vereen Bell—identify as a "vision" variously denominated as "nihilistic" or "existential" (to Bell), religious (to Arnold) or "gnostic" (to Daugherty) has in The Border Trilogy taken the form of a postmodern and commercial fiction.[5] In "Rewriting Modernity," Jean-François Lyotard proposes that postmodernism "is always implied" in modernism's tendency to rewrite itself—a tendency that modern art either successfully or unsuccessfully represses.[6] Lyotard's description of postmodernism as a historical and esthetic revision of modernism's resistance against artistic tradition supplies a new perspective on McCarthy's own rewriting of modernism and of his earlier fiction within The Border Trilogy. First, McCarthy attempts to rewrite Southern fiction within the modern novel; then, in *Suttree,* he both imitates and parodies "great" modern fiction such as Joyce's *Ulysses.* In *Blood Meridian* McCarthy attempts another kind of parody— a postmodern rewriting of the history of the West and the historical romance. Lyotard's conception of the postmodern as a modernism's internal rewriting of itself suggests that the more postmodern novels of The Border Trilogy do not reflect a complete break from the earlier praxis of McCarthy's fiction; rather, they more clearly expose postmodern tendencies already at work within the earlier fiction.

McCarthy's fiction thus divides into two phases: the first is the project to rewrite, revive, or recontemporize modernism within "contemporary" art, the second to create a more popular postmodern fiction within the old popular form of the western. As postmodern fiction, The Border Trilogy's first strategy is to openly imitate the popular western, while the second is to critique from within the western its belief in the autonomous individual. *All the Pretty Horses* and *The Crossing* both reflect and critique the themes of the individual's retreat from society (or the artist's withdrawal into art), of man's relation to nature, and of history's relation to postmodern man.

To more clearly recognize each novel of The Border Trilogy as a postmodern western, we must first distinguish these novels from McCarthy's first western. Besides their common setting within a Southwestern landscape, The Border Trilogy and *Blood Meridian* share the form of the historical romance and the plot of a young protagonist's geographical journey into the borderlands. This journey into nature coincides with the protagonist's exploration of and eventual conflict with other cultures, represented by a series of adversaries—or lovers. This conflict motivates a series of inconclusive acts of violence. Before their conclusions, all three novels depict the now-alienated protagonist as he wanders aimlessly through a newly settled terrain, once a wilderness.

Of course, each narrative uniquely develops and embroiders this essential pattern. In *Blood Meridian* the kid participates in the Apache wars and the Glanton massacres, wanders from California to Fort Griffin after the Yuma massacre, and is murdered by the judge. John Grady Cole, the hero of *All the Pretty Horses,* rides from a modern Texas into the Southwestern borderlands; arrives at a last frontier in the cattle ranges in the mountains of Mexico; enters into an affair with the daughter of his ranch-owner employer; is falsely imprisoned and nearly assassinated in a Mexican prison; and, in the narrative's conclusion, restores his horse to his friend Rawlins. On his return, Cole finds Texas no longer his home, and he rides away on another horse that he feels obliged to return to an unidentified owner.[7] The novel thus divides into three sections: the ride to the Mexican highlands, the scenes on the hacienda and in prison, and the journey home to Texas. The second novel of The Border Trilogy, *The Crossing,* has a similar tripartite structure in the three rides Billy Parham makes from New Mexico to old Mexico and back.[8] In the first ride he seeks to return a wolf to her native range; in the next, with his brother Boyd, he seeks to reclaim the horses stolen during the murder of their parents; in the final ride, Billy attempts to reclaim his brother's corpse from a Mexican grave for burial in his native country.[9] In a series of retrospective conversations, both Parham and Cole repudiate their quests, yet both resume those journeys at the close of their novels.

The exclusion of *Blood Meridian* from The Border Trilogy points to a series of more radical discontinuities behind the surface—discontinuities that largely account for the differences in popular reception of the three novels. As a series title, The Border Trilogy supersedes the titles of the individual narratives, implying a larger historical continuity or other essential link that presumably connects *All the Pretty Horses* to *The Crossing* as phases of a single, larger narrative. Yet the basis of this continuity is not obvious: so far no characters exist simultaneously in both novels of the trilogy (the third novel of the trilogy is not yet published); neither does a forward chronological sequence link the first to the second novel, as is the custom in much popular historical fiction published in series form. *All the Pretty Horses* opens several years after World War II, while *The Crossing* concludes near the close of the same war. If a historical sequence exists, at first glance it would appear to regress back in history toward *Blood Meridian.*

The Trilogy as Romantic Quest

The journeys of John Grady Cole and Billy Parham take the form of the quest, if I and Robert Hass correctly apply the term, signaling an essential difference between *Blood Meridian* and the novels of The Border Trilogy (Hass, 39). Both Cole and Parham begin their narratives as romantic heroes, however problematic, who undertake postmodern versions of a quest, while *Blood Meridian*'s kid is the protagonist of a naturalistic narrative who merely wanders aimlessly, as do McCarthy's earlier protagonists. As a narrative, *Blood Meridian,* like its protagonist, lacks a formal destination, as Vereen Bell and other commentators recognize in criticizing the early novels for their lack of a formal structure or plot

(Bell 1988, 7). The quest motif promises to supply a firmer structure to The Border Trilogy. Nonetheless, in the novels' indeterminate and incomplete conclusions, Cole and Parham regress from romantic heroes to protagonists and the novels transform from romantic to postmodern narratives. Why, then, this use of the romantic quest and hero to achieve a postmodern end? In her study of the romance's anticipation of postmodernism and of postmodernism's reclaiming of the romance, Diane Elam helpfully suggests that "if contemporary writers turn to the romance genre in order to make themselves 'postmodern,' this has less to do with fashion than with the fact that romance, by virtue of its troubled relation to both history and novelistic realism, has in a sense been postmodern all along. . . . The relationship between postmodernism and romance does not allow for any straightforward historical narrative. Postmodernism is not a perspectival view on history; it is the rethinking of history as an ironic coexistence of temporalities."[10] The Border Trilogy returns not to History as a single mononarrative but to histories, the pasts of different people and distinct national cultures. If the quests of Cole and Parham take them across the borders of these cultures, their quests are also temporal, back in time to confront the historical and cultural roots of their identities.

If we look closely, we can trace more muted versions of the postmodern hero and the quest motif in McCarthy's earlier fiction. In *The Orchard Keeper*, Syldar and Uncle Arthur's struggles with the law can be seen as echoes of a heroic rebellion; in *Child of God* Sheriff Tom Davis operates as a traditional hero who crusades against the murderous disorder of the Tennessee White Caps. In fact, this section of the novel is a historical romance revising an obscure history of the White Caps written anonymously in Tennessee in 1896, just as *Blood Meridian* rewrites Chamberlain's *My Confession*.[11] Suttree's wanderings through the Knoxville underground operate as a kind of ironic antiquest for his identity, while his journey from Knoxville promises to initiate a quest affirming life. The clearest version of the quest in the early fiction is Rinthy's search in *Outer Dark* to locate her lost child and regain her identity as mother.

A Pastiche of the Cowboy Myth.   A popular audience for McCarthy's fiction emerges from John Grady Cole's, Billy Parham's, and Boyd Parham's postmodern versions of the quest. All three characters radically revise the characterization of the kid in *Blood Meridian*, who acts as an antiheroic, often violently depraved Westerner. In contrast, John Grady Cole and the Parham brothers function as contemporary versions of the cowboy hero. In fact, Cole and the Parhams function within the novels as a pastiche, a postmodern form of parody, of the sentimental and popular figure of the Last Cowboy. Pastiche, in the formulation of Fredric Jameson, is a postmodern version of parodic satire, with the essential difference that the satire is "blank" or "amputated of the satiric impulse" by failing to provide a coherent ideological alternative to the pastiche. To such critics of the postmodern as Jameson, Jean Baudrillard, and Linda Hutcheon, pastiche functions in postmodern art by resurrecting fragmented elements of history "trapped" within the unhistorical consciousness of the postmodern present. In such Disney films as *Pocohontas,* pastiche history conceals or hides authentic history from our view.[12] Significantly, both novels of The Border Trilogy are set within not the nineteenth but the twentieth century, while as early as the 1890s the cowboy and rancher already were "outmoded" in the West's economy. Mirror opposites of the postmodern audience who escapes in film to a romanticized pastiche past, Cole and the Parhams discover that they are historical anachronisms living within the modern present.

The parody of popular forms within postmodern art reverses modernism's retreat from a commercialized world into art. The commercial popularity of The Border Trilogy in part derives from the presence of this popular figure of the romantic cowboy. Another factor is that McCarthy for the first time adds significant elements of heterosexual romance to his fiction, with the romantic passion of Alejandra and John Grady Cole and the "doomed" love between Boyd Parham and the unnamed peasant girl. Indeed, Boyd's romance with the peasant girl in *The Crossing* further transforms him from cowboy to romantic outlaw, a Southwestern border version of the depression-era outlaws Bonnie and Clyde or Pretty Boy Floyd. A final crucial factor in The Border Trilogy's popular appeal is that John Grady Cole and Billy Parham seem to express a sentimental nostalgia toward the past. To the unhistorical present, stripped of a historical awareness, the American West symbolizes a nostalgia for the putative independence and self-reliance of the past. Nostalgic art, Fredric Jameson argues, builds its appeal on our largely unacknowledged desire to criticize or escape from our imprisonment within the postindustrial capitalism of contemporary society, where identity is mediated through advertising and video images (Jameson, 19–21). Rather than fleeing into art, McCarthy's cowboy heroes make their historical escape away from industrial society and toward a Southwest they envision as an open frontier.

Two Quests to Recover the Past. Given the success of the first two novels of The Border Trilogy, questions arise whether to interpret these heightened romantic elements—the quest, the cowboy hero, the nostalgia toward the frontier past—as a capitulation of McCarthy's art to the commercial. As the sales of The Border Trilogy suggest, these three heroes are or at least can be "consumed" by some readers as commodified romantic heroes who recover a lost past. Such readers wish to reappropriate the West for their own ideological purposes, as in John F. Kennedy's Last Frontier or Ronald Reagan as the Cowboy President. Both novels of the trilogy are instead "serious" parodies of the western—parodies that revise the meaning of the cowboy and the nature of the escape he and the frontier seem to offer to the present. The novels clearly demonstrate that John Grady Cole, Billy Parham, and Boyd Parham cannot successfully embody or "repossess" the nostalgic West of the Hollywood western. In the novels' concluding scenes, the hero's journey, although it parallels the escapist desires of the reader of the popular western, is exposed as a failed attempt to "repossess" an identity based on a mythic and unrecoverable past. John Grady Cole's and Billy Parham's historical nostalgia might be termed the cowboy myth.[13] *All the Pretty Horses* and *The Crossing* subvert the western from within, just as Melville subverted the sea romance in *Benito Cereno* and the female romance in *Pierre; or, The Ambiguities.*

Symbolic Quests. Though John Grady Cole and Billy Parham both seek to found their identity on a shared historical desire to recover the West, as we might expect, the precise symbolic representations of their quests differ. Parham's quest in *The Crossing* is represented in his attempt to restore the Mexican wolf to her home and to recover his own home by repossessing his father's horses. The objects of Cole's version of the romantic quest similarly are captured in two symbols: his maternal grandfather's ranch and the "pretty horses" who roam freely over the Mexican range. The central narrative of *All the Pretty Horses* begins with what appears to be a youthful prank of two Texas schoolboys, Cole and his friend Rawlins, who whimsically cross into Mexico, not by automobile but on horses. The novel's beginning specifies no specific destination or motive for their journey, though several earlier separate conversations between John Grady, his father, and his mother's lawyer suggest that Cole's motivation is supplied by his actress mother, who sells her father's ranch, which her son had planned to work (*APH*, 8–11, 15–18).

In post–World War II Texas, Cole's mother can only "act" her part. The gulf between mother and son is historical, between two versions of the contemporary Texan: the modern (the mother) who repudiates her ranching past for art, and the historicist (John Grady as son) who seeks to revive and repeat that past. Cole desires to supplant his mother by identifying with and occupying the position of her father, the ranch's original proprietor. A later conversation with a *hacendado* (ranch owner) further articulates the symbolic and historical values behind Cole's departure from Texas: "There was two things they agreed upon wholly and that were never spoken and that was that God had put horses on earth to work cattle and that other than cattle there was no wealth proper to a man" (*APH*, 127). Cole's economic and personal values are authentically derived from those of the frontier rancher. Yet from a historical perspective, modernization and market economics have so outdated these values that they can still exist only within the hero in the form of a personal code of behavior.

Stripped of his maternal inheritance, possessing only his knowledge of horses, his horse, and his father's saddle (ironically given to him at the same time as the son learns his mother wishes to sell the ranch), John Grady and his friend Rawlins depart Texas on horseback, their mode of travel an implicit rejection of the mechanized American Southwest of the post–World War II era. Riding southward through Northern Mexico from desert to high plains, then over a mountain divide into a high valley, the two boys attempt to travel historically, finding the open range preserved in the mountain valley to be a modern equivalent of the post–Civil War open range of Texas, Montana, and Wyoming. They will discover that they have not recovered or reopened the frontier but merely have crossed into still another "closed" landscape, possessed by an aristocratic culture impervious to the allure of the cowboy myth.

In despair after his final separation from his lover, Alejandra, Cole reverses the track of his journey into the Mexican range. Capturing the sheriff who had murdered Blevins, then reclaiming the horses belonging to him, Rawlins, and Blevins, Cole flees back to Texas with the sheriff as hostage. The unconscious logic of his actions suggests that if he cannot escape historical change or cultural differences, then by recovering his horses and those of his friends, he symbolically can reverse Blevins's death and his prison experiences and can recover his lost innocence. According to this logic, Cole succeeds, escaping back to Texas and restoring Rawlins's horse, Junior, to his barn. Yet the confusion and guilt that Cole reveals in his conversations with Rawlins, the judge, and the evangelist Blevins suggest that historical events cannot be reversed, that Cole cannot forget his responsibility for his actions, that he cannot remain true to his horseman's code and at the same time live within modernity. Hence his self-imposed exile at the novel's end, wandering with no destination.

Billy Parham's second journey into Mexico to recover his murdered father's horses so closely parallels this conclusion to *Pretty Horses* as to verge on self-parody. After crossing into Mexico to recover the horses, Billy, unlike Cole, comes to recognize the absurdity of his journey. Near the conclusion of his first trip into Mexico with the wolf, Billy is named *huerfano* (orphan) by an old Indian who admonishes him to cease the wanderings that have "estranged" him from other men: "He said that the world could only be known as it existed in men's hearts. For while it seemed a place which contained men it was in reality a place contained within them and therefore to know it one must look there and come to know those hearts . . . and not simply pass among them." Denying the man's analysis of him as an orphan, a few days later Parham cannot "call to mind his father's face," and turns homeward, as if to reassure himself and restore his earlier identity as son (*C*, 134–35). He returns to find the old man's words to be prophetic: his father and mother have been mysteriously killed in his absence; his younger brother, Boyd, taken in by a neighboring family; and his father's horses stolen by the murderers. The murders have an eerie Oedipal structure, as the sheriff recognizes in his initial suspicions of Billy aroused by the boy's inexplicable absence before the murders. The sheriff is unaware of the brothers' secret: a year before the murders they secretly had fed a mysterious Indian who inquired after their father's possessions, then disappeared on foot. Boyd, we learn, is haunted by the fact that the killers attempt to lure him from hiding by calling his name—"They called for me. Called Boyd. Boyd." The brothers keep this incident concealed first from their father, then from the sheriff, as if their act of humanity makes them somehow responsible for the murders (*C*, 166–73).

Postmodern Critiques of the Romantic Quest.   *The Crossing* complicates the earlier novel's structure and its figure of the Last Cowboy. Refusing to relinquish each quest, Billy Parham nevertheless becomes aware of its absurdity, suggesting that Parham is a more self-conscious and postmodern hero than Cole. The absurdity of Billy Parham's attempt to deal with the loss of his father by recovering his horses reveals to him the innocence and inadequacy of his own code.

Recognizing their horse Keno tied outside a "whitewashed" house, the two brothers reclaim him, tracing his sale to a broker in Casas Grandes (*C*, 181–83). About to depart for Casas Grandes, when they request from four old men directions to the town, one draws a map in the dirt that another man immediately dismisses as a "fantasma":

> Billy stood looking at the map. No es correcto? he said.
> The man threw up his hands. He said that what they beheld was but a decoration. He said that anyway it was not so much a question of a correct map but of any map at all. He said that in the country were fires and earthquakes and floods and that one needed to know the country itself and not simply the landmarks therein. . . . His map was after all not really so much a map as a picture of a voyage. And what voyage was that? (*C*, 184–85)

In poststructuralist fashion, this conversation questions the adequacy of man's symbolic representations of the world to signify an exterior reality. Still another speaker counters this criticism by referring to the "good will" of the original mapmaker as an aid in affirming their hopes. Yet interpreting their destination itself as metaphoric, this speaker then regards their proposed journey as a narrative whose meaning cannot be so restricted to intentionality: "there were certainly other dangers to a journey than losing one's way. He said that plans were one thing and journeys another" (*C*, 185).

Given subsequent events, the speaker who first warns against the map proves to have given the Parhams worthy advice. Yet in contradiction of his warning, he next draws them aside and accurately describes to them the road to Casas Grandes. The speaker here enacts a metafictional authorial role, standing in for the authorial McCarthy who at once warns against the novel's tragic events yet compels the youths forward in their journey. With their journey compared to a map's failed attempt to accurately represent and predict the outer world, Billy and Boyd are asked to self-reflexively reconsider their own ambitious "plans" and judge their ability to predict and control the events of the world as narrative. Perhaps the scene also requests its readers to read themselves as self-reflexively as the Parhams, inquiring into the desires that we as readers bring to our journey as readers of the narrative. Reading, narrating, mapmaking, and questing—these are activities that are no longer innocent but reveal our desire to project a fixed structure on a world whose chaos resists such interpretations.

Similar incidents call attention to the theme of their journey as a metanarrative that has already been written before their journey begins. Conversing with the broker Gillian at Casas Grandes, the boys once again receive advice that emphasizes the discrepancy between the intent behind their quest and its consequences. Responding to Boyd's story of their father's death and theft of his horses as "preposterous," the broker appears to self-interestedly question the object of their quest—their father's horses and his murder. If the motives behind his advice are selfish, that advice cannot be so easily dismissed: "It is not such an easy thing to find a man in Mexico. . . . The monte is extensive. . . . A man can be lost" (*C,* 201). Finding them to be young men "far from home," he professes an avuncular responsibility to advise them, stating simply, "Return to your home." Addressing the younger, he explains that the elder Parham "knows what perhaps you do not. That the past cannot be mended. You think everyone is a fool. But there are not so many reasons for you to be in Mexico." He continues: "Your brother is young enough to believe that the past still exists. . . . That the injustices within it await his remedy. . . . What remedy can there be for what is not? You see? And where is the remedy that has no unforeseen consequence? What act does not assume a future that is itself unknown?. . . . You must be sure that the intention in your heart is large enough to contain all wrong turnings, all disappointments. Do you see?" (*C,* 201–202).

Other figures whom Billy encounters—a worker in New Mexico, the prima donna of a traveling theatrical troupe, a blinded revolutionary—similarly will warn against his journey by pointing to its unintended consequences, yet like Oedipus he is blind to the warnings. When Billy asks if his brother understands Gillian's warning, the younger Boyd responds, "Yeah, I know what he was talking about. Do you?" (*C,* 203). Nonetheless, both persist in a journey that succeeds only in that all the horses are temporarily repossessed. Yet Boyd is shot, the brothers are separated, and the younger escapes with a young girl to a life of banditry that ends in his death—one of the unintended consequences against which Gillian warns. Billy's final journey crossing the border into Mexico is a penitential one, to reclaim his brother's body and reclaim Boyd's American identity. In Mexico, Boyd has received a new mythic identity as a romantic, brave, and dead bandit within a *corrido,* or popular folk song (*C,* 381). The contrast between the reality of Boyd's life and his romantic identity in the ballad mirrors that between the Billy who enacts the role of cowboy hero and the confused boy who wanders in and out of Mexico.

The Postmodern Hero's Loss of Self.   John Grady Cole and
Billy Parham both experience a loss of an initially stable identity based
on a mythicized past. This loss of identity mirrors the gap that separates
contemporary man from an authentically historical existence. At the
close of *All the Pretty Horses,* Rawlins invites Cole to stay with him,
asserting, "This is still good country." Cole replies laconically, "Yeah. I
know it is. But it aint my country." To Rawlins's question, "Where is
your country?" Cole's response—and McCarthy's ending—points to the
cowboy's loss of an authentic identity: "I dont know, said John Grady. I
dont know where it is. I dont know what happens to country" (*APH,*
299). At the conclusion of *The Crossing,* Billy Parham also lives as a man
lost within the contemporary world. His quest to return his brother's
body to an American grave is absurd, as the sheriff implies at the cemetery: "Well. You caint just travel around the country buryin people. Let
me go see the judge and see if I can get him to issue a death certificate. I
aint even sure whose property that is you're diggin in" (*C,* 422). If John
Grady Cole's country is "undiscovered," the Shakespearean formulation
for death, *All the Pretty Horse's* ending undermines its quest motif. Cole's
journey to Mexico may have attempted to recover his identity as cowboy
and horseman, but that identity, along with his identity as son and lover,
has been stripped away. Refusing to accept or assign himself an identity
within the contemporary world, he has denied himself an authentic
social identity.

If Cole and Billy Parham are heroes, they are contemporary versions
of the Childe Roland version of the quest. Like the knight, at the close of
their journeys they find themselves not at a "destination" but trapped
within an interiorized wilderness. Both are unable to assign a determi-
nate meaning, stable significance, or unifying agency to the narrative of
their experience. By the novels' conclusions, if not earlier, this motif of
the aimless journey transforms itself into an allegorical figure of the protagonist's loss of innocence and identity. *All the Pretty Horses,* for example, concludes with two short paragraphs describing Cole's four-day ride
from his home. Passing a group of indians (the word pointedly uncapi-
talized in the text), the narrator's description of Cole is at pains to suggest his meaninglessness to these observers: "They had no curiosity
about him at all. As if they knew all that they needed to know. They
stood and watched him vanish upon that landscape solely because he
was passing. Solely because he would vanish" (*APH,* 301). These
observers are exemplary readers of the narrative, ones who simply
regard the passing of a stream of signifiers. One short paragraph later,

Cole and his horses simply vanish for us, his readers, just as he has vanished for these onlookers: "He rode with the sun coppering his face and the red wind blowing out of the west across the evening land and the small desert birds flew chittering among the dry bracken and horse and rider and horse passed on and their long shadows passed in tandem like the shadow of a single being. Passed and paled into the darkening land, the world to come" (*APH*, 302). The string of participial phrases, main clauses, and subjects are only weakly linked by the conjunctive "and." This list is a synecdoche for the narrative as a whole, viewed as an unrelated series of episodes, experiences, and linguistic signifiers.

On the mimetic level, Cole simply rides from the narrative into an unnarrated future at the novel's conclusion. Yet the openly symbolist qualities of the landscape call attention to the ending as a stylized, surrealistic representation of Cole as a historical figure locked into the past, unable to move into the "world to come." This reading of the ending, of course, substitutes a view of Cole as a historical myth for the realistic description of his ride into the landscape. The view of Cole as an elegaicized historical hero furthermore should be opposed to the indians' viewpoint of his ride. To such outside observers unaware of the preceding events, the ride is without significance. If Cole and Parham's wilderness journeys have an allegorized significance, it is derived from a peculiarly postmodern version of allegory: the wilderness journey points only to itself rather than to a final destination or conclusion that would provide the hero with an identity or readers with a fixed meaning for the journey and narrative. Lacking a final destination, Cole and Parham's quests are interminable, their identities undefined, and their stories without satisfactory conclusions. Lacking the finality of typical endings to realistic or modern fiction, McCarthy's inconclusive conclusions to The Border Trilogy suggest, like Vonnegut's multiple endings for *Slaughterhouse Five,* that novelistic endings are arbitrary, merely convenient stopping points.[14]

This instructive "failure" of the concluding passages of *All the Pretty Horses* and *The Crossing* points us again to the postmodern. Lyotard associates the postmodern with a principled refusal of the totalizing *grand récit* or "master narratives" of Marxism, Enlightenment progressivism, or the Freudian unconscious. Such narratives attempt to provide a fixed structure to history and to the self.[15] Similarly, all of McCarthy's novels save *Child of God* close with this figure of the incompleted journey— Culla Holme wandering on a rural path, Suttree following the highway out of Knoxville, the bonepickers of *Blood Meridian* who, near the novel's conclusion, meander across the Texas wasteland collecting the skeletons of bison. *The Crossing* also ends inconclusively: for a year after the burial of his brother, Billy Parham aimlessly rides from ranch to ranch. After chasing away a crippled dog (a faint mirror of the wolf at the novel's beginning), Parham weeps. The novel again ends abruptly: "He sat there for a long time and after a while the east did gray and after a while the right and godmade sun did rise, once again, for all and without distinction" (*C,* 426). The ironic allusion, of course, is to one of modernism's grand narratives, *The Sun Also Rises,* whose title itself connects the sense of the world as meaningless repetition in Ecclesiastes to the loss of meaning in the modern era after World War I. The sunlit ending of *The Crossing* thus critiques the inadequacy of mythic cycles to coherently structure the history of the protagonist's experiences. *The Crossing*'s sun merely rises, like our own, and the ending's final irony is also an allusion, for its sun rises on the just and the unjust alike. This ending thus transumes biblical rhetoric and modernist fragmentation within McCarthy's more postmodern narrative.

Nature and the Heroic Will.   As suggested by this image of the sun's rising (a figure more usually associated with origins and beginnings), *The Crossing* concludes with its hero trapped between the historical and the contemporary. The same is true of John Grady Cole at the ending of *All the Pretty Horses.* In The Border Trilogy a metaphysical gap is opened between nature and consciousness—a gap that mirrors the ones between the will and desire and the conscious and unconscious. As the title of *All the Pretty Horses* implies, the horse is a particularly complex symbolic representation of the relation between the human and the natural: "The boy who rode on . . . sat a horse not only as if he'd been born to it which he was but as if were he begot by malice or mischance into some queer land where horses never were he would have found them anyway. Would have known that there was something missing for the world to be right or he right in it and would have set forth to wander wherever it was needed for as long as it took until he came upon one and he would have known that that was what he sought and it would have been" (*APH,* 23). This passage identifies Cole with the horse, implying that the two share a common symbolic identity. The *vaquero* Luis also suggests this connection: "He told them of horses killed under him and he said that the souls of horses mirror the souls of men more closely than men suppose" (*APH,* 111). In his essay on the novel, Tom Pilkington associates this common identity with the frontier, with the

Western self's desire for freedom and consequent nobility (Pilkington, 311–22). I would add only the necessity of emphasizing how the conclusion undermines Cole's aspirations.

John Grady Cole is a horseman, a horsebreaker, a pivotal figure who on the one hand appears to live a "natural" existence within nature yet who "breaks" nature, in the form of the horse, to the dictates of his will. The rhetorical excesses of a passage describing Cole's riding exemplify this paradox: "While inside the vaulting of the ribs beneath his knees the darkly meated heart pumped of who's will and the blood pulsed . . . and the stout thighbones and knee and cannon and the tendons like flaxen hawsers that drew and flexed and drew and flexed at their articulations and of who's will all sheathed and muffled in the flesh and the hooves that stove wells in the morning groundmist and the head turning side to side and the great slavering keyboard of his teeth and the hot globes of his eyes where the world burned" (*APH,* 128). The grammatical error ("who's") created by attaching the apostrophized *s* to the pronoun *who* suggests a buried question within the description: whose is the will described? While Cole is ostensibly in command of the horse, its heart is not so subservient to his will, as suggested in the analogies to Blake's "The Tyger" in McCarthy's imagery. The "heart pumped of who's will" is comparable to Blake's question "What the hammer?" and the cosmological imagery of the horse's eyes ("hot globes of his eyes") can be matched to the apocalypse at the creation of the tyger, "when the stars threw down their spears."

Cole's domination of the horse in riding evokes reason's imperial desire to subdue the world, bending it to the impulses of the will to write its own destiny. Enlightenment Reason similarly defined itself by first opposing itself to nature and then redefining the natural in its own image.[16] Cole seeks to identify himself with the natural to erase the distinction between himself and the horse. On his first night in jail, he dreams of himself "among the horses running . . . and they flowed and changed and ran and their manes and tails blew off of them like spume and there was nothing else at all in that high world . . . and they ran in that resonance which is the world itself and which cannot be spoken but only praised" (*APH,* 161–62). The dream is of an absolute natural freedom represented by the horses' formlessness—"they flowed . . . and their manes and tails blew off." Cole dreams of crossing over the boundary separating the self from the world. Cole and Rawlins seemingly establish this control over nature when they "greenbreak" (make ridable) 16 horses in four days, "sidelining" the horses (side-roping the hind legs to the front hackamore and thus discouraging their bucking). By this feat, Cole enters into a partnership with the *hacendado* to oversee the breeding of cowhorses for his ranch (*APH,* 103–104, 126–27). Yet it is Cole's affair with the *hacendado*'s daughter, Alejandra, which severs this contract and with it the possibility of Cole's return to a horseman's Eden. In the second half of the novel, he discovers that the natural and social world is not so subject to the dictates of his imperial will as were the horses he has broken.

In two epiphanic passages, Billy Parham first enacts a similar desire to merge with an esthetic idealization of the natural world, then becomes alienated from a world that refuses to reflect his desire. In Stephen Dedalus's epiphany of the girl bathing near the close of *Portrait of the Artist as a Young Man,* Joyce suggests his protagonist's assumption of the role of artist. In Dedalus's perception, the girl takes on a mythic, formalized, even inhuman shape. In a parallel scene in *The Crossing,* Billy Parham walks by the Casas Grandes river early in the morning after he has seen a troupe of actors performing in the countryside. Billy sees the troupe's prima donna bathing: "She bent and caught her falling hair in her arms and held it and she passed one hand over the surface of the water as if to bless it and he watched and as he watched he saw that the world which had always been before him everywhere had been veiled from his sight." The boy's desire would seem to have produced a new, visionary perception of a world sacralized through art, as in Dedalus's epiphany. Yet as the prima donna turns and walks away after seeing the boy, Parham is left with a sense of deprivation rather than heightened imaginative perception: "the sun rose and the river ran as before but nothing was the same nor did he think it ever would be" (*C,* 220). Though perception of the world's beauty stimulates desire, the world, once recognized as an object, frustrates the self's desire for merger with the natural and reveals the self's absolute isolation.

On a second such morning, when Billy recognizes his brother has left his company for the love of the girl they have saved, Billy again recognizes the inhuman distance and antiquity of this old world into which he has crossed: "he looked at the deep cyanic sky taut and vaulted over the whole of Mexico where the antique world clung to the stones and to the spores of living things and dwelt in the blood of men. He turned the horse and set out along the road south. . . . For the enmity of the world was newly plain to him that day and cold and inameliorate as it must be to all who have no longer cause except themselves to stand against it" (*C,* 331). Having earlier denied the Indian's analysis of him as *huerfano* (orphan), on this occasion, while conversing with another old man who asks about his home (*"Esta lejos de su casa"*), Billy now acknowledges that he is both orphan and homeless, to the old man's dismay: "The old man's face grew troubled. . . . The old man said that there was a place for everyone in the world and that he would pray for the boy" (*C*, 236).

The Critique of Idealism: Revolution and Repression

The *hacendado*, Alejandra, and her great-aunt Alfonsita demonstrate to John Grady Cole that this desire to write freely one's own identity must yield to the will of others and to the opposition of historical and cultural forces. Homes construct and imprison the individual. Within prison, Cole is forced to acknowledge the social and historical limits on what he has believed to be his infinite freedom to define his own identity and code of behavior. Here, of course, the novel reflects one of the primary characteristics of postmodernism and poststructuralism—the "constructed" nature of the world. Identity and ethos, nature and society are constructs of culture, not the autonomous self. The boy's conversation with the *majordomo*, the godfather of the prison, begins the process of this discovery. Perez attempts to negotiate with the youth the price of his release, while John Grady at first imperially refuses to negotiate, asking only for knowledge of his friend Rawlins, who has been attacked and injured in prison. Perez criticizes Cole's refusal to negotiate, noting the cultural derivation of his refusal: "Even in a place like this . . . the mind of the anglo is closed in this rare way. At one time I thought it was only his life of privilege. But it is not that. It is his mind. . . . It is that his picture of the world is incomplete" (*APH*, 192).

Perez continues his critique of Cole's moral idealism by noting that identity is not determined by an innate "code" but has a value determined by the world: "Then it can determine your price." When Cole counters, claiming that "some people don't have a price," Perez answers, "That is true. . . . Those people die" (*APH*, 193). If we judge their dispute by the novel's conclusion, Perez's interpretation is the more privileged. For Cole's "price" is determined not by himself but by the transaction between Alfonsita and Alejandra, the latter trading Cole's release for her agreement to end their affair. Immediately before his release, Cole is required to violate his code by killing a youth who has been hired—probably by the *hacendado*—to kill him: "The chuchillero spoke no word. His movements were precise and without rancor. John Grady knew he was hired. . . . He looked deep into those dark eyes and there were deeps there to look into. A whole malign history burning deep and cold" (*APH*, 200). Cole can transcend neither history or society but is situated within, limited by, and constructed by both forces.

Alfonsita: Class Conflict, Revolution, and Nihilism.

Cole's release places him and Alejandra into the aunt's debt, obliging both lovers to acknowledge the constraints of history and society. In her dialogue with Cole, Alfonsita acknowledges their similarity as uncompromising individualists and their absolute difference as cultural Others. In that the narrative refuses to restrict the great aunt to the role of a villain, it emerges as an authentic "border" novel, acknowledging at the same time that their separate cultures construct Alfonsita and Cole as enemies yet they are merged in that the desire of each—Alejandra—mirrors that of the other.

The autobiography that Alfonsita narrates to explain her actions against Cole clarifies that she herself once had occupied her niece's position as rebel against the conventions and restrictions of society. Alfonsita's rebellion was a political romanticism, supporting the program of economic equalization proposed by her youthful lover, Gustavo Madera: "When I was a girl, the poverty in this country was very terrible. What you see today cannot even suggest it. And I was very affected by this. . . . In all cases I refused to believe in a God who could permit such injustice as I saw in a world of his own making. I was very idealistic" (*APH*, 231–32). If Cole's idealism seeks to nullify history in his belief that he can relive the roles of rancher, horseman, stockbreeder, and romantic lover, then Alfonsita's idealism had consisted of her acquiescence in the belief of Francisco and Gustavo Madera that they could sever Mexican politics from its history and culture. Their political revolution could achieve economic justice, they believed, by ending the aristocracy's and industrial monopolies' domination of Mexican politics. Invited to the Maderas' house, she explains, "it was in that house that I first heard the full expression of those things closest to my heart. I began to see how the world must become if I were to live in it"—live, that is, as what she considers to be "a person of value" (*APH*, 233–35). As a young woman, she had believed, as Cole does, that the individual is able to determine her value existentially, superior to historical and cultural restraints. On the contrary, her father would soon forbid her engagement to Gustavo, banishing her to Europe. Meanwhile, the counterrevolution would dispose of the Maderas' political revolution (and cruelly dispose of the Maderas themselves), anticipating Franco's fascist counterrevolution in Spain.

Two Revolutionaries in *The Crossing.* Paralleling Cole and
Billy's desire for power over the natural world, Alfonsita's revolt against
economic injustice seeks the power to change the social and economic
world. *The Crossing* expands Alfonsita's interpolated tale with two similar tales—that of the girl who becomes Boyd's lover and the longer tale
of the blind revolutionary. The girl's tale is of her grandmother's life,
one that mirrors Alfonsita's: her grandmother while still in her teens
had married three revolutionaries, each killed in the wars. Like Alfonsita, the grandmother responds with skepticism toward such "rash
men," yet she acknowledges them as a romantic "temptation." Earlier,
during a dispute with a *gerente* (foreman) over the ownership of their
father's horse, Billy had spooked the *gerente*'s horse, who unseats his
rider, accidentally breaking his back. After Boyd is killed, the folk song
of his life rewrites the conflict with the *gerente* to suit the shape of the
audiences' desire: the *gerente* is not killed in an accident but shot by Boyd
as romantic *güerito.* Envisioning herself a romantic, the girl falls in love
with Boyd. Learning of Boyd's stillborn twin sister, the girl imagines
herself in the role of the missing twin; Boyd is the male form—or
twin—of her own idealized identity.

Throughout the novel, Boyd enacts the role of the skeptical hero—
one who acts or loves in spite of his skepticism. He is skeptical of Billy's
wishes to rescue the peasant girl from rape ("What do you want to do,
said Boyd" [*C,* 206]); to aid the prima donna stranded by the road
("Let's go, he said. If they aint nothin else will satisfy you" [*C,* 225]);
and to recover their father's horses ("You think maybe we ought to of
stayed back yonder?" [*C,* 234]). After their claim to the horses is denied
by the *gerente,* Billy argues to continue on in pursuit: "We come too far
down here to go back dead." Boyd's response betrays his more realistic
assessment: "You think there is a place that far?" Yet Boyd allows the
older brother to define their quest and, by it, his own identity (*C,*
248–49). Although his abandonment of Billy may seem an uncharac-
teristically assertive act of self-definition, here, too, Boyd enacts a role
assigned to him—that of folk hero, *hombre de la gente,* and revolutionary—by the girl's desire to repeat her grandmother's history (*C,*
322–23). This reenactment allows Boyd to claim a Mexican home and
his identity within the folk song of the gringo *güerito.* Such a home is
denied Billy, who enacts the exile of the *huerfano* (orphan).

The blind man's interpolated tale in *The Crossing* reinscribes and critiques the girl's revolutionary desires, yet his position is not identical
to Alfonsita's skeptical realism that privileges the opposition of "the

world" over the desire to revise history and politics. The blind man and Alfonsita are maimed by history in both the literal sense and the figurative (she suffers a disabling accident to her hand before falling in love with Madera). If Alfonsita experiences a social alienation that takes the paradoxical form of reaffirming the world's opposition to the affair between her niece and Cole, the blind man suffers a more radical and metaphysical version of her alienation. A soldier for the revolution, he remains loyal to the cause after the town he defends is captured and his comrades are shot as traitors. He is blinded by the German mercenary Wirtz, who sucks out the soldier's eyes. On his journey home, the blinded soldier must acknowledge the radical alienation that is the metaphysical consequence of his idealism and consequent blinding: "He said that the light of the world was in men's eyes only for the world itself moved in eternal darkness and darkness was its true nature and true condition and that in this darkness it turned with perfect cohesion in all its parts but that there was naught there to see" (*C*, 283). His new disassociation from the once-visible world reveals a new metaphysics in which the world is not divided between illusion and reality but between two worlds—the "dark" world outside of human comprehension and the world that is the product of human perspective. The blind man's tale, like Alfonsita's, again warns the boy against his quest to find justice by repossessing his father's horses and relocating his brother. His blindness prefigures Billy's own blind disassociation from the world at the end of his quest.

"Those whom life does not cure death will."   Alfonsita's rebuke of John Grady Cole similarly opposes the world to the human spectator, yet she assumes the adequacy of the reason to see the world as it is and act correctly on that vision. Speaking of the counterrevolution against the Maderas, concluding in Gustavo's torture and execution, Alfonsita concludes, "In the end we all come to be cured of our sentiments. Those whom life does not cure death will. The world is quite ruthless in selecting between the dream and the reality, even where we will not. Between the wish and the thing the world lies waiting" (*APH*, 237–38). Her opposition to Alejandra and Cole's love, then, is a self-critique of her own earlier idealism. Her wish to bound Alejandra's sexuality to conventional constraints ironically rehearses her own father's decision to sublimate her political desire for revolution and her sexual desire for Gustavo. Alfonsita's vision assumes the power of the Reason—a belief in its adequacy to see the world and a denial that fate determines her choices. The blind man's recognition of the visible world as illusion critiques her faith in our ability to perceive and to choose within a world that restricts our desire.

Other motives determine Alfonsita's behavior toward Cole and Alejandra. Stating that societies are "largely machines for the suppression of women," her desire is to gain power over the story of her life through controlling the life of her niece, for whom she plans an "unconventional" marriage (*APH*, 240). Ostensibly the aunt seeks freedom for her niece, yet we discover in Cole's final interview with Alejandra that the aunt had attempted to subject Alejandra to her will by threatening to reveal the affair to the father. Just as ironically, to free herself from her aunt's control Alejandra confesses the affair to her father at the cost of losing Cole and her own freedom: "I couldnt stand for her to have that power. I told him myself" (*APH*, 250). Attempting to control her own fate, Alejandra loses control to her father and to her aunt, who alone has the power to release Cole. Yet the fundamental drive determining the aunt's actions is a will to power that is ultimately metaphysical, rather than political or personal: "the question for me was always whether that shape we see in our lives was there from the beginning or whether these random events are only called a pattern after the fact" (*APH*, 230). While she appears to represent a hardheaded realism against the idealism of the young, the aunt remains a radical idealist who denies fate by emphasizing the possibility of the individual to define herself, even in the face of the disastrous constraints of culture and history that have scarred her own life: "It's not so much that I dont believe in it [fate]. I dont subscribe to its nomination" (*APH*, 241). She attempts to play the role of fate in relation to Cole and Alejandra. Aware of the constraints of culture, history, and gender, Alfonsita seeks to rewrite her earlier rebellion by living a vicarious second youth through rewriting her niece's life.

Border Crossings and Cultural Conflict

The dialogue between Alfonsita and Cole operates as a paradigmatic border crossing—a crossing in which the desire of a young Westerner (an innocent of an almost Jamesian variety) is opposed by a different culture and history. *The Crossing,* aptly titled to identify its major theme of a series of transgressive border "crossings," is a revision that fully plots this theme by more closely examining the ironic tension between the heroic individual and the limiting constraints of culture and history. It hardly can be accidental that on the novel's first page (describing the year of the Parham family's crossing into New Mexico), the ecological range of the wolf is shown to overlap the national boundary and the property line of the Parham ranch. The novel's first page thus contains three crossings: the family's crossing from Texas into New Mexico; the consequent crossing or demarcation of nature into an individually marked possession of the family ("The new country was rich and wild. You could ride clear to Mexico and not strike a crossfence"); and the crossing over of the wolf, whose existence dictates that she traverse all such human boundaries.

The Wolf as Embodiment of the Border Crossing.   The wolf apparently operates as a symbolic embodiment of the hero's freedom in much the same manner as the horse in *All the Pretty Horses*. Early in Billy Parham's childhood, a vision of the wolf's crossing will determine his very identity: "On a winter's night in that first year he woke to hear wolves in the low hills to the west of the house and he knew that they would be coming out onto the plain in the new snow to run the antelope in the moonlight." Looking out over the scene where the wolves have "crossed" before him, the child Billy glimpses a perception of another world—a world whose contours are radically different from the human. The wolf's identity is one unalienated from the natural and its own predatory nature: "They were running on the plain harrying the antelope and the antelope moved like phantoms in the snow and circled and wheeled and the dry powder blew about them in the cold moonlight and their breath smoked palely in the cold as if they burned with some inner fire and the wolves twisted and turned and leapt in a silence such that they seemed of another world entire" (*C*, 3). That the wolves, in mirrorlike fashion, "know" Billy is clear in their returned gaze at their return from the hunt, passing within 20 feet of the boy (*C*, 4).

This repressed memory will return when his glance next crosses that of a wolf—the female wolf he traps years later: "He was in no way prepared for what he beheld. . . . He . . . took up the reins and mounted up and turned the horse and headed out to the road. The wolf was watching him as before. He sat the horse a long time. The sun warm on his back. The world waiting. Then he rode back to the wolf" (*C*, 53). This glance, and the repressed memory of his youth that it releases, determines Billy's decision to "cross" into Mexico with the wolf. Billy Parham's adolescent view of the wolf has transformed radically. Originally viewing the wolf as an economic threat and as an intellectual challenge, the 16-year-old Parham had assumed from his father the task of trapping the wolf. Yet as the dreamlike incident from the novel's start suggests, he from the beginning has held a contradictory view of the wolf as his own double, representing the desire for an intellect unalienated from the natural.

Using the wolf as the symbolic representation of the natural, the first section of *The Crossing* has a far more contemporary reference than at first may appear. Indeed, this beginning historicizes the acrimonious and well-publicized contemporary debate over the reintroduction of wolves into the United States. Since the 1970s, the federal government has planned to reintroduce the Mexican wolf into federally owned areas of Southern Arizona and New Mexico—ironically the same territories in which the animal was trapped into extinction from the 1920s to 1940s. This extinction was accomplished with the support of federal and state government bounties, as the novel suggests through the two old men, Echols and Don Arnulfo, who have made their living trapping wolves. In his study of the Southwestern lobo, Burbank James examines this historic extinction of the lobo, estimating that in the early 1980s only 30 animals were left in the Southwest. His book probably is one of McCarthy's primary sources on the lobo, since Burbank's introduction recounts not only a "first encounter" enacted "face to face" with a wolf but a dream with several similarities to Billy's own dream. We know also that McCarthy was a friend of the environmental writer and activist Edward Abbey and had discussed with Abbey the issue of the reintroduction of the Mexican lobo into the Southwest in the year of Abbey's death, 1989.[17]

Once he finds the wolf in his trap, Billy is caught upon the horns of an adolescent dilemma: "My daddy wanted me to come and get him if I caught her but I didn't want to leave her cause they's been some vaqueros takin their dinner over yonder and I figured they'd probably shoot her so I just decided to take her on home with me" (C, 59). Chastized earlier by his father for breaking his promise to return before dark, Billy first decides to follow the letter of his father's law, bringing the live wolf directly before his father's sight.

In contrast to the consummate seriousness of the wolf's tragic end, two of the more comic scenes in all of McCarthy's fiction sketch the reactions of the two ranchers who encounter Billy, roped wolf in tow. Billy's comic encounter with the first rancher is a paradigmatic intergenerational encounter between the Old and New West, but the encounter is arranged ironically, with Billy riding a horse and the rancher driving a Model A, which he leaves at idle because of its "refusal" to be restarted. Other than Twain, few writers have displayed a mastery of the Southwestern idiom and Western dead-pan humor in so pithy a set of comic dialogue:

> That's a damn wolf.
>   Yessir, it is. . . .
>   What are you doin with him?
>   It's a she.
>   It's a what?
>   A she. It's a she.
>   Hell fire, it dont make a damn he or she. What are you doin with it?
>   Fixin to take it home.
>   Home?
>   Yessir.
>   Whatever in the contumacious hell for? (*C*, 58–59)

Both ranchers instinctively identify with the mixture of radical individualism and stubbornness implicit in the boy's journey to deliver the wolf alive; both immediately sense the absurd humor in their decision to aid the boy. When Billy informs him of his decision to return the wolf to Mexico, the second rancher, Stephens, responds dryly,

> What have you got against the Mexicans?
>   I don't have nothing against em.
>   You just figured they might could use another wolf or two. . . . How are they fixed for rattlesnakes down there do you reckon? (*C*, 68)

The novel reconstructs the terms of the contemporary debate over the reintroduction of wolves, questioning the automatic opposition of ecological and ranching interests. The wolf, Billy Parham, and the rancher Stephens embody an older, less capitalized West where decisions are not always determined by economic self-interest. In light of *The Crossing*'s critique of individualism and its analysis of culture and identity as constructions, Burbank's comments on the hiring of wolf trappers could act as a thematic gloss of the first third of the novel:

> When wolf kills became more than cowhands could rightly handle, ranchers hired a "wolfer" to pursue and destroy the hated wolves. . . . Like individuals, cultures determine their meaning. . . . Ranching was simply an extension of this process that viewed restless expansionism as an inevitable journey toward total dominance. . . . The wolf had found its

symbolic home in this wilderness of spirit, a profound emptiness at the
root of consciousness, a desolation and isolation that yawned in a great
chasm separating Western man from natural circumstance. (Burbank,
88–89)

As belated Westerners, faced with the implications of man's "total
dominance" over nature and the accompanying closure of the frontier,
Billy and Stephens repudiate their own economic, cultural, and historic
interests. Deciding not to seize Billy and return him to his father,
Stephens acts in sympathy with Billy's mastery of the contradictory
roles of respectful youth and defiant individualist, interpreting the
youth's decision to return the wolf as the act of a sane adult. A more
crucial motive is Stephens's understanding of the event as historical:
when Billy states that he came with his family into New Mexico a "long
time" ago, "goin on ten years," Stephens interjects, "Ten years, the man
said. Time just flies, don't it?" (C, 69). With the old West about to
transform into the modern West, Stephens finds his economic interests
less important than his sympathy for the wolf and Billy.

The supreme representation of the Other in *The Crossing* is thus the
wolf, embodying an alternate consciousness to that of the human, one
inhabiting "another world" that is unfallen. The figure of the wolf
reveals the Enlightenment's separation of ourselves from a world located
outside the self. Just as Billy's world is constructed out of the world of
family, of society, of the economic, the national, the historical, the wolf's
world is also a construct—constructed first out of the senses, then by
the pack and the biological imperative to kill. The wolf's world is one
constructed primarily out of the single sense of smell, as Billy learns on
his trip to the dying Mexican trapper. Frustrated by the wolf's unerring
ability to sense his traps, Billy asks the trapper about the bottles of
"matrix" or scent that he has borrowed from the absent trapper Echols.
The dying trapper answers by contending that the matrix cannot be "so
easily defined. Each hunter must have his own formula" (C, 45). While
Billy's question is intended as a practical question, the old trapper
defines the question as epistemological. The wolf's world differs from
the human, a difference built in part on its reliance on smell to construct
its world.

But the difference between the world of the wolf and the human is
also metaphysical: "The old man said that no man knew what the wolf
knew. . . . The old man went on to say that the hunter was a different
thing than men supposed. . . . He said that the wolf is a being of great
order and that it knows what men do not: that there is no order in the

world save that which death has put there" (*C*, 45). The wolf's vision is thus a tragic one (one that echoes that of the judge in *Blood Meridian*); and through the death first of the trapped wolf, then of his parents and finally of his brother, Boyd, Billy's perspective will eventually coincide with it. If Alfonsita locates her "world" of disillusion between the "wish and the thing," the trapper notes a more radical disjunction between human perception and the real, which is unknowable: the world is not a Lockean collection of apperceived "things" but an invisible, unknowable matrix. The world is a matrix similar to the matrix of the wolf's scent-knowledge: positioned between man's vain "acts and ceremonies," constructed by culture, the real is "invisible," untouchable, only a "breath" (*C*, 46). The narrative refuses to privilege either the constructed world of the human (Western rational) mind or the alternative visions of the invisible matrix of the old wolf trapper or the blind man's dark world. In reading the narrative, we, like Billy Parham, are poised on the borders between these constructs for the world.

Borders and the Deconstructed Identity: Family, Nation, Property.

Near the close of *The Crossing*, the *gerente* of the Barbícora, a man named Quijada, argues for a final version of this theme of the world as the Other. He has treated Billy with humanity throughout the novel, first in the leap of faith that allows him to recognize the boy's claim to his father's horses as a "true claim" despite the boy's lack of papers, later in his attempts to redirect the lost young American to his home. Quijada attempts to end Billy's quest humanely, by revealing the story of Boyd's death and burial place. To Quijada, the "real" does not lie poised between the "wish" and the "thing" but is a construct of society. While he earlier had restored the boys' horses, acknowledging their claims of possession, to Billy's attempt to reclaim his brother's body based on the proposition that kin have "nationality," he responds, "The world has no name. . . . The names of the cerros and the sierras and the deserts exist only on maps. We name them that we do not lose our way. Yet it was because the way was lost to us already that we have made those names. The world cannot be lost. We are the ones. And it is because these names and these coordinates are our own naming that they cannot save us" (*C*, 387). The passage is one of great poignancy, analyzing Billy's predicament—his homelessness in the world—with analytic precision. Historians of the Age of Discovery have acknowledged the relationship between the technology of mapping and the growth of the transcendental reason. Mapping requires a transcendentally detached perspective—one that requires the separation of consciousness from the exterior world. In metaphysics, this mapping reaches its fullest expression in the transcendental reason of Kantian philosophy, with the reason's requisite empowerment in the midst of its alienation from the natural. To Quijada, Billy and all men are lost because of this gap between the world and its representations, whether in mathematical, graphic, or verbal languages. The world, which can be known only through its representations, is ineffable, and man loses himself within his various representations of the world.

If his diagnosis is clear, Quijada's solution is not. Remarking that Boyd "should have gone home," he reproves Billy for not taking care of his brother. Despite the folk song's romantic portrayal of Boyd's death, he asserts that it, not Billy, has defined Boyd's identity. Quijada concludes, "Your brother is in that place which the world has chosen for him. He is where he is supposed to be. And yet the place he has found is also of his own choosing. That is a piece of luck not to be despised" (*C*, 387–88). In similar fashion, the *hacendado* upbraids John Grady Cole in a puzzling conversation before Cole's imprisonment: "Our country is not another country. Mexico is not Europe" (*C*, 145). In context, he is reproving Alfonsita's youthful revolutionary ideas as European, therefore inapplicable to Mexico. On a second reading, given that we know he has already learned of his daughter's affair, the *hacendado* is warning Cole against his egalitarian idealism. As Cole learns in prison, his freedom and even his identity are constructs of culture. In their search for a more natural or historic identity, Cole and Billy Parham exile themselves from home and identity.

If mapping is an arbitrary construct of culture, so is the concept of home; Boyd is as much home in his grave in Mexico as he ever was in New Mexico. Billy, of course, denies Quijada's insights, dooming himself to be forever homeless on the border. His insistence to reaffirm the border between Mexico and the United States by reclaiming Boyd's body and restoring his "American" identity denies the lesson of the wolf. As Cole learns in prison and as Boyd's death illustrates, identity cannot be maintained solely by one's own power; the choice of identity is limited by the influences of personality, geography, and culture. In McCarthy's border fiction, identity at first appears to be an inheritance of family, culture, and history. But such a historical identity is lost all too easily in the postmodern present of The Border Trilogy. Crossing the border allows Cole and the Parhams to strip away the layers of the historical, the familial, and the person, only to discover that on the border authentic identity can only be lost, not found.

Chapter Six

The Rhetoric of McCarthy's Fiction: Style, Visionary Landscapes, and Parables

Cormac McCarthy's critics often display a curious ambivalence toward his narratives, acknowledging their imaginative power while registering discomfort with their violence or nihilistic vision. This chapter analyzes the "rhetoric" of McCarthy's novels in an attempt to more systematically account for their esthetic and imaginary power.[1] This power, I suggest, is located predominently in several recurring characteristics of his novels: their repertoire of stylistic registers; their adroit merging of symbolic and mimetic landscapes in representing the natural world; their use of allegory and parable; and their elusive and idiosyncratic vision of man's relation to and apprehension of the world—a vision variously termed nihilistic, existential, or gnostic. Responding to a series of ethical critiques, I conclude by sketching connections within McCarthy's fiction between the motif of the visionary journey and the impulse to tell tales.

The Rhetorical Elements of McCarthy's Style

Frequently cited in reviews of McCarthy's works is an appreciation of their powerful command of language and prose style. At its best the language of McCarthy's fiction exhibits characteristics of what Longinus in antiquity termed the sublime. In *On the Sublime* Longinus identifies the sublime by its power to "uplift" the reader into an esthetic awareness of the text's linguistic and imaginary greatness, authority, or power. Admittedly, such esthetic uplift is now acknowledged to be as much a function of the readers' culturally determined response to stylistic features as an intrinsic power of the text. Many of McCarthy's most striking passages—those frequently cited in reviews or in criticism—are selected for discussion because they momentarily shift from a prosaic to a more lyric, rhetorical, or oratorical style.

Two representative passages from *Child of God* illustrate this tendency to shift, at least momentarily, into a lyrical register of discourse through the use of a striking or unexpected word, image, or trope. After Ballard is introduced to us as a "child of God," our next vision of him is bathetic, with him urinating inside the barn. The narrative perspective then shifts quickly away from Ballard to an apparently random catalog of the barn's interior: "Wasps pass through the laddered light from the barn-slats in a succession of strobic movements, gold and trembling between black and black, light fireflies in the serried upper gloom. . . . Buttoning his jeans he moves along the barn wall, himself fiddlebacked with light, a petty annoyance glickering across the wallward eye" (*CG,* 4). The apparently unrelated image of the wasps is the type of seemingly irrelevant detail that Eric Auerbach in *Mimesis* (1968) found to mark mimetic narrative. Yet such apparent irrelevancies often invite and reward further analysis of the text. This image of the "strobic" apparitions of wasps, which momentarily appear in the "gold" light only to disappear "black and black" into darkness, is indicative of an esthetic, lyric, and perhaps epiphanic view of the natural, which opposes itself to the scatological naturalistic detail of Ballard urinating. Of course, in contrast to our and the narrator's perspectives, Ballard himself is blind to this lyrical perception of the natural. Finally, in the passage's striking detail of the annoyance in his "wallward eye," Ballard's characteristic alienation is momentarily underlined, reinforced by the dramatic presentation of him placed apart inside the barn, while we, the narrative perspective, and the rest of Sevier country are arranged outside, voyeuristically gazing barnward and inward at him. These esthetic, naturalistic, and psychosocial perspectives on Ballard and his world are integrated within the passage's lyric style.

Another, more pronouncedly lyric passage a few chapters later summarizes the passage of the seasons and outlines the intensification of Ballard's alienation as he retreats from society within the natural: "The hardwood trees on the mountain subsided into yellow and flame and to ultimate nakedness. . . . Alone in the empty shell of a house the squatter watched through the moteblown glass a rimshard of bonecolored moon come cradling up over the black balsams on the ridge, ink trees a facile hand had sketched against the paler dark of winter heavens. A man much for himself" (*CG,* 40–41). Competing for the reader's attention are the alliterative repetitions in the last half of the description ("come cradling," "black balsam," "man much") and the imagery: the leaves' subsiding "flame," the moon as a rimshard of broken china, the trees as ink-sketch. From Ballard's day and nighttime perspective out the window of the "empty" shack, these "naked" trees and "rimshard" moon mirror his corresponding psychic nakedness as his social self disintegrates: the moon, of course, is traditionally associated with madness or "lunacy."

In a stylistic analysis of *All the Pretty Horses,* Nancy Kremle observes a division in McCarthy's narration between what she terms an "opaque" and a "transparent" style. To Kremle, this "transparent" narration is emphatically prosaic, employing a predominantly simple Anglo-Saxon diction. Because it is stripped of narrative commentary and representations of character consciousness, the style is open to varying readerly interpretations. In contrast, the "opaque" style employs a more "literary" language (marked by use of metaphor, alliteration or assonance, intensive subordination, and other forms of syntactic connectives) and draws from a lexicon of radically diverse idioms.[2] What I have termed the "sublime" style largely overlaps Kremle's description of this "opaque" style; no matter which terminology is used, the figurative language and poetic devices draw readerly attention, both favorable and unfavorable, to such passages. Placed even in the midst of McCarthy's most shocking material, these opaque passages display a lyric, poetic, or esthetic sensibility on the part of the narrator's perspective, which often clashes with the novels' violent or mundane subject matter.

Such passages function as a kind of "covert rhetoric" that Seymour Chatman defines as a technique that works "to esthetic ends" and that "suades us to something interior to the text, particularly the appropriateness of the chosen means to evoke a response appropriate to the text's intention."[3] That response, in part, is a sheer pleasure in language itself and in language-play. I suggest in Chapter 5 that the stylistic and language-play of the early fiction is characteristic of the "modern" concept of the author and text and is partly responsible for preventing a popular reception of McCarthy's early fiction. To the literary reader, on the other hand, such manipulation of language and styles produces a sense of the authority of McCarthy's texts as "literary" novels—works of "high" literature. Yet through Judge Holden, the most linguistically gifted character besides Suttree in all of McCarthy's fiction, readers who revel in such language-play implicitly are warned against language's blandishments. Tobin remarks of the judge, "Him and the governor they sat up till breakfast and it was Paris this and London that in five language, you'd have give something to of heard them. The governor's a learned man, but the judge . . . " (*BM,* 123). Judge Holden, an avatar for death and the devil, is also—like Suttree—an avatar of the rhetorician and artist (Holden is gifted at sketching), perhaps of McCarthy as author. Language's esthetic appeals can be wielded for good or for ill.

Besides the lyric and opaque stylistic registers discussed by Kremle, an important component of McCarthy's rhetoric is a set of passages, usually written in a form of intrusive narrative commentary, that critics, reviewers, and readers often identify as crucial to the interpretation of the fiction. Such commentary can be brief or gnomic, as in the terse and ambiguous "A man much for himself" that concludes the passage already quoted from *Child of God* describing winter's onset. The most prolonged passage of intrusive narrative commentary extends through *Suttree*'s first three pages, which serve as the primary evidence for the four critical analyses of the novel by Frank Shelton, Thomas Young, Jr., Vereen Bell, and D. S. Butterworth. The striking italicized description of Knoxville in the novel's first page is quoted by the first two critics: *"This city* [Knoxville, in McCarthy's italics] *constructed on no known paradigm, a mongrel architecture reading back through the works of man in a brief delineation of the aberrant disordered and mad. A carnival of shapes upreared on the river plain"* (S, 3–4).[4] Bell and Shelton center their analysis of the novel's thematics of death and alienation on the memorable image, a page later, of the city as a *"camp before battle, . . . beset by a thing unknown. . . . The murengers have walled the pale, the gates are shut, but lo the thing's inside and can you guess his shape?"* (Bell 1988, 69; Shelton, 82). In these opening pages of *Suttree,* the comparisons between Knoxville and a "mongrel architecture," a "carnival of shapes," a battle "camp," and later a theatrical stage by no means sketch a realistic representation of the city. Instead the viewpoint of the city is mythopoeic, conveyed through these metaphoric tenors, encompassing within itself and extending Suttree's own imaginative perception of Knoxville as a modern version of a Dantean underworld. To this narrative voice, we suspect, Knoxville operates as a further synecdoche, representing contemporary urban life in contemporary America.

Stylistic Criticisms.   Such mythopoeic fragments and the apparently stilted rhetoric accompanying them disturb many reviewers who dismiss the former as disruptions or interruptions of the novels' realism or react to the rhetoric as uncontrolled, inartistic language conflicting with the more prosaic and restrained narrative voice or with the lyric styles discussed earlier. Although she admits the power of *Suttree*'s language, dialogue, and comic characters and scenes, Dorothy Wickenden in a *New Republic* review criticizes its opening passages as "a ponderous narrative voice," dismisses the narrative style as "convoluted" and "labored," and finds the novel's many "scenes of surreal horror" merely to be "gratuitous indulgences," like the novel itself.[5] In a caustic review of *Blood Meridian,* Terence Moran similarly dismisses Judge Holden as "The Man Who Never Shuts Up" and associates the judge's "pseudo-philosophic palaver" style with that of the narrative.[6] And against admiring reviews of the language and style of *Outer Dark* by Guy Davenport in the *New York Times Book Review* and Robert Coles in the *New Yorker,* Patrick Cuttrell dissents, charging that the novel's dialogue is "thickly picturesque," the sentences "interminable" and "shapeless," the descriptions strewn with "literary epithets," and the archaic vocabulary "pointless."[7] Moran's conflation of the narrative's rhetoric with that of the judge isolates a stylistic register that Cuttrell and Wickenden also criticize: a type of formal, oratorical address closely associated with Southern political or religious rhetoric. Such oratory is seen as both uncontrolled and excessive and is usually associated in early reviews with an undigested influence of Faulkner's style on McCarthy. Implying that this style detracts attention from the narrative events or characters, these criticisms are founded on a mimetic conception of novelistic language as representation and on a preference for the austere narrative style developed from modern journalism and typical of post–World War II fiction.

In his study of nineteenth-century romantic fiction, Edwin Eigner responds to criticisms that such passages interrupt mimetic representation in the fiction of Melville, Dickens, and Hawthorne. Such "projections" of the mythopoeic imagination along with romantic, fantastic, visionary, or imaginary elements are used by these romance writers, Eigner argues, to impel readers toward a philosophical apprehension of the world that transcends the worldview of empiricism, logical positivism, or the deterministic materialism of nineteenth-century realism.[8] Although Vereen Bell's book-length study rightly celebrates McCarthy's talent for mimetic description, this aspect of his fiction is deceptive, for the frequent rhetorical interruptions and lyrical imagery remind us that the fictional landscape is not mimetic but imaginative, often symbolic or even symbolist. Of course, the narration, as Kremle suggests in her analysis of *All the Pretty Horses,* tends to limit such "commentary" in the form of formal, direct addresses to the reader; thus the mimetic function of the narrative predominates over the mythopoeic. Hence, after its italicized opening, *Suttree* mutes our awareness of this narrative voice, incorporating briefer mythopoeic passages that momentarily rupture the mimetic description. The metaphysical vision of Knoxville in the novel's opening thus eerily extends itself throughout the narrative, like the sewers Harrogate explores underneath Knoxville, to reemerge in the mythic conclusion.

The oratorical narrative commentary of McCarthy's fiction, whether brief or lengthy, powerfully invokes the elusive presence of the narrative voice and the ghostlike authorial presence evoked by or "residing" in that voice. The stylistic comparison to Faulkner is inevitable, given their common Southern heritage, and the comparison helpfully situates McCarthy's fiction within the Southern folk tradition. Yet this inevitable comparison is also misleading: in his infrequent interviews, McCarthy invariably lists Melville and Joyce as the "great" novelists. In one such interview, shortly after the publication of *Outer Dark,* McCarthy mentions liking Joyce, Faulkner, O'Connor and "particularly" Melville (Jordan, 6). The influence of Melville's style may better account for narrative intrusions such as the prolegomenon to *Suttree,* with its apparently portentous rhetoric and formal, even oratorical, diction. Both qualities often characterize Melvillean narrative, earning him the hostility of his American reviewers and eventually driving Melville's narrator "underground" in a series of subversive fictions—*Pierre,* "Bartleby the Scrivener," "I and My Chimney"—that satirize the publishing world and middle-class American readers. McCarthy's own notable disregard for the marketing publicity and the social scene of the literary world might be viewed as a Melvillean contempt for popular public authorship, not a Salingeresque obsession with his own privacy. More crucially, the formal style of the intrusive narrative passages functions in Melvillean fashion to expose fictional language as a rhetorical illusion—a writerly or written fictive language that points our attention toward itself, not toward an "outside" world that it represents. Readers are thus distanced—sometimes subtly, sometimes more violently—from a faith in narrative language as mimetic representation. Narratologists such as Seymour Chatman in discussing narrative discourse revive the Platonic distinction between *mimesis* (showing) and *diegesis* (telling) (Chatman, 32). Diegetic passages such as this instrusive narrative commentary are crucial in attracting readerly and critical consciousness to the McCarthy "voice" and situate McCarthy's narrator in the role of tale-teller.

Voice, Orality, and the McCarthy Narrator.   As a direct address to the reader, passages such as *Suttree*'s beginning apostrophe to its readers—"Dear Friends"—direct our attention toward the tale as a fiction, a linguistic construct of the narrator who relates the tale. Identifying his interlocutors as "Dear Friends," this narrator affiliates himself with the American folk tradition extending from the Southern oral tale to Faulknerian fiction and with the Western tall tale incorporated within Twain's narratives. We recall that Huck's narration, though written, mimics the form of a direct oral address to his interlocutors, while the implied Twainian author directly addresses readers in the famous preliminary author's note: "Persons who find a moral will be banished." In *The Orchard Keeper* Arthur Ownby's tall tale of the "wampus cat," told to entertain a group of boys, reflects the desire of McCarthy's contemporary narratives to affiliate themselves with a past regional or Southern oral tradition. In similar fashion, Twain's realism from *Roughing It* to his late fiction subsumed within itself the regional Western tall tale. Yet this tradition is "buried" within the past, just as Arthur's tale is interpolated within the narrative. Similarly, *Blood Meridian* and *All the Pretty Horses* are allied to the Western tall tale through tales such as Tobin's recount of how the judge supplied gunpowder to Glanton's troop or Cole's story of his misadventures to the judge and jury. Through such interpolated tales and by the use of regional dialects within the fiction, McCarthy's narratives—despite their modernist and postmodern elements—strongly identify themselves with regional fictional traditions of the South and Southwest.

Southern and Southwestern Dialect in McCarthy's Fiction.

McCarthy's novels reflect the oral dimensions of language most clearly in the characters' diction (the fiction is an archaeology of communal speech registers) and in the introjection of regional and archaic speech within the larger narrative voice. In "Cormac McCarthy and the Text of Jouissance," which draws on Roland Barthes's theories of textual erotics, Nell Sullivan notes the disturbing tension between a "high" or literary register of style and a "low" style that accompanies the often predominately "low" characters and subject matter of the fiction (Hall and Wallach, 116–17). A literary parallel is to the development of the Wordsworthian style (with *Lyrical Ballads*' program to reinvigorate a corrupt poetic diction with the infusion of popular speech), from the pastoral pathos of "Michael" to epiphanic scenes such as that of the lowly leech-gatherer in "The Prelude."

Most characters speak in distinctive dialects that reflect their regional origin and educational background or class status. The speech of the characters of *The Orchard Keeper* betrays their rural origins in Red Branch, not only a rural backwater but a time capsule of regional idioms made possible only by the village's isolation from urbanized modernity. "Well, you don't care for me to ride that fer with ye, do ye," says Kenneth Rattner, hitching a ride at the novel's opening; his benefactor, from Austell, another small hamlet, responds in kind, "Be proud to hep ye out that fer" (*OK*, 10). Regional idioms—"be proud"—are combined with regional pronunciations—"hep" and "fer" for "help" and "far." On the other hand, Marion Syldar, who has worked in the outside world for five years before returning to Red Branch, can vary his speech by employing a range of regional idioms and profanities suited to his listeners.

A Twain-like sensitivity matching dialect and idiolect to character is displayed in McCarthy's first novel, as we see when Syldar and his friend June laugh at the country girl's use of the euphemism "needled" for intercourse (*OK*, 21). Yet the joke is also on Syldar and June (not only in the substitution of needle for phallus), for Syldar's use of the idiomatic "nigger shithouse" evokes from the reader the same sense of social and ethical superiority that the girl's "impure" speech evokes in the two men. Viewed in the sociolinguistic perspective that associates Standard English with purified language, Uncle Arthur's speech, given the dominant role of regional and archaic idioms, would place him at the bottom of the linguistic and moral register. But in his later conversation with the county welfare agent, Arthur's moral stature has so increased that his idioms and archaicisms now seem representative of a "pure" dialect, a standard by which we judge all other dialects, perhaps even that of the narrative. A masterful tragicomic scene ensues with Arthur's failure to comprehend the agent's purpose in asking him questions to qualify him for federal benefits. To the agent's explanation of "welfare" ("You see, we help people"), Arthur responds by assuming the agent abashedly is requesting a donation: "Well, I ain't got nothin. I don't reckon I can hep yins any" (*OK*, 219). Suspecting next that the questions are a prelude to charging him with the destruction of the government tank, he defies the agent, "Why not jest up and ast me," and is met with a politely mannered response: "I beg your pardon?" (*OK*, 221).

The mutual incomprehension caused by the clash of their dialects reveals a conflict of ethics and worldview between the rural past and urban modernity; this conflict corresponds to the clash within the narrative between a Southern and postmodern fiction. Arthur's use of "jest" for "just" is incomprehensible to the agent; the word's signification within Arthur's dialect is replaced by an opposed signification within Standard

English as jest or comedy, and the scene's function as a kind of grim social comedy is thus underlined in the friction between spoken (dialect) and written significations of jest. Imprisoned within his dialect, Arthur nonetheless tragically is as aware of the agent's victory as we are. The jailer's dismissal of him as "onery" or "mean as a snake" and the agent's modernistic diagnosis as "definitely an anomic type" are revealed as simplistic, meaningless clichés drawn from the vocabulary of regional and clinical dialects.

In *Suttree* the various levels of oral language are most complexly interwoven in the collisions between the middle-class dialect of Suttree, the street talk of the underworld he inhabits, and the formal rhetoric of its narrative voice. Harrogate and the Reese family reflect the idioms of Arthur Ownby and the rural characters of the first three novels, while Suttree's repartee with his black friends reflects an inventive mixture of ribald street jive and Black English. Nig, one of Suttree's drinking friends, memorably describes their whiskey: "Lord honey I know they make that old splo in the bathtub but this here is made in the toilet" (*S*, 24). Such conversations supply a necessary comic relief to the darkness of the novel. In contrast is Ab Jones's rendering of Black English in his paternalistic musings to Suttree: "You see a man, he scratchin to make it. Think once he got it made everthing be all right. but you dont never have it made. Dont care who you are" (*S*, 203). A bewildering panoply of characters—Daddy Watson, J-Bone, Oceanfrog, the transvestite Trippin through the Dew—are memorably rendered primarily through their creative mixtures of regional and ethnic dialects, underworld cant, profanity or ribald sexual innuendo, and nicknames (indeed, characters bewilderingly assume new street names or are renamed by others throughout the novel). In *Suttree* McCarthy's fond indulgence of the language of the street is reminiscent of the freedom Dickens extended to his own underworld and lower-class characters: Sam Weller, Fagin, the Dodger, Quilp, Mrs. Gamp, and Uriah Heep.

With the shift to the Southwest in *Blood Meridian,* the oral dimensions of the narrative are reoriented toward the regional patterns of Southwestern speech, although several members of Glanton's gang, including the kid, are from Tennessee, and their speech reflects their Southern origins. The judge is the troop's only rhetorician, fluidly adjusting his discourse among various stylistic registers, all formal variations of the high style. Thus in one of his addresses to the Glanton troop, on the question of intelligent life on Mars, the judge pontificates, "Had you not seen it [the world] from birth and thereby bled it of its strangeness it would appear to you for what it is, a hat trick in a medicine show, a fevered dream, a trance bepopulate with chimeras having neither analogue nor precedent, an itinerant carnival" (*BM*, 245).

Within the frame of this argument, he employs a catalog of florid images, littered with the vocabulary of logic ("analogue," "precedent") and medicine ("bled"). He concludes his argument with a thinly disguised allusion to Hamlet's rebuke of Horatio: "Even in this world more things exist without our knowledge than with it and the order in creation which you see is that which you have put there, like a string in a maze, so that you shall not lose your way. For existence has its own order and that no man's mind can compass, the mind itself being but a fact among others" (*BM*, 245). The judge's rhetoric betrays him, for the allusion to *Hamlet* ("more things exist without our knowledge") hardly fits the new context, contradicting both his premise, which denies the existence of intelligent life besides man, and his argument with Toadvine a few days earlier, in which the judge, as biologist, claims the sufficiency of the reason to encompass all of the natural world: "that man who sets himself the task of singling out the thread of order from the tapestry will by the decision alone have taken charge of the world" (*BM*, 199). The contradictory elements of the judge's discourse reveal the pettifogger or debater—one who merely pleads a case or argues an assigned position and, furthermore, one who has fallen in love with his own manipulations of language.

In contrast, the terse, laconic speech of the other members of the troop suggests their distrust of language. As the primary character, the kid's discourse is distressingly monosyllabic. In response to the invitation to filibuster in Mexico, he responds with the hilariously incomprehending double negative, "I aint lost nothin down there" (*BM*, 29). Perhaps his most inspired pieces of dialogue take the form of questions: after the Comanche attack, he inquires, "What kind of indians was them?" (*BM*, 56) and, in response to Tobin's tale of the judge's preternatural gifts, he perspicuously asks, "What's he a judge of?" (*BM*, 135). Were it not for the judge's rhetorical skills, we might suspect that the origins of the Glanton troop's violence lie in this failure of language, for they—Glanton in particular—prefer to communicate through their actions, in their deeds of war. Yet a wry, often blackly comic language-play is articulated by several members of the troop. Toadvine's first words after his brawl with the kid in Nacogdoches are to ask, "Are you quits? . . . Cause if you want some more of me you sure as hell goin to get it" (*BM*, 10). Tobin's meditation on the enigma of the judge combines the vocabulary of evangelical Christianity and business: "The gifts of the Almighty are weighed and parceled out in a scale peculiar to himself. It's no fair accountin" (*BM*, 123).

Dialect and the First-Person Narration of *Child of God*.   Even the narrator's discourse absorbs the region and class dialects of these characters. This phenomenon is most marked in *Child of God*: on occasion the discourse of a third-person narrator is interrupted by various anecdotes involving Ballard—anecdotes that take the form of direct speeches, unattributed and unexplained, from various Sevier townspeople. These speeches of communal commentary, usually involving moral judgments of Ballard, are placed in separate chapters, detached from the discourse of the third-person narrator, whose perspective appears considerably more sympathetic to Ballard. We are introduced to this device of the choruslike communal narrators in the second chapter, which begins with an unnamed townsman commenting on the resolution of Lester Ballard's threats against the sheriff and auctioneer of his property: "Lester Ballard never could hold his head right after that. It must of thowed his neck out someway or another. I didn't see Buster hit him but I seen him layin on the ground. I was with the sheriff. He was layin flat on the ground lookin up at everbody with his eyes crossed and this awful pumpknot on his head" (*CG*, 9).

This device of unmarked, incorporated first-person narrators again is reminiscent of Faulkner. The Faulkner novel, we recall, invokes the Southern oral tale by enfolding narrators and interlocutors within its narration. In *Absalom, Absalom!* Aunt Rosa tells Sutpen's story to Quentin, Quentin adopts Rosa's role to Shreve, and so on. Through such momentary narrative allusions, the McCarthy novel acknowledges Faulknerian narrative yet appears to avoid the trap of imitation or parody by projecting its own "individual" voice, unlike more direct imitations of Faulkner's oral rhetoric by writers such as Walker Percy in *Lancelot* or T. R. Pearson in his novels *A Short History of a Small Place* and *Off for the Sweet Hereafter*. But these communal narrators of *Child of God* play a further role, supplying a necessary comic relief to the dark events by invoking the existence of an alternate moral universe beyond that of Ballard and the McCarthy narrator's studious avoidance of moral commentary or judgment. Noting that CB, the auctioneer, continues the auction of Ballard's family property "like nothin never ever happent," the townsman remarks that the purchaser is from a different county, "Not sayin nothin against him but he was" (*CG*, 9). The implication is that only someone from outside the community would buy at the auction after Lester's protest. Against this fiction of the moral force of the community stands the enigmatic figure of Ballard, who is born within but is not restricted by the moral approbation of the Sevier community. The narrator sometimes shares in this linguistic community. The glimpse of a boy's face in the bus, we are told, gave Ballard "the fidgets," and through this idiom Ballard's perspective and dialect become part of the narrator's own discourse (*CG,* 191).

Other, more momentary examples of the integration of "lower" dialect within the narrative discourse occur throughout the Southwestern fiction. Unlike the preceding example, these cannot be explained as indirect quotations of characters' mental speech. In *Blood Meridian,* for example, referring to a group of itinerant magicians, the narrator remarks, "they looked a set of right wanderfolk cast on this evil terrain" (*BM,* 89). The diction—"right wanderfolk"—and the use of "looked" as a transitive verb employ a regional dialect; just as crucially, the use of "evil" supplies a momentary ethical expansion that overlaps the medieval romance and its association of wilderness, magic, and evil. In a similar passage early in *The Crossing,* as Billy Cole rides up on a wolf-kill, the narrator comments idiomatically that "the horse wanted no part of it" (*CR,* 32). Such idioms seem narrative comments that incorporate the regional dialect. McCarthy's narratives thus adroitly, if momentarily, shift between lyric prose, mimetic representation, an oratorically "high" style of the direct address, and various "low" dialects of region, class, and profession.

The style of McCarthy's fiction does not reflect the unified, relatively unvaried, or monologic narrative style characteristic of mannered writers such as Updike but is a divided style composed of textual or stylistic registers that dialectically oppose one another. Nell Sullivan contends that the "conformist" language within McCarthy's fiction is opposed or "embattled" by the vernacular, and she perceptively connects this stylistic violence to its violent subject matter (Hall and Wallach, 117). In "Discourse in the Novel" Bakhtin explains such violent shifts between various stylistic and linguistic registers as characteristic of novelistic language, which ideally should reject the unified language of poetry. Criticizing the linguist's notion of language as a unified system, Bakhtin argues for a complex coexistence and combinations of different languages within a society: "each generation at each social level" and "every age group has as a matter of fact its own language, its own vocabulary, its own particular accentual system that, in their turn, vary depending upon social level, academic institution . . . and other stratifying factors." Based on this model of social communication among coexisting languages rather than on a monolithic community based on a shared language, he generalizes, "at any given moment, languages of various epochs and periods of socio-ideological life cohabit with one another."[9]

Terming this coexistence of languages *heteroglossia,* Bakhtin argues that these languages are incorporated within fictional language: "these dialects, on entering the literary language and preserving within it their own dialectological elasticity, their other-languagedness, have the effect of deforming the literary language; it, too, cease[s] to be . . . a closed socio-linguistic system." Yet in the process of their incorporation within fiction, he notes, dialects are also transformed, losing "the quality of closed socio-linguistic systems" (Bakhtin, 294). McCarthy's fiction exhibits a similar *heteroglossia* in which its profusion of styles and dialects (the languages of region, class, street, ethnicity, and profession) war against or cohabit with one another and exert their own influence on the literary language of the fiction, deforming or reconstituting it into a unique narrative discourse.

Bilingualism and the Dialogic in the Southwestern Border Novel.

This conflict between the monologic style of the normal, transparent mimetic representation of McCarthy's narratives, the formal or oratorical styles, and the lower dialects and character idiolects becomes most apparent from *Blood Meridian* to *The Crossing,* for in the Southwestern fiction untranslated Spanish (the Spanish of the Northwestern Mexican border) plays an increasingly important role in the fiction. Spanish plays so important a role in *The Crossing* that an otherwise sympathetic reviewer from the *Wall Street Journal* condemned the fiction for its "pretentiousness" indicated in part by its "infuriating new trick" of using Spanish dialogue, though somewhat contradictorily the novel's "authentic" rendering of Southwestern dialogue is singled out for praise.[10]

Bakhtin's notion that fiction should contain a wide diversity of social languages and ideologies can be usefully applied to all of McCarthy's fiction, most notably to the frequent linguistic confrontations that reflect social or ideological confrontations. We might refer to a long scene early in *The Crossing* when Billy Parham enlists the aid of a Hispanic trapper in his attempt to trap the wolf. The clash between the English and Spanish dialogue mirrors the confrontation in age and worldview between the characters; the man's extreme age and infirmity contrast

strikingly with Billy's youthful vigor and naïveté. The trapper's view of
the wolf is metaphoric and ethical: *"El lobo es una cosa incognoscible. . . . Lo
que se tiene en la trampa no es mas que dientes y forro. El lobo propio no se puede
conocer. Lobo olo que sabe el lobo. Tan como preguntar lo que saben las piedras.
Los arboles. El mundo* [The wolf is a thing unknowable. . . . What you got
in the trap is only just teeth and fur. The wolf cannot be known. The
wolf's scent smells just like the wolf. We might as well ask the rocks
what they know. The trees. The world]" (*CR*, 45). If the boy seeks to
gain knowledge of the wolf as a step toward trapping it, the old man's
view is that the wolf can be known only by another wolf. Yet the old
trapper next animizes the wolf, characterizing its vision (though he
insists it cannot be known) as that of the hunter, in which order is created through the death blood of the prey. This wolf's knowledge he
opposes to man's parodic imitation of that truth in the Christian communion. Concluding his discourse to Billy, he argues that the wolf, like
the world, "is made of breath only" (*CR*, 46).

A third perspective is supplied by the earthy religiosity of the old
man's daughter-in-law, who, reflecting the views of her orthodox community, warns Parham that the man is considered a *brujo* (witch) and has
"the sin of orgullo [pride]. You know what is orgullo?" (*CR*, 48). In similar fashion, midway through the dialogue, the old man is unsure of
their ability to communicate as members of different language commu-
nities, asking Billy, "Me entiendes?" The narrator both comments and
translates, "the boy didn't know if he understood or not" (*CR*, 45). This
narrative commentary dramatizes the issue in its gnomic skepticism:
just as biology separates man's knowledge from the wolf's, so language,
class, ethnicity, religion, and life experience prevent a secure understanding between the boy, the man and the daughter-in-law. Nor do we
know if the narrator knows whether the boy knows. The novel's *heteroglossia* establishes McCarthy as a writer with a masterful control of a
unique literary language that merges the dialects of the South and the
languages of the Southwestern United States.

Landscape and Perception in McCarthy's Fiction

McCarthy's landscapes are as powerfully rendered as the language of the
fiction. Landscape is often a primary, if inhuman, character, haunting
the background of the novels as does Fate in Greek tragedy. Yet
McCarthy's landscapes receive surprisingly little mention, save in Vereen
Bell's attentive reading of *Suttree*'s almost photographic renderings of

the natural world of the river, the slum, and the countryside of Knoxville. In a more recent article, Brian Evenson provocatively analyzes the semiotic function of those landscapes, arguing that McCarthy's characters are primarily either "tramps" who move along the fringes from one society to another or "nomads" who travel primarily within the "smooth space" or unsettled border countries of the fiction (Hall and Wallach, 41–42). Yet Evenson's approach to these landscapes functions as an aid more to a structural analysis of the characters than to an analysis of McCarthy's landscapes in their own right.

While McCarthy's landscapes often do supply a symbolist commentary on his characters or their drama, those landscapes fulfill another function—that of rehistoricizing an old myth of American national self-consciousness. In this myth the "American" contradictorily is defined as "natural man" yet receives identity in the consciousness of his or her exile from nature. The Massachusetts Bay Puritans had read New World nature as a fallen wilderness that nonetheless typologically revealed God's design for the new nation, the New Jerusalem, as a redemptive correction of the Old World. In *Nature,* Emerson's transcendentalism begins by identifying with and negotiating between these opposed national definitions, stripping away American history (particularly its emulation of European art) in order to empower creativity within the American present. Many of McCarthy's characters are similarly stripped of their identities and of their security to be thrust, naked and unprotected like Adam, into the unhomely surroundings of American nature.

The description in *Outer Dark* of Rinthy's preparation to set out into the wilderness in search of her child transforms her into an allegorical figure of the American Eve/Madonna: "Of the shift she made a package in which lay rolled her small and derelict possessions and thus equipped she took a final look about to see what had been forgotten. There was nothing. She tucked the package beneath her arm and set forth, short-gaited" (*OD,* 53). With her "shift" (hence not quite "shift-less") she is "thus equipped" for her journey into the landscape. We know that she is instead pathetically unequipped for that journey. The hopefulness of Rinthy's initial departure, smiling childlike at the sky, must be opposed to the rivetingly pathetic conclusion to her "errand" into the Tennessee wilderness: "Late in the afternoon she entered the glade, coming down a footpath where narrow cart tracks had crushed the weeds and through the wood, half wild and haggard in her shapeless sundrained cerements, yet delicate as any fallow doe, and so into the clearing to stand cradled in a grail of jade and windy light, slender and trembling and pale with wandlike hands" (*OD,* 237). By novel's end, Rinthy's consciousness of the distinction between herself and the natural has so nearly disintegrated that it has become absorbed by the natural; here she, dehumanized, *is* the landscape.

The Luminist Vision of American Nature.   The complex landscapes of McCarthy's fiction are rendered in realistic detail, alluring in imagery, esthetically appealing yet threatening. The fictional landscapes, sketched in language not oils, derive from the American landscape tradition, luminism, which extends from Emerson to Frederic Church, then from Church to the landscape painters and seaside photographers of the late nineteenth century and early modernism, and which culminates in Ansel Adams's black and white photographic landscapes. Discussing the crucial role of Emerson's influence in shifting the national landscape art from a Kantian and European romanticism to a national and American mode of luminism, Earl Powell explains that "this art related . . . the overriding influence of Kant in a wholly unique way. What luminist art achieved, in Europe and America, was a reformulation, under the impact of transcendentalist philosophy, of the formal appearances of nature into a new vocabulary of religious symbols. . . . Luminist paintings attempt . . . to visualize an intuited experience of nature through the stylistic confluence of color, light, and space and the supra-reality of silence."[11]

Early in *The Orchard Keeper* we encounter a fictional landscape that is McCarthy's first incorporation of luminism. Our perspective resembles that of Frederic Church's mid-career landscapes of the 1850s—*Mount Ktaadn, Twilight (Sunset), Twilight in the Wilderness*—in which the viewer often is stationed on a highland vista whose horizontal extension draws the spectator's gaze "into" the landscape and outward to the farther heights of a distant panorama. McCarthy's narrator first orients us geographically, pointing us east of Knoxville to Red Mountain, which marks the beginning of the "Appalachians that contort the outgoing roads to their liking" (*OK,* 10). We are invited to participate in the fiction by extending our vision from our foreground vantage point at Red Mountain southward to the Appalachian summit, then to look downward and feel the heat of the red clay. The narrative perspective includes fully rendered close-up details of the foreground scene: "The red clay banks along the road are crested with withered honeysuckle, peavines dried and sheathed in dust. By late July the corn patches stand parched and sere, stalks askew in defeat. All greens pale and dry" (*OK,* 11). Our vision then is redirected from the defeated roadside vegetation of the foothills outward to mountain forests: "In the relative cool of the timber strands, possum grapes and muscadine flourish with a cynical fecundity, and the floor of the forest—littered with old mossbacked logs, peopled with toadstools strange and solemn . . . —has about it a primordial quality" (*OK,* 11).

Just as Church often drops tiny signs of human presence at the periphery of his grandiose natural landscapes, the description points our attention toward human encroachment into the natural: "Under the west wall of the mountain is a community called Red Branch" (*OK,* 11). Opposed to the human-centered world of much of the novel is this natural frame of the Smoky Mountains that encompasses Red Branch; but this is more than a frame, as it constitutes an alternate reality that interpenetrates the world of the human. McCarthy's representations of the landscape continually remind readers of the natural world within our sight, if only we expand our vision. In similar terms, Emerson in *Nature* opposes the transcendental vision of the poet to that of most contemporaries who "do not see the sun," save with a "superficial seeing." McCarthy's fiction might be termed an environmental fiction, constantly reinserting human society and human reality within a largely ignored yet alien natural environment.

Under the influence of Emersonian transcendentalism, American luminist landscapes, according to Powell, replaced the vertical extension of height in the Burkean European landscapes with a "new emphasis on space" created by a lateral extension along a horizonal axis and an extension of the perspective of depth along the vertical plane: "in luminist painting the viewer does not experience nature from outside the picture but from within as an intuited phenomenon: the plane of a luminist canvas extends toward the viewer to encompass his presence in the conceptualized space of the landscape itself." Luminism's other emphasis is on silence, conveyed by still water or the extended light or bands of color of the sky (Powell, 72). In the shift of McCarthy's fiction to the arid Southwestern mountain plains, this emphasized horizontal axis and extended depth perception become more pronounced than in the Southern fiction. In *Blood Meridian* several descriptive passages of the journey of White's filibusterers into the "howling wilderness" emphasize the vast depths of the Western mountain plains: "They set forth in a crimson dawn where sky and earth closed in a razorous plane. Out there dark little archipelagos of cloud and the vast world of sand and scrub shearing upward into the shoreless voice where those blue islands trembled and the earth grew uncertain, gravely canted and veering out through tinctures of rose and the dark beyond the dawn" (*BM*, 50).

The description of the kid and Sproule's journey after the Comanche massacre diminishes the two into the vastness of Western space by emphasizing two perspectives. The first is a wide-angle perspective down from the cliffs toward the kid in the distance: "They set forth in the afternoon down the valley following the war trail and they were very small and they moved very slowly in the immensity of that landscape." Next we view, from the kid's panoramic perspective, the cliffs overlooking the valley: "Come evening they hove toward the rimrock again and Sproule pointed out a dark stain on the face of the barren cliff. It looked like the black from old fires. The kid shielded his eyes. The scalloped canyon walls rippled in the heat like drapery folds" (*BM*, 56). The landscape passages in the Southwestern novels produce a sublime in which characters and the reader's consciousness are engulfed in the immensity of the landscape.

McCarthy's novels, not content with recording characters' social interaction, thus insist on the significance of the human encounter with the natural. I would not argue that the role of landscape in McCarthy's fiction is uncritically transcendental, for McCarthy's characters, as well as his narrative perspective, ultimately resist the mystical ideal in luminism. Even Emerson, in "Experience," revises the Calvinist and Puritan concept of the Fall to acknowledge the contemporary crisis of the fall into self-consciousness, into science, into alienation from nature, into modernity: "It is very unhappy, but too late to be helped, the discovery we have made, that we exist." It is Rinthy's brother Culla who verges on a recognition of this fall at the novel's close, as he enters the swamp described as "a spectral waste," a "landscape of the damned," and finally "a faintly smoking garden of the dead" (*OD*, 242). Culla's response is to "wonder" why this is the road's destination and why the blind man he encounters is headed there. While McCarthy's landscapes hold significance, their meanings are indeterminate.

A Postmodern Revision of Transcendentalism.   In McCarthy's fiction, particularly the Southwestern fiction, characters must resist the temptation to identify with the landscape. In *Blood Meridian* the dying Sproule represents this resistance: "He was wounded in an enemy country far from home and although his eyes took in the alien stones about yet the greater void beyond seemed to swallow his soul. . . . They reached the valley floor at dusk and set off across the blue and cooling land, the mountains to the west a line of jagged slate set endwise in the earth" (*BM*, 65). This greater void beyond reflects, finally, not an Emersonian or luminist contemplative merger of the soul, but death, man's fundamental alienation from his natural environment. In *Moby-Dick* Melville's Ishmael slips into a similar dreamy identification with the rocking sea below, yet self-consciousness returns to him "in horror" when he almost falls from the mast to his death. In McCarthy's Southwestern desert, Sproule's dying vision resists a visionary merger with the "alien" landscape. This alienation differs from the postmodern commodification of the natural, which has resulted in recent declarations of the "end of nature." A Melvillean analogy once again is instructive, for in his sea fiction the ocean supplies a series of mimetic, symbolic, and mythic landscapes for his drama. In *Moby-Dick*'s opening, Ishmael suggests that the decision to go to sea is a suicidal repudiation of normal existence on "land" in order to quest after the oceanic mysteries in the psyche. McCarthy's characters wander, like Ishmael, from their homes, relinquishing the safety of American normalcy of the highway and town for the Smoky Mountain countryside, the 1950s underworld of McAnally Flats, or a lonely death in the Southwestern desert.

Emerson and Church—perhaps luminist art as a whole—project a historical myth of national identity in which American society, pushing westward, "progresses" by continually encountering then civilizing nature. At the end of the luminist tradition, Ansel Adams's great landscapes of the Yosemite repress the modern triumph over nature by excising man and technology from his photographic frame. Yet the completeness of this repression of modernity testifies all the more powerfully to the contemporary eclipse of American nature. We and Adams know that the Yosemite valley preserved in his photographs is an artistic fiction, an atavism about to be engulfed by the urbanization to the south and west. McCarthy's landscapes, particularly his Southwestern panoramas, part company with Church in resisting this national myth of historic progression from nature to civilized domination of nature, implying that such progression is an interpretive projection and illusion. Sometimes apparently hostile, other times merely indifferent to the characters, the Southwestern deserts and mountains are the Other, representing the nonhuman faculty of the self projected outward into the landscape and opposed to the ego. If the Emerson and luminist doctrine is to identify the natural with the godhood of the self, McCarthy's landscapes reflect an Other whose final frontier is within the human heart, within the Lester Ballards, the Judge Holdens, the Joel Glantons, the

Boyd Parhams. The unselfconscious violence of all these characters (save
the judge) reflects "natural" man stripped of his civilization. Hence they
are children of God, "like ourselves," but rejected by us in horror of the
natural without and within.

The Rhetoric of McCarthy's Fictional Form

A few early reviews voiced criticisms of the shape of McCarthy's novels,
particularly their plots. Referring to his "modernistic, elliptical narrative
technique" of working through short "small anecdotal units that tend
not to connect," Vereen Bell suggests that "Subjects exist, *données,* and
chronological advance is always perceptible; but plots in the conventional sense, complicated stories with appropriate resolutions or out-
comes, do not prevail" (Bell 1988, 7). Bell, of course, is aware of the narrative assumptions behind his critique, defining plot and "appropriate
resolution" in terms of drama and English realistic fiction. While
McCarthy's fiction is often so highly episodic and anecdotal as to appear
composed of narrative fragments, his plots are linear, primarily shaped
by his protagonists' movements across the landscapes of his fiction.
Rather than the great tradition of Jane Austen or Henry James, the
picaresque would seem a better model for analyzing McCarthy's plots
and narrative form, given their tendency toward the episodic; their
resemblances to travel narrative; and their themes of delinquency, crim-
inality, alienation, or marginality. Juxtaposed to the picaresques of
Sterne, Defoe, Dickens, Twain, and Melville, the episodic movements of
McCarthy's characters might seem less problematic. Indeed, the self-
conscious modernity of his picaresque travel narrative is evident; to a
large degree the road and the journey are metaphoric, delineating the
protagonists' search to find an identity external to their given "social"
identity. This metaphoric and psychological dimension to the plots is
already suggested in *The Orchard Keeper* in Syldar's love of fast cars and
fast driving and in Arthur's more atavistic attempt to flee the sheriff by
retreating into the Smoky Mountains or the "Harrykin." With *Outer
Dark,* this metaphoric link between journey and identity is firmly established in the divergent paths—and chance intersections—of Culla,
Rinthy, the tinker, and the outlaws.

**Interpolated Tales and the Self-Reflexive Form of McCarthy's
Fiction.**   If the unique quality of McCarthy's fiction derives in part
from its style and uncanny landscapes, the parablelike tales interpolated

throughout the novels are another crucial component. Within the Southern novels, the interpolations take the form of either italicized stream-of-consciousness narratives or first-person tales related in dialogue. The stream-of-consciousness fragments provide exposition for the plot, often supplying both a historic context and a momentary insight into the consciousness of characters. Such exposition could be supplied by the narrator or through dialogue, and character consciousness could be supplied by the omniscient narrator in free indirect narration ("he thought that . . ."). But McCarthy prefers to supplement the main narrative, using italicized fragments that directly represent or quote a character's thoughts. Most italicized sections of *The Orchard Keeper,* for example, interrupt the main narrative to reveal a series of Arthur Ownby's memories: of his estranged wife who has run off with a drummer, of his discovery of Kenneth Rattner's corpse, and finally of his old home in Red Branch and Rattner's gravesite. As we have seen, in *Child of God* such italicized passages are replaced by separate interludes narrated directly by nameless Sevier townspeople, while in *Suttree* the protagonist's thinking is conveyed to the reader through free indirect narrative, abandoning the use of italics save in the long prolegomenon. After his quarrel with his girlfriend, Joyce, Suttree speculates in this fashion about the color of memory and of life: "And what is is the color of grief? Is it as black as they say? And anger always red? The color of that sad shade of ennui called blue is blue but blue unlike the sky or sea, a bitter blue. . . . The color of this life is water" (*S,* 415).

Although the italicized passages diminish as we proceed chronologically through the fiction, the significance of first-person tales increases, beginning with *Child of God*'s oral tales about the exploits of Ballard and the historic sheriff Tom Davis, who rids Sevier of the White Caps. Such oral tales are closely integrated into *Suttree* in the form of character dialogue, like Trippin through the Dew's tale of the "crazy" reverend who "trimmed hisself" with a razor: "Just sliced em off honey, what they tell me" (*S,* 111). Similarly, the old railroader tells Suttree of burning up a train in the Colorado winter. Ab Jones tells Suttree of his "first acquaintance of the wrath of the path" when he is arrested and falsely accused of the murder of a white man he had bested in a fight; he is released by his nemesis the police only because the murderer proudly and publicly displays in a shoebox the head of his victim (*S,* 182, 204). As in the italicized passages of the earlier fiction, such tales supply exposition and supplement characterization. The tales of Jones and the railroader, in fact, function as life stories—events that have shaped and fixed the identities of the tellers. While the reverend's act is a mutilation that symbolizes both the insanity of his religious belief and his repudiation of the world of the flesh, paralleling Suttree's own psychological self-mutilation in his narcissism and alcoholism, in contrast, Trippin through the Dew's bemused, comic rendition of the reverend's self-mutilation reveals his comfortable acceptance of his own sexual roles as transvestite and prostitute.

Detached from their usefulness in alluding to the oral tradition, or delineating character, or highlighting the fiction's thematic concerns, these interpolated tales comment obliquely on the larger narrative that can "contain" them only uneasily. The tales sketch events that ironize the dramatic plot and develop character viewpoints often opposed to the worldviews of the protagonists. At the same time, such tales inquire into the purpose, form, and craft of narrative art itself, construed as a dialogue between teller and listener, writer and reader.

Interpolated Tales, Narrative, and the Witness. The first interpolated tale in the Southwestern fiction is Judge Holden's tale of the dead father, told as an elliptical answer to a question about the Anasazi builders of the ruins within which the troop is encamped. The tale is mythic, unadorned, told almost in outline form by the judge. A harnessmaker in the Alleghenies, meeting a young traveler, invites him home. Paid with two gold coins, the harnessmaker covets more, is lectured by the traveler, and seemingly repents. On the road, he murders, robs, and buries the traveler, pretending to his family that the two have been robbed by thieves and the traveler murdered. The story first offers itself as an explanation of the social source of the Glanton troop's violence, if members are placed in the position of the harnessmaker's son, for the judge suggests that the tale's significance is located not in the two fathers but in the two sons. Resenting his father's deathbed confession, the harnessmaker's son flees to the West to become a "killer of men," while the traveler's son discovers his life to be "broken" before the myth of his dead father's perfection. The troop's response to the tale is significant, for in quarrelling with particular details, all indicate their familiarity with a version of the tale, suggesting their own identification with the sons' quarrels against the legacy of the fathers. More important, the story associates the judge with the role of storyteller and artist, for the tale immediately follows a debate with Webster who has refused to allow the judge to sketch his likeness in the judge's memorandum book. To the end of the parable, the judge adds a commentary in which he identifies himself with the Anasazi and the artist: in contrast to the fate of those who build shelter of "reeds and hides" is the mason, who "seeks to alter the structure of the universe and so it was with these masons however primitive their works may seem to us" (*BM*, 146). Tales, sketches, masonry—all are arts that are patriarchal monuments whose preservation haunts the consciousness of later generations.

Parables of Art: *The Stonemason* and the Ex-Priest's Tale.

Whether or not we are to identify the judge with the Anasazi masons is unclear, for his role within *Blood Meridian* is that of killer and destroyer, not the builder of a monumental artistic legacy. Nevertheless, the story gives voice to a motif echoed in The Border Trilogy and reshaped into McCarthy's *The Stonemason,* a play unsuccessful when judged in purely dramatic terms but worthwhile for the sidelight it casts on the fiction. A drama that traces the interrelations between four generations of an African-American family in Louisville, the play focuses on the tensions between father and son that eventually destroy the family. At the play's conclusion, Ben Telfair, the play's narrator and protagonist, is the only male survivor remaining after the death of his grandfather Papaw, the suicide of his father, Big Ben, and the death by overdose of his young nephew Soldier. But the internal conflict of the play lies elsewhere, in the conflict between Ben's humanity and the call of his art. That humanity is represented in his family obligations to his sister, his delinquent nephew, and his father; Ben's art is the craft of freestone masonry, embodied in his grandfather, the master craftsman. Near the play's end, Ben betrays his sister by paying his nephew to leave town secretly, then attempts to conceal the nephew's identity after he dies of an overdose purchased with Ben's money.[12] Ben also repudiates his father's request to borrow $6,000, presumably to repay a gambling debt, offering only his unsecured credit rather than the mortgage on the ancestral stone house that Ben and Papaw are rebuilding (*SM*, 76–78). But the play's essential conflict is between grandfather or grandson, craftsmen married to their own art, and the son and father Big Ben, who sees his own masonry business merely as a means for the accumulation of money.

Viewed in the context of similar passages in McCarthy's fiction, the play ironically bespeaks McCarthy's commitment to his own craft, the costs of that commitment, and the purposes of that craft. As Henry James's similar architectural image of the house of fiction suggests, both grandfather and grandson speak for a Jamesian conception of the art of fiction in which the novelist painstakingly builds for immortality, placing words and sentences like the mason places his stones. In the grand-father's view, masonry is "the craft," emulating the Maker's craft in building the world; depicted as constantly reading his Bible, the grand-father can hardly be innocent of the Pauline doctrine of Christ's identity as the cornerstone of the new Tabernacle (Ephesians 2:20). Discussing the ownership of unpaid stonework, Papaw states what Ben calls the "labor theory of value": "The man's labor that did the work is in the work. . . . Even if it's paid for it's still there. If ownership lies in the ben-efit to a man then the mason owns all the work he does in this world and you caint put that claim aside nor quit it and it dont make no dif-ference whose name is on the paper" (SM, 30–31). Against his grandfa-ther's view of the inherent moral value of work, Ben emphasizes the esthetic value of the final product: "In form and design and scale and structure and proportion I've yet to see an example of the old work that was not perfectly executed" (SM, 91). For McCarthy, writing seems a commensurate "old work," and the novel a kind of monument built and "owned" by its literary mason. If the play emerges from McCarthy's own experience in working stone in the counties south of Knoxville, its tragic dénouement cautions against young Ben's and perhaps McCarthy's own overestimation of art as a sacred labor.

The long interpolated tales in *The Crossing,* especially the one told by the ex-priest, place less emphasis on this conception of fiction as an esthetic object or monument. These tales instead stress that narrative is a means of establishing identity, of lending at least a provisional mean-ing to one's existence—an existence that is completed only in the lis-tener's reception of the tale. This narrative cycle is inscribed within the ex-priest's tale, which deals only tangentially with himself. In the ruins of Huisiachepic, the ex-priest retells the life story of a man from that vil-lage, in answer to Billy Parham's question of how he came to be in the abandoned village. Orphaned when his parents are killed in the cannon-ade of the church at Caborca during the Mexican War, the man leaves his child with relatives in Bavispe, where it is killed by a building that collapses in an earthquake. These disasters cause him to question Provi-dence, become a heretic, and in his old age to "beard" God by living in the ruins of the church in Caborca and disputing with its priest: "What we seek is the worthy adversary. For we strike out to fall flailing through demons of wire and crepe and we long for something of substance to oppose us. . . . Otherwise there were no boundaries to our own being and we too must extend our claims until we lose all definition" (C, 153).

To the ex-priest, his tale is a means of establishing these boundaries and his identity. The tale is not concluded, even with the heretic's death and the priest's fall into heresy and subsequent retreat to live as a hermit in Huisiachepic. For it and the ex-priest to have existence, the tale must be told to Billy Parham: "Acts have their being in the witness. Without him who can speak of it? In the end one could even say that the act is nothing, the witness all" (*C*, 154). The ex-priest reverses the mimetic view of fictional language, the conviction that language can represent the world, claiming that world is itself merely a tale containing myriad others: "For this world also which seems to us a thing of stone and flower and blood is not a thing at all but is a tale. And all in it is a tale and each tale the sum of all lesser tales and yet these also are the self-same tale and contain as well all else within them" (*C*, 143). Through the ex-priest's narration, Billy Parham's own tale intersects the tales of the heretic and ex-priest.

Of course, this narrative circle is duplicated in our own reading of *The Crossing*—a reading that thereby fixes the identities of the man, the ex-priest, and Billy Parham. To what degree the ex-priest here and elsewhere speaks as narratologist for McCarthy's own art cannot be established. As the implied maker of his world of fiction, McCarthy stands as elusively outside his fictional creations as God stands elusively outside the world of the heretic and ex-priest: "Nothing can be dispensed with. Nothing despised. Because the seams are hid from us, you see. The joinery. The way in which the world is made. . . . And those seams that are hid from us are of course in the tale itself and the tale has no abode or place of being except in the telling only and there it lives and makes its home and therefore we can never be done with the telling. Of the telling there is no end" (*C*, 143). The ex-priest here, as in the judge's tale and in Ben Telfair's monologues, again uses the conceit equating the mason, the world's maker, and the tale-teller. Listening to the heretic's tale, the priest may lose his priesthood but gains his identity as tale-teller. McCarthy's fiction may stem from a mystical or sacred questioning, but it must take a secular form. Or perhaps the ex-priest's insistence on the necessity of all the tale's details reflects the implied author's rejoinder to all criticisms of his character, plots, and bleak narrative vision, by declaring that all is necessary. Yet the witness, interlocutor, or reader of these tales plays as crucial a role as the teller: there can be no tale without the witness. After *Suttree,* McCarthy's fiction places an increasing emphasis on interpolated tales, exhibiting thereby a pronounced self-consciousness about narrative and the function of the novel within the postmodern world.

Interpolated Dream Narratives.   In *Suttree* and The Border Trilogy dreams play a crucial role similar to that of the tales. The frequent dreams in McCarthy's fiction further connect the visionary impulse of McCarthy's wandering anti-heroes to the theme of the world as narrative. *Suttree* suggests that dreams act as a visionary state, an alternate apocalyptic vision in which the world and the identity of the self are deconstructed and reconstructed. While Suttree's dreams perform a role similar to that of the dream mechanism or unconsciousness in Freud's *The Interpretation of Dreams* (1900), many of the dreams in the novel's final sections are waking dreams dealing with an alternate, visionary consciousness, not the classic unconscious. The final chapters of *Suttree,* beginning with his drugging by the witch-woman and culminating in his hospital visions, relate a series of dream visions of himself and the world. While drugged, his visions continually begin with the the phrase "He saw," suggesting this passage from one visionary state to another. While these visions may be dismissed as simple hallucinations, the culminating visions of Suttree's imaginary trial and his apocalyptic vision of the birth of a new city arising in lava under "some eastern sea" are crucial factors in his rebirth in the novel's conclusion. John Grady Cole's dream of horses running free, Boyd Parham's dream of a burning lake and his accompanying premonitions, and Billy Parham's dream of the faceless messenger with invisible writing on a "ledgerscrap" all function as narrative foreshadowing and depict the dreamers as visionaries (*CR,* 82–83). While Billy's dream presages the death of his father, the dream also envisions his future life as empty pages, an unwritten narrative. Such dreams compare with the cryptic but foreboding fortunes rendered to Glanton's troop by the gypsy in *Blood Meridian;* both dreams and the cards function as divinations or forevisions of the stories that are to come (Sepich, 106–112, 115).

The Ethos of McCarthy's Visionary Narratives: Divination, Existentialism, and Nihilism

As I argue in Chapters 4 and 5, McCarthy's Southwestern fiction coincides with a movement away from a modernist and purely esthetic model of fiction and toward the acknowledgment of a popular audience in *All the Pretty Horses.* The Border Trilogy parallels the visionary quests of the protagonists John Grady Cole and Billy Parham to a series of visionary interpolated narratives. Despite the claim of the ex-priest that all men's tales are one, such visions or tales are individual, highly particularized, hence the necessity for the interpolated tales, each containing a unique vision of the world. In *The Crossing* the stories of Billy and Boyd Parham are to be juxtaposed to the narratives of the visionary journeys of the ex-priest and blind man. Like McCarthy's questors Suttree, John Grady Cole, and Billy Parham, these interpolated tales mediate between the nihilistic worship of force (represented by the judge, Lester Ballard, the outlaws of *Outer Dark,* and Alfonsita) and a limited social morality (represented by the communal narrators of *Child of God,* the legal authority of Sheriff Gifford in *The Orchard Keeper,* or the worship of money and respectability of Suttree's father). These fictions allow readers to choose the vision with which they will identify.

Such multiplicitous character perspectives, given the omniscient narrator's studious disinclination to use moral commentary, have given impetus to a persistent strain of moral criticism. The violent struggles within McCarthy's fiction are by no means confined to the characters or to the linguistic levels of its rhetoric. The McCarthy novel is not only stylistically divided in its narration and in its inclusion of regional and professional dialects, but it is also divided among contradictory ideological, philosophical, and ethical visions that resist easy integration into a unified ideology by readers or critics. Bakhtin's discussion of the novel is again helpful in resisting our temptation to seek a unified ideology or ethos in the novelistic discourse. He argues that distinctive ideologies that characterize social, generational, regional, and ethnic groups first are expressed within their dialects or languages, then achieve ultimate expression within the novel as it incorporates these languages and viewpoints within itself. The novelist, as opposed to the poet, "welcomes" into the novel the diverse ideologies and "socio-ideological cultural horizons" expressed within the characters' sublanguages (Bakhtin, 299). In contrast with the ideal of the unified moral vision of the English tradition, small wonder that two of McCarthy's earliest critics, Walter Sullivan and Vereen Bell, attempt readings of the moral vision of McCarthy's fiction only to recoil at the implications of their readings, dismissing the moral world of McCarthy's fiction as gnostic or nihilistic.

Critics of *Blood Meridian* such as Terence Moran and Peter Josyph focus on the issue of violence, identifying the fiction's ethos with the violence represented within the fiction or purveyed by McCarthy's violent protagonists, all of whom repudiate social mores. Thus Josyph argues that, despite the masterful prose of *Blood Meridian,* the ethos of the novel "is so admiring of the quick over the dead that it is ethically bereft" and positions us outside any law save that of force. In the form of a question, Josyph memorably states this reading of *Blood Meridian,* a reading that is often applied to McCarthy's entire corpus: "Must we . . . check our *ethos* at the door to fully enjoy McCarthy's *epos?*" (Hall and Wallach, 185, 187). Similarly, a feminist critique of the fiction would surely note the relative absence of fully imagined female characters and the relegation of important female characters (for example, Rinthy Holme in *Outer Dark)* to the function of maternal object. Such a feminist critique of McCarthy's fiction has not yet been written and no doubt would take a different shape to the one I have outlined. But the essentially patriarchal shape of McCarthy's characterizations, plots, and style can hardly be questioned, although the portrayal of women in The Border Trilogy would require a reassessment of feminist critiques, given the crucial role of Alfonsita in *All the Pretty Horses* and the novel's ironizing of Cole's romantic conception of Alejandra as the beloved. Perhaps this novel can be said to initiate McCarthy's self-criticism of the characterization of women in his earlier fiction.

While legitimate, these moral critiques of McCarthy's fiction allow only a relatively restricted range of discourses, representations, ethics, and ideologies within the novels and within novelistic discourse. On the contrary, to Bakhtin the novel *must* incorporate semi-autonomous language-play and character speech, often making use of tales narrated by characters or framed genres such as diaries or dreams, all incorporated within the larger novel in order to emphasize, rather than suppress, the tensions between "language borders" and their accompanying ideologies. Such ideologies have been created by "history and society," and their tension reaches expression in both society's and the novel's "relativized consciousness" (Bakhtin, 323–24). Bakhtin's critique of unified discourse and McCarthy's fiction suggest that we flee to the novel, requesting it to express a unified moral vision in order to impose that language or vision on a disunified world, even while we demand that fiction represent the world. Perhaps what we fear most in the judge and Ballard is that their worship of violence suggests how the world resists our moral imperatives.

Yet many of McCarthy's other characters supply ideologies that counter nihilists such as the judge or Lester Ballard. Even the visionary wanderers of The Border Trilogy, John Grady Cole and Billy Parham, recognize legitimate restrictions of conscience and society on desire and the will. Hence Cole's confession to the judge of his bad conscience over his killing of the assassin in prison and his recognition of his own bad conduct with the hacendado and Alfonsita. While Cole and Parham may wander outside the law on the borders of society, they do recognize an alternate ethos beyond the law of force. When he traps the wolf, Billy is presented with three choices, making decisions that either can be praised as heroic or criticized as romantically foolhardy. In the first choice, as he gazes at the wolf caught in his trap, Billy can solve his dilemma easily and shoot the wolf or obey his father's injunction to keep the wolf alive unless its leg is broken. Second, viewing the homeward road north versus the "open country" to the south, he can choose either to return to the safety of home or to disobey his father in restoring the wolf to her own home in that idealized open country. Finally, already having chosen the southward path and disobedience, once he realizes that the mountains of Mexico are not open but subject to the law of the hacendado's will, he chooses to bow to the hacendado's authority and ride home. Significantly, he then changes his choice, returning to shoot the wolf before she is baited and torn apart by the airedales for sport. This decision is made knowing that his own death is a likely result.

While obvious parallels can be drawn with Hemingway's celebration of the cult of ceremonial death in his analysis of bullfighting in *Death in the Afternoon,* I would note several important distinctions. Parham's first two choices are not to kill, even when killing is the most convenient of alternatives. When the final choice is merely between alternate modes of killing, Parham opts for the wolf to die unceremoniously; this repudiation of death as ceremony must be opposed to Hemingway's bullfights. Parham's decisions to free the wolf, to feed the Indian without alerting his father, and to return to Mexico for his brother's body are made at the cost of much personal suffering. Such decisions, like many made by John Grady Cole in *All the Pretty Horses,* rightly cannot be termed nihilistic celebrations of force. The ethos represented here is instead an acknowledgment of the individual's ability, power, and right to choose, including the right to choose conduct that absurdly is opposed to one's own social and economic self-interest. Furthermore, while such choices are shown to define an authentic identity as opposed to the socially determined or given identity within society (for example, that Billy is merely "Will Parham's boy"), the inexorable costs of such visionary choices— the manner in which the exterior world and society resist such choices— are also emphasized unmistakably. In fact, the judge in *Blood Meridian* reads the kid's refusal of violence along similar lines, interpreting his choices not to shoot or to kill as a repudiation of the judge's nihilistic code of violence. As a faint precursor of the visionary protagonists of the Border Trilogy, the kid, despite his murders, represents something different from Josyph's and Moran's readings of the novel as a nihilistic praise of force.

Within McCarthy's Southwestern fiction, *The Crossing*'s interpolated tale of the blind man most clearly connects the theme of the journey of the visionary hero (or antihero) to narrative's purpose of expressing a vision that mediates between the exterior world and the interior world of the self. Despite the darkness of his vision—a darkness that verges close to nihilism—the blind man critiques, if momentarily and provisionally, the vision of nihilists like the judge. His wife plays the role of primary narrator, retelling his tale, while Billy Parham and the blind man himself act as interlocutors. His tale deals with the loss of his normal vision, his forgetting of that vision, and its replacement with the new world of his dark vision. The loss of his vision, his wife emphasizes, is the result of a heroic choice to remain at his position as cannoneer despite the failure of his fellow rebels to capture Durango. Ironically, he is saved from execution by a German captain named Wirtz, who blinds him by sucking out his eyes.

More horrifying, perhaps, than any of the bloodshed in *Blood Meridian* is the brutally naturalistic description of the rebel's physical suffering: "He cried out in his despair and waved his hands about before him. He could not see the face of his enemy. The architect of his darkness, the thief of his light. He could see the trampled dust of the street beneath him. . . . He could see his own mouth. . . . The red holes in his skull glowed like lamps" (*C,* 277). But as the imagery of seeing and blindness, light and darkness suggests, more horrible still is the psychological effect of the slow dimming of the lamp of the world, submerging him into a slowly progressing blindness: "The eyes dried and wrinkled and the cords they hung by dried and the world vanished and he slept at last and dreamt of the country through which he'd ridden in his campaigns in the mountains and the brightly colored birds thereof and the wildflowers" (*C,* 277).

The remainder of the tale is concerned with the blind man's attempts to explore his blindness, to determine its significance, to understand his new vision of the world, to comprehend a world in which such blinding could occur. The tale is simultaneously realistic in its representation of the man's journey home; surrealistically absurd in scenes like the one in which he attempts to drown himself in knee-deep water; and symbolist in its allegorical presentation of characters, events, and the imagery of light and darkness. The plot and the imagery of blindness self-consciously allude to the blinding of King Lear and Kent and their reluctant revision of their worldviews after their blinding. The blind man's journey home is a realistic parallel to his inner quest for meaning or enlightenment. Just as obviously, his tale parallels and ironically comments on Parham's own "blind" journeys, which form the novel's main plot.

In the same fashion, the blind man's tale revises and comments on all the journeys that form the basis of McCarthy's plots. By telling his tale, the blind man attempts to order the true darkness of the world that he has only begun to recognize: "He said that the light of the world was in men's eyes only for the world itself moved in eternal darkness and darkness was its true nature and true condition and that in this darkness it turned with perfect cohesion in all its parts but that there was naught to see" (*C*, 283). While the blind man's vocabulary and imagery allude to Christian discourse, in which the "light of the world" is associated with Christ, the vision is not Christian. Although he uses the term loosely in his reviews to refer simply to an abandoning of fixed communal beliefs, Walter Sullivan's term "gnostic" surprisingly is more applicable than it would at first appear. Historic gnosticism, a version of Christianity that was finally proscribed as heresy, in several points closely resembles the blind man's vision, for gnosticism saw the world as the darkened creation of the flawed demiurge, preferred mystical interpretations of the parables, and opposed the imagery of light as knowledge to darkness as ignorance.[13] Wirtz's violence expresses another tale of blindness, a moral darkness that differs from the blind man's version of darkness. Wirtz gives order to the darkness of the world by reflecting its darkness within his own actions. Speaking of Wirtz, the blind man explains, "The man of whom we speak will seek to impose order and lineage upon things which rightly have none. He will call upon the world itself to testify as to the truth of what are in fact his own desires. In his final incarnation he may seek to indemnify his words with blood" (*C*, 293).

Violence can be interpreted as a type of narrative that reveals our attempt to project our own desire not only on the darkness of the world but on others who oppose our will. The victim is a symbolic replacement for the darkness of the world, its resistance to the narrative of our will. Wirtz thus represents the way or vision that the blind man unhesitatingly characterizes as evil, although he does not use the term in the Christian sense. Furthermore, the blind man's analysis of Wirtz's vio-

lence as a metaphysical response to the world comments ironically on
Billy Parham's earlier sympathy for the wolf's vision of the world, that
of the pure killer, with the crucial distinction that to men such as Wirtz
violence has not a biological imperative but a metaphysical one. The
wolf's killings lack the philosophical motive and choice of Wirtz, who by
blinding the rebel seeks to inflict pain on him by lending him a physical
version of Wirtz's dark knowledge of the world. Clearly, the blind man's
tale repudiates the vision both of his earlier self and of Wirtz; he tells his
tale implicitly to warn Billy Parham against the world's darkness. Yet
the hospitality offered Parham by the blind man and his wife, as well as
the hospitality shown to the blind man and Parham by the many people they encounter on their journeys, points toward a different narrative
vision of this dark world and an ethos beyond that of violence for
McCarthy's fiction: "For the sharing of bread is not such a simple thing
nor is its acknowledgment" (C, 161).

This interpolated tale finally can be read as as a parodic reinterpretation of the theme of the journey in McCarthy's fiction. Through his
blinding, the man is forever alienated from the world: "Nothing would
ever come again to touch him out of that estrangement that was the
world. Not in love, not in enmity." At the same time, he paradoxically is
imprisoned within the world of his new perception of touch: "The bonds
that fixed him in the world had become rigid. Where he moved the
world moved also and he could never approach it and he could never
escape it" (C, 279). The blind man's tale is his response to his blinding,
expressing his new vision of the dark world; yet he is also aware that his
vision is a relative one, and that the world to all people takes the shape
of a picture that we represent to ourselves: "The picture of the world is
all the world men know and this picture of the world is perilous" (C,
293). The blind man's tale thus cautions against Billy's journey, against
the visionary impulse toward absolute knowledge, and against the perils
of narrative itself. McCarthy's visionary wanderers are here so complicated and ironized as to transform into the antiheroic. In the retelling of
this tale told by the blind man to his wife, who tells it in turn to
Parham, the tale's ownership transfers from the blind man to
McCarthy's narrator and warns us against the perilous force and vision
of McCarthy's fiction.

The interpolated tales of the judge, the blind man, and the ex-priest
and the journeys of John Grady Cole, Billy Parham, and McCarthy's fiction itself all spring from a radical questioning of the meaning of the
world or self that corresponds to the current age of uncertainty, whether

scientific, religious, interpretive, or epistemological. While this questioning cannot rightly be termed religious, mystical, or even metaphysical, McCarthy's narratives early were termed either existential or nihilist because this quest for meaning never is resolved authoritatively. Hence the unresolved endings of *Suttree,* with Suttree's departure from Knoxville that can be construed as either an ending or a new beginning; of *All the Pretty Horses,* with Cole's departure to locate an unspecified "my country"; or of *The Crossing,* with Parham's weeping on the road under the sun that rises "without distinction" (*C,* 426). Nor can the quest for meaning be resolved, at least within secular fiction like McCarthy's.

If McCarthy's fiction springs from a desire to assign meaning and value to the self and world, this desire cannot be fulfilled either by the journeys of McCarthy's protagonists or by fiction itself. Nonetheless the protagonists' tales must be told—and told responsibly. Near the conclusion of his tale, the ex-priest meditates on the relationship between narrative and the world: "He [the tale-teller] sets forth the categories into which the listener will wish to fit the narrative as he hears it. But he understands that the narrative is itself in fact no category but is rather the category of all categories for there is nothing which falls outside its purview. All is telling" (*C,* 155). What belief that can be registered in McCarthy's fiction is first a belief in in the significance of the choice of linguistic style and a belief that fictional and human identities are both not fixed but derive from choice. Second, McCarthy's fiction expresses a belief—a highly qualified belief—in narrative as a replacement for the older verities of divine narrative. If knowledge of the darkness of the world and the self is a perilous knowledge, what knowledge we can have must be expressed in the form of narrative: "All is telling." Beyond their considerable range of language and style, McCarthy's narratives gain their power largely through the intensity of this belief in narrative and narrative alone.

Notes and References

Chapter One

1. Knoxville, Tenn., *City Register,* 1937, 1941, 1962.

2. Don Williams, "Cormac McCarthy," *Knoville News-Sentinel,* 10 June 1990, E2; hereafter cited in text.

3. *Volunteer Moments: Vignettes of the History of the University of Tennessee, 1794–1994* (Knoxville: Office of the University Historian, University of Tennessee, 1994), 45 (hereafter cited in text); Pat Fields, "Knoxville Author Gets Award for Writing," *Knoxville Journal,* 19 May 1965, n.p.; hereafter cited in text.

4. Richard Jordan, " 'Just Write' Says Successful Author," *University of Tennessee Daily Beacon,* 30 January 1969, 6; hereafter cited in text.

5. See Gregory Jaynes, "The Knock at the Door," *Time,* 6 June 1994, 63; hereafter cited in text. A Peggy Lee Holleman is listed as a freshman in the University of Tennessee *Student Directory* from 1957–58 until 1960–61.

6. Edwin T. Arnold and Dianne C. Luce, Introduction to *Perspectives on Cormac McCarthy* (Jackson: University Press of Mississippi, 1993), 4; hereafter cited in text.

7. Pat Fields, "Knox Native McCarthy"s *Outer Dark:* Second Novel Gets Good Reviews," *Knoxville Journal,* 7 October 1968, A8.

8. Don Williams, "Annie DeLisle," *Knoxville News Sentinel,* 10 June 1990, E1–2.

9. Pat Fields, "Novel by Knoxvillian Wins Award," *Knoxville Journal,* 12 March 1966, n.p.

10. Robert Coles, "The Empty Road" (review of *Outer Dark), New Yorker,* 22 March 1969, 133–39 (hereafter cited in text); Patrick Cruttwell, "Plumbless Recrements" (review of *Outer Dark), Washington Post Book World,* 24 November 1968, 18.

11. "A Star Is Born," *Book World,* 8 May 1994, 15 (hereafter cited in text); Jaynes, 62.

12. Alan M. Kriegsman, "Public TV's 'Visions' of Expanded Dramatic and Creative Horizons," *Washington Post,* 16 January 1977, E5.

13. Richard B. Woodward, "Cormac McCarthy's Venomous Fiction," *New York Times Magazine,* 19 April 1992, 36.

14. Jerome Charyn, "Doomed Huck" (review of *Suttree*), *New York Times Book Review,* 18 February 1979, 14; Edward Rothstein, "A Homologue of Hell on a River of Death" (review of *Suttree*), *Washington Post,* 19 March 1979, B2.

15. "After the Windfall: How 'Geniuses' Make Out with No-Strings Grants," *Wall Street Journal,* 19 November 1981: A1; Woodward, 30.

155

16. "A Star Is Born," 15; Walter Sullivan, "About Any Kind of Meanness You Can Name" (review of *Blood Meridian*), *Sewanee Review* 93 (Fall 1985): 653, 650.

17. Gary Wallace, "Meeting McCarthy," *Southern Quarterly* 30 (Summer 1992): 135; Jaynes, 64.

18. "Ex-Knoxville Author Given Fiction Honor," *Knoxville News-Sentinel*, 20 November 1992, 1; *Knoxville News-Sentinel*, 30 September 1990, People Section, 1.

Chapter Two

1. Orville Prescott, "Still Another Disciple of William Faulkner" (review of *The Orchard Keeper*), *New York Times*, 12 May 1965, 45–46.

2. Walter Sullivan, "Worlds Past and Future: A Christian and Several from the South" (review of *The Orchard Keeper*), *Sewanee Review* (Autumn 1965): 720; hereafter cited in text.

3. Allen Tate, *Essays of Four Decades* (Chicago: Swallow Press, 1968), 533; hereafter cited in text.

4. Louis D. Rubin, Jr., *The Wary Fugitives: Four Poets and the South* (Baton Rouge and London: Louisiana State University Press, 1978), 42–45, 187; hereafter cited in text.

5. *I'll Take My Stand* (New York: Harper & Brothers, 1930); reprinted as *I'll Take My Stand: The South and the Agrarian Tradition* (New York: Harper Torchbook, 1962).

6. Walter Sullivan, *A Requiem for the Renascence: The State of Fiction in the Modern South* (Athens: University of Georgia Press, 1976), 63–73.

7. Louis Rubin, Jr., "Is the Southern Literary Renascence Over?: A Sort of Cautionary Epistle," in *The Rising South,* vol. 1, ed. Donald R. Noble and Joab L. Thomas (University of Alabama: University of Alabama Press, 1976). In this essay Rubin directly responds to Sullivan's thesis of the death of the renaissance and repudiates his own earlier attempt to link contemporary writers to antebellum Southern tradition, arguing that critics should instead read backwards from contemporary writers to the earlier tradition, stressing discontinuities.

8. *The Orchard Keeper* (New York: Random House, 1965; reprint, New York: Vintage, 1993), 10; hereafter cited in text as *OK*.

9. Joseph Blottner, *Faulkner: A Bibliography* (New York: Random House, 1974).

10. *Outer Dark* (New York: Random House, 1968; reprint, New York: Vintage, 1993), 57–77; hereafter cited in text as *OD*.

11. John Irwin, *Doubling and Incest/Repetition and Revenge: A Speculative Reading of Faulkner* (Baltimore and London: Johns Hopkins University Press, 1976), 4.

12. Jefferson Humphries, ed., *Southern Literature and Literary Theory* (Athens and London: University of Georgia Press, 1990), ix–x.

13.   Patrick Crutwell, "Plumbless Recrements" (review of *Outer Dark*), *Washington Post Book World*, 24 November 1968, 18.

14.   Cleanth Brooks, *William Faulkner: The Yoknapatawpha Country* (New Haven and London: Yale University Press, 1963), 1, 10–28.

15.   Neal R. Peirce, *The Border South States: People, Politics, and Power in the Five Border South States* (New York: W. W. Norton, 1975), 16.

16.   V. O. Key, Jr., *Southern Politics* (New York: Alfred A. Knopf, 1950), 75.

17.   Vereen Bell, *The Achievement of Cormac McCarthy* (Baton Rouge and London: Louisiana State University Press, 1988), 2, 7, 11; hereafter cited in text.

Chapter Three

1.   *Suttree* (New York: Random House, 1979; reprint, New York: Vintage, 1992), 457; hereafter cited in text as *S.*

2.   *Child of God* (New York: Random House, 1973; reprint, New York: Vintage, 1993), 4; hereafter cited in text as *CG.*

3.   Andrew Bartlett, "From Voyeurism to Archaeology: Cormac McCarthy's *Child of God*," *Southern Literary Journal* 24 (Fall 1991): 4; hereafter cited in text.

4.   Increased incorporation of a viewpoint or "focal" character—to use Henry James's term—within omniscient third-person narration is characteristic of the realistic novel as it develops into the modern novel. Paralleling this development is that of the accompanying discourse of the indirect free style, which indirectly merges the narration with the "untagged" or unidentified focal character's mental statements or perceptions. For an analysis of these terms, consult Seymour Chatman, *Story and Discourse: Narrative Structure in Fiction and Film* (Ithaca, N.Y., and London: Cornell University Press, 1978), 198–209; hereafter cited in text. With stream-of-consciousness discourse, Joyce, Faulkner, and modern novelists would supplement or replace omniscient third-person narration with the interior monologue of this focal observer. In *Child of God*, commentary on Ballard by other characters takes the form of free untagged monologues, separated from the larger narrative perspective and placed in separate chapters. By primarily adopting the viewpoint of Ballard as focal observer, the novel's discourse seems to critique the perspective of the residents of Sevierville, though this is not to suggest that the implied author's perspective is synonymous with Ballard's.

5.   R. W. B. Lewis, *The American Adam: Innocence, Tragedy, and Tradition in the Nineteenth Century* (Chicago: University of Chicago Press, 1955), 20–27.

6.   Eric J. Sundquist, *Home as Found: Authority and Genealogy in Nineteenth-Century American Literature* (Baltimore: Johns Hopkins University Press, 1979).

7.   Mark Royden Winchell, "Inner Dark; or, The Place of Cormac McCarthy," *Southern Review* 26 (April 1990): 293–309.

8.   Vereen M. Bell. "The Ambiguous Nihilism of Cormac McCarthy," *Southern Literary Journal* 15 (Spring 1983): 38–39.

9.   Bell, "Ambiguous Nihilism," 37–38, and John Lewis Longley, Jr., "Suttree and the Metaphysics of Death," *Southern Literary Journal* 17 (Spring 1985): 86.

10.   Frank W. Shelton, "Suttree and Suicide," *Southern Quarterly* 29 (Fall 1990): 71–72; hereafter cited in text.

11.   Thomas D. Young, Jr., "The Imprisonment of Sensibility: *Suttree*," *Southern Quarterly* 30 (Summer 1992): 72–91; hereafter cited in text.

12.   Ellie Ragland-Sullivan, *Jacques Lacan and the Philosophy of Psychoanalysis* (Urbana and Chicago: University of Illinois Press, 1986), 14–16.

13.   Jacques Lacan, "The Mirror Stage," in *Ecrits: A Selection,* trans. Alan Sheridan (New York and London: W. W. Norton, 1977), 1–7.

Chapter Four

1.   Portions of the argument in this chapter were first published in my article "Revisioning the Western?: Three Recent Cases," *Cañon: The Journal of the Rocky Mountain American Studies Association* 2 (Spring 1995): 24–51.

2.   *Blood Meridian or the Evening Redness in the West* (New York: Random House, 1985; reprint, New York: Vintage, 1992), 3; hereafter cited in text as *BM*.

3.   See Leslie Fiedler's discussion of the American hero's escape and Huck, Jim, and the raft in *Love and Death in the American Novel,* rev. ed. (New York: Stein & Day, 1966), 25–26.

4.   William Faulkner, *Go Down, Moses* (New York: Vintage, 1940), 245–49.

5.   I restrict my remarks to the divested social identity of the male hero in the "masculine romance," not the American romance in general. In Stowe, Warner, Jewett, Chopin, identity formation in the nineteenth-century female romance is quite different. Chopin's Edna of *The Awakening* craves a romantic escape into both the self and art, an escape found only in suicide.

6.   Discussing *Huckleberry Finn*, Leo Marx states that "freedom in this book specifically means freedom from society and its imperatives" (*The Pilot and the Passenger* [Oxford: Oxford University Press, 1988], 49).

7.   Jerome Loving, *Lost in the Customhouse: Authorship in the American Renaissance* (Iowa City: University of Iowa Press, 1993), ix.

8.   John McGowan, *Postmodernism and Its Critics* (Ithaca, N.Y. and London: Cornell University Press, 1991), 4–12.

9.   Franklin Kelly, "A Passion for Landscape: The Paintings of Frederic Edwin Church," in *Frederic Edwin Church Exhibition Catalogue* (Washington, D.C.: National Gallery of Art, 1989), 43, 53; hereafter cited in text. Church's

1860 *Twilight* is termed a "supreme moment of cosmic time" or "a natural apocalypse" by David Huntington (*The Landscapes of Frederic Edwin Church* [New York: 1966], 82).

10. Frederick Merk, *Manifest Destiny and Mission in American History: A Reinterpretation* (New York: Alfred A. Knopf, 1963), 25, 32, 124; hereafter cited in text.

11. Albert K. Weinberg, *Manifest Destiny: A Study of Nationalist Expansionism in American History* (Baltimore: Johns Hopkins University Press, 1935; reprint, Gloucester, Mass: Peter Smith, 1958), 39–41, 100, 211–12; hereafter cited in text.

12. Merk, 227, and Thomas R. Hietala, *Manifest Design: Anxious Aggrandizement in Late Jacksonian America* (Ithaca, N.Y.: Cornell University Press, 1985), 11, 122–27, 164, 167–69; hereafter cited in text.

13. John Sepich, *Notes on Blood Meridian* (Louisville: Bellarmine College Press, 1983), 27, 29–31, 53–55, 129–39; hereafter cited in text.

14. Emily Miller Budick, *Fiction and Historical Consciousness: The American Romance Tradition* (New Haven, Conn.: Yale University Press, 1989), ix.

15. Hayden White, *Metahistory: The Historical Imagination in Nineteenth-Century Europe* (Baltimore: Johns Hopkins University Press, 1973), 1–42.

16. Fredric Jameson, *The Political Unconscious: Narrative as a Socially Symbolic Act* (Ithaca, N.Y.: Cornell University Press, 1981), 104.

17. Richard Chase, *The American Novel and Its Tradition* (Garden City, N.Y.: Doubleday, Anchor, 1957).

18. Jane Tompkins, *Sensational Designs: The Cultural Work of American Fiction, 1790–1860* (New York and Oxford: Oxford University Press, 1985), 94–95, 101–103.

19. Leonard Thompson and Howard Lamar, eds., *The Frontier in History: North America and Southern Africa Compared* (New Haven, Conn.: Yale University Press, 1981), 7.

20. Paying close attention to the origins and development of Puritan "covenant" theology is Perry Miller's early and influential study *Errand into the Wilderness* (Cambridge, Mass.: Belknap Press of Harvard University Press, 1956).

21. Urizen is portrayed as a Satanic figure in Blake's rewriting of *Paradise Lost* in the mini-epic *Milton,* so Tobin's interpretation of the Judge as devil and the Judge's Enlightenment rhetoric can be reconciled by this analogy to Blake's character.

22. Donald Worster, *Rivers of Empire: Water, Aridity, and the Growth of the American West* (New York and Oxford: Oxford University Press, 1985), 129–30, 172–79, 264–79, 300–302; hereafter cited in text.

23. Patricia Limerick, *The Legacy of Conquest: The Unbroken Past of the American West* (New York: W. W. Norton, 1987), 27–29, 214–58; hereafter cited in text. While I attend to the revisionary aspects of her theme of conquest, Limerick's history also is revisionary in surveying topics that traditional histo-

ries have either underemphasized or ignored, particularly the contributions of women and ethnic minorities in the settling of the West.

24. A patient listener likened McCarthy's violence to pornography (or a sadography) in response to an early, brief version of this argument, delivered at the national American Studies Association meeting in Boston, 5 November 1993.

25. Richard Slotkin, *Gunfighter Nation: The Myth of the Frontier in Twentieth-Century America* (New York: Atheneum, 1992), and *Regeneration through Violence: The Mythology of the American Frontier, 1600–1860* (Middletown, Conn.: Wesleyan University Press, 1973), 21–24.

26. Richard Drinnon, *Facing West: The Metaphysics of Indian-Hating and Empire Building* (Minneapolis: University of Minnesota Press, 1980), xvii–xviii.

Chapter Five

1. See Kurt Tidmore, "Lighting Out for the Territory" (review of *All the Pretty Horses*), *Washington Post Book World,* 3 May 1992, 1–2, calling McCarthy "one of America's finest writers."

2. Jürgen Habermas, "Modernity—an Incomplete Project," in *Postmodernism: A Reader,* ed. Patricia Waugh (London and New York: Edwin Arnold, 1992), 160–70.

3. Andreas Huyssen, *After the Great Divide: Modernism, Mass Culture, Postmodernism* (Bloomington: Indiana University Press, 1986); McGowan, *Postmodernism and Its Critics,* 8–10.

4. Tompkins, 3–39; Richard Brodhead, *The School of Hawthorne* (New York: Oxford University Press, 1986).

5. Edwin Arnold, "Naming, Knowing and Nothingness: McCarthy's Moral Parables," *Southern Quarterly* 30 (Summer 1992): 31–50; Leo Daugherty, "Gravers False and True: *Blood Meridian* as Gnostic Tragedy," *Southern Quarterly* 30 (Summer 1992): 122–33; Bell, 2, 34, 120–22.

6. Jean-François Lyotard, *The Inhuman: Reflections on Time*, trans. Geoffrey Bennington and Rachel Bowlby (Stanford, Calif.: Stanford University Press, 1991), 33–34.

7. *All the Pretty Horses* (New York: Alfred A. Knopf, 1992), 298–300; hereafter cited in text as *APH*.

8. See the discussion of the novel's three-part structure by Robert Hass in what may be the most insightful review essay of McCarthy's Southwestern fiction, "Travels with a She-Wolf: Cormac McCarthy's Border Hero Returns to Mexico's Mythic Sierra" (review of *The Crossing*), *New York Times Book Review,* 12 June 1994, 2; hereafter cited in text.

9. *The Crossing* (New York: Alfred A. Knopf, 1994), 72–127 (first ride), 177–273 (second ride), 393–423 (burial ride); hereafter cited in text as *C*.

10. Diane Elam, *Romancing the Postmodern* (London and New York: Routledge, 1992), 3.

11. *The White-Caps: A History of the Organization in Sevier County* (Knoxville: Bean, Workers, 1899; reprint. Gatlinburg, Tenn.: Buckhorn Press, 1989), 11–13, 23–27, 35–46.

12. Jean Baudrillard, *Selected Writings*, ed. Mark Poster (Cambridge: Polity Press, 1988), 170–74; Jameson *Postmodernism*, 16–18; Linda Hutcheon, *The Politics of Postmodernism* (New York and London: Routledge, 1989), 13–14. In "Simulacra and Simulations" Baudrillard uses Disneyland as an exemplary representation of the historical that erases the real, operating as a "hyperreality" or as "its own pure simulacrum."

13. Tom Pilkington, "Fate and Free Will on the American Frontier: Cormac McCarthy's Western Fiction," *Western American Fiction* 27 (February 1993): 311–22; hereafter cited in text.

14. Roland Barthes, *Mythologies,* trans. Annette Lavers (New York: Hill & Wang, 1972), 113–17.

15. Jean François Lyotard, *The Postmodern Condition,* trans. R. Durand (Manchester: Manchester University Press, 1986), 72, 82.

16. Michel Foucault, *The Order of Things: An Archaeology of the Human Sciences* (New York: Vintage, 1973), 50–58.

17. Luther Burbank, *Vanishing Lobo* (Boulder, Colo.: Johnson Books, 1990), 40, 4–12 (hereafter cited in text); Woodward, 30.

Chapter Six

1. The notion of a fictional rhetoric, of course, alludes to Wayne Booth, *The Rhetoric of Fiction* (Chicago: University of Chicago Press, 1961).

2. Wade Hall and Rick Wallach, eds., *Sacred Violence: A Reader's Companion to Cormac McCarthy* (El Paso: Texas Western Press, 1995), 140–43; hereafter cited in text.

3. Seymour Chatman, "The 'Rhetoric' of 'Fiction,'" in *Reading Narratives: Form, Ethics, Ideology,* ed. James Phelan (Columbia: Ohio State University Press, 1989), 52.

4. Shelton, 74; Young, 72; Bell, 69; D. S. Butterworth, "Pearls as Swine: Recentering the Marginal in Cormac McCarthy's *Suttree*," in Hall and Wallach, eds., *Sacred Violence,* 95.

5. Dorothy Wickenden, review of *Suttree, New Republic,* 10 March 1979, 46.

6. Terence Moran, "The Wired West" (review of *Blood Meridian), New Republic,* 6 May 1985, 37–38.

7. Guy Davenport, "Appalachian Gothic," *New York Times Book Review,* 29 September 1968, 4; Coles, 133–37; Patrick Cruttwell, "Plumbless Recrements (review of *Outer Dark*)," *Washington Post Book World,* 24 November 1968, 18.

8. Edwin Eigner, *The Metaphysical Novel in England and America* (Berkeley: University of California Press, 1978), 5–11, 62–65.

9.   M. M. Bakhtin, "Discourse and the Novel," in *The Dialogic Imagination: Four Essays by M. M. Bakhtin* (Austin: University of Texas Press, 1981), 290–91; hereafter cited in text.

10.   Brooke Allen, "Back West: High Wind in the Cottonwoods" (review of *The Crossing*), *Wall Street Journal*, 10 June 1994, A8.

11.   Earl A. Powell, "Luminism and the American Sublime," in *American Light: The Luminist Movement, 1850–1875* (Princeton, N.J.: Princeton University Press, 1989), 79–80; hereafter cited in text.

12.   *The Stonemason* (Hopewell, N.J.: Ecco Press, 1994), 117, 121; hereafter cited in text as *SM*.

13.   James M. Robinson, ed., *The Nag Hammadi Library in English* (San Francisco: Harper, 1988), 3–6.

Selected Bibliography

PRIMARY WORKS

All the Pretty Horses. New York: Alfred A. Knopf, 1992.

Blood Meridian or the Evening Redness in the West. New York: Random House, 1985; reprint, New York: Vintage, 1992.

Child of God. New York: Random House, 1973; reprint, New York: Vintage, 1993.

The Crossing. New York: Alfred A. Knopf, 1994.

The Orchard Keeper. New York: Random House, 1965; reprint, New York: Vintage, 1993.

Outer Dark. New York: Random House, 1968; reprint, New York: Vintage, 1993.

The Stonemason. Hopewell, N.J.: Ecco Press, 1994.

Suttree. New York: Random House, 1979; reprint, New York: Vintage, 1992.

SECONDARY WORKS

Bibliography

Luce, Dianne C. "Cormac McCarthy: A Bibliography." *Southern Quarterly* 30 (Summer 1992): 143–51.

Books on McCarthy

Arnold, Edwin T. and Dianne C. Luce, eds. *Perspectives on Cormac McCarthy.* Jackson: University Press of Mississippi, 1993. Reprint of articles in Cormac McCarthy special issue of *Southern Quarterly* (Summer 1992).

Bell, Vereen M. *The Achievement of Cormac McCarthy.* Southern Literary Studies, edited by Louis D. Rubin. Baton Rouge and London: Louisiana State University Press, 1988.

Hall, Wade and Rick Wallach, eds. *Sacred Violence: A Reader's Companion to Cormac McCarthy.* El Paso: Texas Western Press, 1995.

Sepich, John. *Notes on "Blood Meridian."* Louisville: Bellarmine College Press, 1983.

Sullivan, Walter. *A Requiem for the Renascence: The State of Fiction in the Modern South.* Mercer University Lamar Memorial Lectures, No. 18. Athens: University of Georgia Press, 1976.

Related Books

Bakhtin, Mikhail Mikhailovich. "Discourse and the Novel." In *The Dialogic Imagination: Four Essays by M. M. Bakhtin,* 259–422. Austin: University of Texas Press, 1981.

Brooks, Cleanth. *William Faulkner: The Yoknapatawpha Country.* New Haven, Conn., and London: Yale University Press, 1963.

Chamberlain, Samuel E. *My Confession: The Recollections of a Rogue.* New York: Harper, 1956.

Drinnon, Richard. *Facing West: The Metaphysics of Indian-Hating and Empire Building.* Minneapolis: University of Minnesota Press, 1980.

Habermas, Jürgen. "Modernity—an Incomplete Project." In *Postmodernism: A Reader,* edited by Patricia Waugh, 160–70. London and New York: Edwin Arnold, 1992.

Hietala, Thomas R. *Manifest Design: Anxious Aggrandizement in Late Jacksonian America.* Ithaca, N.Y.: Cornell University Press, 1985.

Humphries, Jefferson, ed. *Southern Literature and Literary Theory.* Athens and London: University of Georgia Press, 1990.

Hutcheon, Linda. *A Poetics of Postmodernism: History, Theory, Fiction.* New York and London: Routledge, 1988.

I'll Take My Stand. New York: Harper & Brothers, 1930. Reprinted as *I'll Take My Stand: The South and the Agrarian Tradition.* New York: Harper Torchbook, 1962.

Jameson, Fredric. *Postmodernism; or, The Cultural Logic of Late Capitalism.* Post-Contemporary Interventions, edited by Stanley Fish and Fredric Jameson. Durham, N.C.: Duke University Press, 1991.

Lacan, Jacques. "The Mirror Stage." In *Ecrits: A Selection,* translated by Alan Sheridan, 1–7. New York and London: W. W. Norton, 1977.

Lamar, Howard, and Leonard Thompson, eds. *The Frontier in History: North America and Southern Africa Compared.* New Haven, Conn.: Yale University Press, 1981.

Limerick, Patricia Nelson. *The Legacy of Conquest: The Unbroken Past of the American West.* New York: W. W. Norton, 1987.

Rubin, Louis D., Jr., *The Wary Fugitives: Four Poets and the South.* Baton Rouge and London: Louisiana State University Press, 1978.

Simpson, Lewis P. *The Brazen Face of History: Studies in the Literary Consciousness in America.* Baton Rouge and London: Louisiana State University Press, 1980.

Slotkin, Richard. *Gunfighter Nation: The Myth of the Frontier in Twentieth-Century America.* New York: Atheneum, 1992.

Tate, Allen. *Essays of Four Decades.* Chicago: Swallow Press, 1968.

Waugh, Patricia, ed. *Postmodernism: A Reader.* London and New York: Edward Arnold, 1992.

The White-Caps: A History of the Organization in Sevier County. Knoxville: Bean, Workers, 1899; reprint, Gatlinburg, Tenn.: Buckhorn Press, 1989.

Weinberg, Albert K. *Manifest Destiny: A Study of Nationalist Expansionism in American History*. Baltimore: Johns Hopkins University Press, 1935; reprint, Gloucester, Mass.: Peter Smith, 1958.

Worster, Donald. *Rivers of Empire: Water, Aridity, and the Growth of the American West*. New York and Oxford: Oxford University Press, 1985.

Articles and Book Chapters

Arnold, Edwin. "Naming, Knowing and Nothingness: McCarthy's Moral Parables." *Southern Quarterly* 30 (Summer 1992): 31–50. Reprinted in Arnold and Luce, eds., *Perspectives on Cormac McCarthy, 43–67*.

"A Star Is Born." *Book World,* 8 May 1994, 15.

Bartlett, Andrew. "From Voyeurism to Archaeology: Cormac McCarthy's *Child of God*." *Southern Literary Journal* 24 (Fall 1991): 3–15.

Bell, Vereen. "The Ambiguous Nihilism of Cormac McCarthy." *Southern Literary Journal* 15 (Spring 1983): 31–41.

_____. "Between the Wish and the Thing, the World Lies Waiting." *Southern Review* (Autumn 1992): 920–27.

Cheuse, Alan. "A Note on Landscape in *All the Pretty Horses*." *Southern Quarterly* 30 (Summer 1992): 140–42.

Daugherty, Leo. "Gravers False and True: Blood Meridian as Gnostic Tragedy." *Southern Quarterly* 30 (Summer 1992): 122–33. Reprinted in Arnold and Luce, eds., *Perspectives on Cormac McCarthy, 157–72*.

Grammer, John. "A Thing against Which Time Will Not Prevail: Pastoral and History in McCarthy's South." *Southern Quarterly* 30 (Summer 1992): 19–30. Reprinted in Arnold and Luce, eds., *Perspectives on Cormac McCarthy, 27–42*.

Jarrett, Robert L. "Revisioning the Western?: Three Recent Cases." *Cañon: The Journal of the Rocky Mountains American Studies Association* 2 (Spring 1995): 24–51.

Jaynes, Gregory. "The Knock at the Door." *Time,* 6 June 1994, 62–64.

Longley, John Lewis, Jr. "Suttree and the Metaphysics of Death." *Southern Literary Journal* 17 (Spring 1985): 79–90.

Luce, Dianne E. "Cormac McCarthy's First Screenplay: *The Gardener's Son*." *Southern Quarterly* 30 (Summer 1992): 51–71. Reprinted in Arnold and Luce, eds., *Perspectives on Cormac McCarthy, 69–94*.

Morrison, Gail Moore. "*All the Pretty Horses:* John Grady Cole's Expulsion from Paradise." In Arnold and Luce, eds., *Perspectives on Cormac McCarthy, 173–93*.

Pilkington, Tom. "Fate and Free Will on the American Frontier: Cormac McCarthy's Western Fiction." *Western American Fiction* 27 (February 1993): 311–22.

Powell, Earl A. "Luminism and the American Sublime." In *American Light: The Luminist Movement, 1850–1875,* 69–94. Princeton, N.J.: Princeton University Press, 1989.

Ragan, David Paul. "Values and Structure in *The Orchard Keeper.*" *Southern Quarterly* 30 (Summer 1992): 10–18. Reprinted in Arnold and Luce, eds., *Perspectives on Cormac McCarthy,* 15–25.

Rubin, Louis D., Jr. "Is the Southern Literary Renascence Over?: A Sort of Cautionary Epistle." In *The Rising South,* vol. 1: Changes and Issues, edited by Donald R. Noble and Joab L. Thomas. University of Alabama: University of Alabama Press, 1976.

Sepich, John. "A 'Bloody Dark Pastryman': Cormac McCarthy's Recipe for Gunpowder and Historical Fiction in *Blood Meridian.*" *Mississippi Quarterly* 46 (1993): 547–63. Reprinted in Sepich, *Notes on Blood Meridian,* 119–28.

_____. "The Dance of History in Cormac McCarthy's *Blood Meridian.*" *Southern Literary Journal* 24 (Fall 1991): 16–31.

_____. " 'What kind of indians was them?': Some Historical Sources in Cormac McCarthy's *Blood Meridian.*" *Southern Quarterly* 30 (Summer 1992): 93–110. Reprinted in Arnold and Luce, eds., *Perspectives on Cormac McCarthy,* 121–41.

Salter, Susan. "McCarthy, Cormac." In *Contemporary Authors,* vol. 10, edited by Ann Evory and Linda Metzger, 314–15. Detroit: Gale Research, 1983.

Shaviro, Steven. " 'The Very Life of the Darkness': A Reading of *Blood Meridian.*" *Southern Quarterly* 30 (Summer 1992): 111–21. Reprinted in Arnold and Luce, eds., *Perspectives on Cormac McCarthy,* 143–56.

Shelton, Frank W. "Suttree and Suicide." *Southern Quarterly* 29 (Fall 1990): 71–83.

Young, Thomas D., Jr. "The Imprisonment of Sensibility: *Suttree.*" *Southern Quarterly* 30 (Summer 1992): 72–91. Reprinted in Arnold and Luce, eds., *Perspectives on Cormac McCarthy,* 95–120.

Winchell, Mark Royden. "Inner Dark: or, The Place of Cormac McCarthy." *Southern Review* 26 (April 1990): 293–309.

Wallace, Gary. "Meeting McCarthy." *Southern Quarterly* 30 (Summer 1992): 134–39.

Richard B. Woodward, "Cormac McCarthy's Venomous Fiction." *New York Times Magazine,* 19 April 1992, 28–40.

Reviews

Allen, Brooke. "Back West: High Wind in the Cottonwoods." Review of *The Crossing. Wall Street Journal,* 10 June 1994, A8.

Charyn, Jerome. "Doomed Huck." Review of *Suttree. New York Times Book Review,* 18 February 1979, 14–15.

Coles, Robert. "The Empty Road." Review of *Outer Dark. New Yorker,* 22 March 1969, 133–39.

_____. "The Stranger." Review of *Child of God. New Yorker,* 26 August 1974, 87–90.

Cruttwell, Patrick. "Plumbless Recrements." Review of *Outer Dark*. *Washington Post Book World*, 24 November 1968, 18.

Davenport, Guy. "Appalachian Gothic." Review of *Outer Dark*. *New York Times Book Review*, 29 September 1968, 4.

Hass, Robert. "Travels with a She-Wolf: Cormac McCarthy's Border Hero Returns to Mexico's Mythic Sierra." Review of *The Crossing*. *New York Times Book Review*, 12 June 1994, 1+.

Kriegsman, Alan M. "Public TV's 'Visions' of Expanded Dramatic and Creative Horizons." Review of *Gardener's Son*. *Washington Post*, 16 January 1977, E5.

Moran, Terence. "The Wired West." Review of *Blood Meridian*. *New Republic*, 6 May 1985, 37–38.

Prescott, Orville. "Still Another Disciple of William Faulkner." Review of *The Orchard Keeper*. *New York Times*, 12 May 1965, 45–46.

Rothstein, Edward. "A Homologue of Hell On a River of Death." Review of *Suttree*. *Washington Post*, 19 March 1979, B2.

Sullivan, Walter. "About Any Kind of Meanness You Can Name." Review of *Blood Meridian*. *Sewanee Review* 93 (Fall 1985): 649–56.

_____. "Worlds Past and Future: A Christian and Several from the South." Review of *The Orchard Keeper*. *Sewanee Review* 73 (Autumn 1965): 719–26.

Tidmore, Kurt. "Lighting Out for the Territory." Review of *All the Pretty Horses*. *Washington Post Book World*, 3 May 1992, 1–2.

Wickenden, Dorothy. Review of *Suttree*. *New Republic*, 10 March 1979, 46.

Newspaper Articles

Fields, Pat. "Knoxville Author Gets Award for Writing." *Knoxville Journal*, 19 May 1965, n.p.

_____. "Knox Native McCarthy's *Outer Dark:* Second Novel Gets Good Reviews." *Knoxville Journal*, 7 October 1968, A8.

_____. "Novel by Knoxvillian Wins Award." *Knoxville Journal*, 12 March 1966, n.p.

Jordan, Richard. " 'Just Write' Says Successful Author." *University of Tennessee Daily Beacon*, 30 January 1969, 6.

Williams, Don. "Annie DeLisle: Cormac McCarthy's Ex-wife Prefers to Recall the Romance." *Knoxville News-Sentinel*, 10 June 1990, E1–2.

_____. "Cormac McCarthy: Knoxville's Most Famous Contemporary Writer Prefers His Anonymity." *Knoxville News-Sentinel*, 10 June 1990, E1–2.

Index

The Author

Robert L. Jarrett is associate professor of English at the University of Houston–Downtown. He has recently published articles on the revisionary western and on the use of computerized data bases in teaching English composition. He is currently writing a study of contemporary western authors.

The Editor

Frank Day is a professor of English and head of the English Department at Clemson University. He is the author of *Sir William Empson: An Annotated Bibliography* (1984) and *Arthur Koestler: A Guide to Research* (1985). He was a Fulbright lecturer in American literature in Romania (1980–1981) and in Bangladesh (1986–1987).